"MY DEAR AND ONLY SON"

Letters to a Heartland Pioneer

Edited and with an Introduction by

Carolyn Grattan Eichin

Heritage Books
2025

HERITAGE BOOKS

AN IMPRINT OF HERITAGE BOOKS, INC.

Books, CDs, and more—Worldwide

For our listing of thousands of titles see our website
at
www.HeritageBooks.com

Published 2025 by
HERITAGE BOOKS, INC.
Publishing Division
5810 Ruatan Street
Berwyn Heights, MD 20740

Cover photo: Albert G. Williams as a young man.

Cover design courtesy of the author.

International Standard Book Number
Paperbound: 978-0-7884-5052-5

To Joe, Heather, and Sarah

Table of Contents

My Dear and Only Son

Preface

History contains more than just the stories of the wealthy and well-known. It encompasses the narratives of the countless men and women whose experiences have created the dynamic backdrop of national and world events. The letters in this collection provide an intimate portrait of a family populated by ordinary people challenged in many ways by extraordinary circumstances. For historians, the collection is somewhat unusual in documenting atypical situations. Most nineteenth-century letter collections detail married spouses forced to live apart either because of the Civil War or other military relocations; or more distant family members reporting on travels or temporary arrangements. Rarely do intimate nineteenth-century letters exist from divorced parents to their estranged child. For this family, the dissolution of the nuclear family forged a backdrop for other events. The writings document individual experiences of space and time; the day-to-day struggles that facilitated survival and fashioned the lives of mid-nineteenth century Americans. The collection's foremost value may lie in its ability to help stimulate ideas about how ordinary people perceived, articulated, and succeeded in their world.

The Albert Williams' collection provides a window into Iowa's 19th century pioneer period, illuminating much about the people who called Iowa home. Luke Newton and Annginette Hall (Williams) Sherman are considered among the first permanent settlers in an area that became Chester Township, Poweshiek County, about five miles north of modern Grinnell's town center.[1] The collection contains four letters from Annginette, Albert's older sister. Her last two letters informed Albert's move to Iowa, where he remained for almost forty years. Albert's move to Chester township, Grinnell, in 1856/57, only months after his sister and brother-in-law, posits him, also, as among its earliest settlers.

Most of the letters originate from Albert's divorced parents, Stephen Williams, Jr. and Melinda (Hall) Williams, reaching him after his move. Fourteen letters date from 1857 and 58. We can almost hear Stephen's Yankee drawl with his vernacular speech patterns carried into writing. His "a goin'", "pertemuch", "a doin'", and the occasional homespun metaphors flavor the gossipy letters that relate little of Stephen's emotional circumstance. He does demonstrate a concern for alienating his adult children, and his loss of their presence in New Hampshire is keenly felt in his iterations on local gossip. For Albert, the letters tie him to his natal community in New Hampshire and offer him a basis for comparisons of his situation with the lives of others. These letters preserved family ties and the cultural framework of no-nonsense, socially conservative, rural lifestyles.

The majority of letters in the collection were written by Stephen Williams, Jr., to Albert. His letters sketch a hardscrabble life of subsistence farming, usually only three acres planted a year, as well as his independent financial pursuits through shingle-making, temporary work on nearby farms, and wage employment in the gun manufacturing industry. Stephen's writing is at its best in letters describing his youngest daughter, Francis[2], and her activities and emotional states. Stephen's precise observations of Francis' behavior, facilitated by a legal system that valued father's rights over those of mothers, provide insight into the Victorian cultural thoughts and practices related to children, as well as grounding the family's narrative. In 1861, Francis was spirited away from New England by Uncle Worthin Hall and his wife, to settle in Iowa with her mother and siblings.

Albert's mother, Melinda (Hall) Williams, in contrast to her ex-husband Stephen, wrote painful, heart-wrenching epistles to her son. For her time, she exemplifies a well-educated and literate woman. Underneath the emotion she begged for forgiveness for forcing Albert into a life neither of them could control. An underlying message was one of the confidence she had in Albert to sort through the chaos of his early years, and still continue to love her, while succeeding in life. At about 12 years old, subsequent to his parents' separation, Albert was bound out, signaling the beginning of communication between mother and child through letter writing to supplement intermittent personal visits. Her letters seek to tie Albert emotionally to her, reflecting the critical reality of the distance between them created by the separation and divorce. Although at first only a few miles away, in reality, Melinda could not function as a mother to her children, and an obsessive quality surfaces in some letters through her painful separation. Letter writing allowed her to express an unhappiness that was prohibited in public expression.

Melinda found it necessary to pursue wage labor, an uncommon avenue of relief for respectable women of the mid-nineteenth century. She struggled financially and emotionally with conflicting responsibilities, even as she enjoyed a modicum of independence. Her six letters provide the historian insight into a world rarely documented, a divorced woman's plight in the 1850s. Melinda's voice is strong and illuminates a time and situation not well known. In general ways, the letters enforce the concepts of men tied to a market economy and women tied to domesticity and the household economy.[3] Her letters are in sharp contrast to Stephen Williams' letters in both execution and in focus. The family was split, and these parents lost the ability to present a united front, common goals, and consistent interpretations for their children. As they write about daily happenings, they define those situations and compose a world formed by their perceptions. They were individuals. That individualism is a benefit for historians wanting to piece together the lives of nineteenth-century folk.

As historian Jill Lepore believes: Microhistories of unknown people find their lives serving as allegories for the larger American culture; a microhistory of one life takes us closer to the lives of many. The value is not in uniqueness, but in exemplariness.[4] Thus, this collection offers paradigms on daily life in the mid-nineteenth century; a portrait of a family undergoing change. For readers, the collection serves as a resource for those interested in nineteenth-century history, especially the lived experiences of women and children. For the authors and recipients, the letters offered emotional strength. The letters were a substitute for a conversation between father and son, mother and son, and Albert with other relatives and friends. Albert would draw strength from the knowledge that his family cared about him and were confident that he could negotiate life's many challenges. Most letters sent to Albert in Iowa provided a continuation of the community, the local, personal and informal interactions he had left in New Hampshire and also of the cultural parameters – honesty, sobriety, hard work – of the life he led. The religious morality, the family values even in the face of divorce, the concern for relatives not to be forgotten by the physical distance between them, and the perpetuation of values important to a culture which helped frame the mid-west, all underscore the communications. It is the quotidian, delicate, intimate quality of these letters that makes them so extraordinarily revealing, and valuable.[5] The letters are more than just biographical frameworks of the authors, and more than just historical "raw material." They form an "illusion of individuals telling their own stories," an autobiographical form of artistry, and a bridge between mutually absent correspondents.[6] Moreover, they contribute to the conversation about middle America's heartland and cultural values.[7] If we only knew these people by the recorded documents of life, such as birth, marriage, and death records, they would be almost invisible. These letters breathe life into this family.

The Albert Williams' collection consists of 35 letters, and two contemporary documents labeled in chronological order with the letters. The two contemporary documents, a deed for Albert's Iowa farm and his wife's teaching certificate, were incredibly important to preserve. Their existence elevates the preservation of these letters. They were personally of great significance to Albert. The oldest letter is dated February 20, 1853, and the most recent April 18, 1872. Aside from parents' letters, three from Albert's uncle George Philander Williams, and two from childhood friends were included. Only one letter written by Albert himself remains in the collection, and it was co-authored by a college friend, Albert W. Hobbs, who lost his life in service to the North during the Civil War. The letters are organized chronologically, with the exception of one letter to Albert's wife from her cousin, and her teaching certificate transcription which appear after all others. One appendix includes the memories of Albert's daughter Lavinia who was born in Iowa, lived much of her life there, and ultimately died in the house in which she had been born. Appendix II is an advertisement for the Chester Nursery business that Albert established and owned on his farm. Appendix III was written by Albert late in life in response to his wife's suffragist activities.

Any epistolary collection is incomplete and cannot convey the true experience of reading original, handwritten historic artifacts. The letters represent relationships that disappeared or changed over time, and one can only speculate on the reasons why Albert kept these letters, carefully tied with a snippet of old ribbon, when in reality he must have received others that were not kept. An introduction to Albert's life and family helps explain the possible answers. Genealogy websites have been used extensively to locate people mentioned in the letters, determine their relationships and vital statistics, and are generally not footnoted. Most of the people mentioned in the letters have been identified, and standard sources have been footnoted. Albert had close to 50 first cousins, plus uncounted numbers of second cousins and more distant relatives, making identification challenging in some instances.

The goal of presenting the text of the letters as accurately as possible, while still creating a readable text, has been facilitated by correcting spelling and capitalization, adding punctuation where missing, and the use of modern paragraph formatting when appropriate. Each letter is numbered and a heading for each letter provides the letter's recipient, the letter writer, and place of origin, if missing from the main text. There has been a minimum use of [*sic*]. Brackets are used when information is incomplete [pages torn, etc], or words illegible, or when information has been added to clarify meaning. When unsure of an illegible word, the presumed word with a question mark has been used in brackets. Original underlining in the text has been preserved. The placement of dates, salutations and closings have been standardized, and all alterations were made with a focus on making the letters more accessible to readers.

---

[1] Leonard Fletcher Parker, *History of Poweshiek County, Iowa; A History of Settlement, Organization, Progress, and Achievement*, (Chicago: S. J. Clarke Publishing Company, 1911), 227, Chester Township was organized in 1860.

[2] Francis Williams [Hays] [1851-1899] spelled her name with an "i" in one of the following letters, although her mother's letters and her tombstone reflect the use of e in Frances, a more traditional spelling for females. The spelling has been standardized to Francis herein.

[3] Nancy Woloch, *Women and the American Experience*, (New York: McGraw Hill: 2011), 216, for 10.2 % of the free labor force in 1860 were women.

[4] Jill Lepore, "Historians Who Love Too Much: Reflections on Microhistory and Biography," *Journal of American History*, Vol. 88, Issue 1, (June 2001), 133.

[5] Few Iowa family letter collections providing insight into their daily lives exist. One collection is John Kent Folmer, ed. *"This State of Wonders", The Letters of an Iowa frontier Family, 1858-1861*, (Iowa City: University of Iowa Press, 1986).

[6] William Merrill Decker, *Epistolary Practices, Letter Writing in America before Telecommunications*, (Chapel Hill and London: University of North Carolina Press, 1998), 9, 160.

[7] For a recent discussion of the mid-west as heartland see Eric Arnesen, "Inventing a Heartland," *Middle West Review*, Vol 9, no. 2, (Spring 2023): 91-104.

Acknowledgements

Many people assisted with research, and all deserve recognition. Primarily, Worthin E. and Maretta Grattan need to be thanked for their encouragement of this project and for the use of the original letters, family bible, and photos. Thanks also go out to: Barbara Kresse, Croydon Historical Society; Peter Larsen and Bonnie Stewart for use of their ancestor William Foster's letters to his wife (Foster letters); Mark D. Procknik, Librarian, Grimshaw-Gudewicz Reading Room, New Bedford Whaling Museum; Kerry Perkins and Anna Rosenbluth, Campbell Museum; Molly Rowe, Mission House Museum Library, Honolulu; Poweshiek County Recorder's Office and Historical Society; Christopher Jones, Special Collections, Grinnell College; Steven Delassio, American Precision Museum, Windsor, Vermont; Chris Klosterman, Poweshiek County Clerk of Court, Montezuma, Iowa; Pat Rowell, Poweshiek County Historical and Genealogical Society; Craig Farnham, Vermont Historical Society; Peabody Essex Museum; Tasha Caswell, Connecticut Museum of Culture and History; and Dublin, NH Historical Society. Special thanks go out to those who read and commented on early drafts: Chris Eichin, Brian Grattan, and Jeanette Knight. My heartfelt thanks and gratitude go out to my husband Chris, without whose help this volume would not have been possible.

Introduction

Albert Gordon Williams was born November 18, 1840 in Cornish, New Hampshire, the only son of Stephen Williams, Jr. and Melinda (Hall) Williams. Albert's challenging early life in New Hampshire was shaped by his parent's turbulent relationship. They separated in 1852, divorcing in 1856. Albert was "bound out" during this interim period, eventually leaving New Hampshire for Iowa slightly after his sixteenth birthday, following his oldest sister and her husband who had left on their wedding day, less than a year before. His arduous childhood encouraged the development of skills later used for survival. He grew up, as did Iowa, itself.

The story of Iowa's pioneer period found people struggling in the new environment; building up equity through personal labor and making the most of the fertile plains. Albert succeeded in Iowa through hard work, familial support, and persistence, establishing a farm in Poweshiek County and ultimately a nursery business offering fruit and vegetable plants to neighbors. He remained among the earliest settlers of what became Chester Township, Poweshiek County, Grinnell, Iowa. Escaping chronic asthma, in 1893 Albert, his wife, children and his father relocated to Campbell, California in the Santa Clara valley, at a time when Campbell was populated by only a few hundred persons. Albert passed away in 1922 at almost 82 years after attaining political positions in the Campbell community including Justice of the Peace. At 5'9" of medium complexion, Albert's piercing blue eyes had read and perhaps reread the letters coveted in his collection. Clearly, they sustained his journeys, both emotionally and physically through life.

In 1900, a friend of Albert's drew conclusions about the poor boys of Grinnell – Albert included – who had attained success in their chosen fields. He searched for "the conditions and causes of their financial success" that revealed "several that have been common to them all." They are as follows:

> 1. They have had fairly good health.
> 2. A fair degree of good fortune.
> 3. Business sense.
> 4. If on a salary they earned what they received.
> 5. The spirit of push that will find a way or make one.
> 6. A business character so made up of intelligence and integrity as to win the confidence of patrons.
> 7. Economy. They were careful to spend a dollar only for what was worth a dollar to them, and then spent less than their income.[1]

Success was measured financially, and the analysis sustained the "great man" theory of history, but failed to credit Albert with a loving support system including parents, siblings, and wife. However, his observations prompt questions: What were the influences on Albert that led to his success, as measured by the society in which he lived? How does this epistolary collection provide answers to questions about the value system and culture of that time, and more generally, about early mid-western settlement?

Albert's natal state, New Hampshire, exemplified the hinterland of New England absorbing Boston's liberal influences but mixing them with conservative rural notions.[2] The population grew significantly during the late 1700s so that by 1790 New Hampshire had a population of 141,885 enjoying a density of fifteen people per square mile. It was a world of small towns – none over 5,000 – and resourceful people.[3]

Albert's birthplace, Cornish, settled in 1765, boasted of 13 families only two years later.[4] At the time of Albert's birth, the Cornish population stood at 1,726, slightly more than the current number. Typically, small town in attitude, everyone knew their neighbor's business; a fact reflected in the letter collection. Most families were interconnected by marriage.[5] All of the letters, with the exception of one, sent to Albert from his father originated in Cornish, or Cornish Flat, a village in the northeastern part of Cornish. Other small towns in the region – Claremont, Newport, Plainfield, and Croydon – housed other family members.[6] These New England roots impelled Albert's life and career, and established parameters to his beliefs and behavior. This influence continued even in death as his tombstone reads "Native of New Hampshire."

Williams Family

Albert was a ninth generation American on his father's side and seventh generation American on his mother's side. Both families stretched back to the Puritan Great Migration when thousands of settlers from England came to America. Albert's ancestors were dominated by farmers, but a sprinkling of other occupations included deacons and ministers of the Puritan, Congregational church, as well as businessmen and politicians. Every known line of ancestry originated in the British Isles.

There were several waves of immigrants after the landing of the Mayflower in 1621, and much research has been done on the Puritan Migration from England to America in the mid-1600s which created and defined what American culture would become.[7] Migration from England was central to growth in the American colonies. By the mid-1600s between 20,000 and 30,000 people immigrated with more than thirteen thousand Puritans arriving in New England during the 1630 to 1640 decade.[8] Puritans were generally from the middling ranks, neither poor nor wealthy. They moved to New England in large numbers for religious freedom, for personal growth and knowledge, and in broad terms for economic prosperity.[9] England under Charles I had become corrupt and restrictive of the Puritan religion, a situation which pushed people to emigrate.[10] Movement to New England facilitated their service to God and their ability to lead productive, as well as profitable lives.

The Williams' line can be traced with surety to Albert's great-grandfather, Samuel Williams [1751-1799], a revolutionary soldier. It is believed that this Samuel Williams was the son of Samuel and Hannah (Chandler) Williams of Roxbury, Massachusetts where Samuel was likely born. If this is the correct lineage, and by process of elimination it seems to be, then this Williams' line descends from Puritan Robert Williams' [1607-1693] and his son Samuel's [1632-1698] immigration in 1637.[11] Hannah Chandler's [1728-1804] line also dates to a 1637 migration.[12]

Robert Williams, presumably from County Norfolk, England, immigrated to America on the *John and Dorothy* with wife and children, settling in Roxbury, Massachusetts.[13] These 1637 families were made up mostly of mid-career tradesmen who settled in an uncertain New England to pursue farming.[14] Albert's line descended through Robert's son Samuel.[15] The child immigrant Samuel married Theoda Park whose family had unloaded from the ship *Lyon* in 1631.[16]

It is painful and deeply troubling to find slaveowners on the Williams family tree, however, historians estimate that 1,600 enslaved Africans lived in New England by 1700; and by 1770, two percent of Massachusetts' population of 250,000 people were enslaved. Both the Park and Williams family contained slaveowners. Theoda Park's father, William Park [1607-1685], created an eight-year indenture in 1673-4, of an enslaved man, Silvanus Warro, continuing a system which deprived Silvanus of his liberties for most of his life.[17] Slavery had existed legally in Massachusetts from the early 1640s until an April 1783 legal opinion rendered slavery inconsistent with the Massachusetts constitution and thereafter illegal. Eleazer Williams [1695-1768], whose will transferred title of "a Negro man Bristone" to a son, died only a few years before the end of slavery in Massachusetts.[18] Both Eleazer Williams, Albert's great-great-great grandfather, and William Park had extensive land holdings. Evidently the prosperity of Albert's ancestors in New England of the 1600s and 1700s depended, to some degree, on their abuse of others.

Samuel Williams [1751-1799] settled in Amherst, one of the larger New Hampshire towns of that time, established as early as the 1730s.[19] New Hampshire offered up 2,000 un-uniformed men by the 23rd of April 1775 for the battles near Cambridge and Medford,[20] among them, Samuel Williams. Poorly equipped, lacking in uniforms, and ill-prepared for the fight against seasoned British troops, approximately 1200 New Hampshire men subsequently served in the infamous Battle of Bunker Hill.[21] Amherst had 328 men of fighting age at that time and about 100 went to Bunker Hill for the June 17, 1775, battle there. The battle of Bunker Hill saw a few wounded from Captain Josiah Crosby's regiment, and specifically noted that Samuel Williams lost a shirt, handkerchief, and gun as a result of the battle.[22] Starting April 23, Samuel Williams of Amherst served three months and 16 days in 1775, for which he was paid seven pounds, two shillings, and ten pence for his service.[23] Captain Crosby's company was present, as was Samuel Williams as a part of this company, when George Washington took possession of the army on July 2, 1775.[24] In October, 1775, Samuel Williams appears to have received four pounds for his service, signing the roster with an X, indicating illiteracy.[25]

After returning home, Samuel Williams quickly moved to Dublin, New Hampshire, population roughly 305, where he signed an April 12, 1776, resolution against the British, and later again actively served in the Revolution.[26] Having recently married, Samuel Williams' first child, Abijah, was born in 1776 in Dublin. By the time of Samuel's death in 1799, he and Louise added seven children to the one thousand residents who called Dublin home, as others had moved in from Massachusetts and neighboring towns in New Hampshire.[27]

A diarist and member of the Dublin community, Abner Sanger, recorded his thoughts on the daily life of Dublin where he befriended Samuel Williams. Only a few of the early years of the 1790s remain of the journal, but those few crumbs provide a glimpse into life there. The two men, Sanger and Williams, exchanged work, loaned items, and Samuel compassionately retrieved the local doctor for Sanger's wife in childbirth.[28] Barn raisings, mowing hay, loaning cows, and tidbits of gossip shaped agrarian life based on barter and self-reliance. Sanger specifically noted that Samuel made shoes for his family and perhaps others and hired out his and Abijah's labor during haying season. His oldest daughter Hannah sewed clothes. Life was based on the struggle to earn a living from the bounty of the land; barter and reciprocity with neighbors influenced their personal successes.[29] From other sources it is known that Samuel's family consistently hosted the local teacher as a live-in guest and showed a keen interest in the school his children attended.[30]

After a harsh winter, Samuel Williams died at 47 years old and was buried in Dublin in 1799. The words "Life is a span, a fleeting hour, how soon the vapour flies, Man is a tender, transient flower, that in the blooming dies," adorn his tombstone. Samuel's probate record gives his wife's first name as Louise or Louisa, but as she signed the proceedings with an X, few details of her life remain in the historic record; her maiden name unknown. She is listed as head of a household of six children in the 1800 census.[31]

New England enjoyed a literate population throughout the eighteenth and nineteenth centuries, with male literacy at about 85 percent and female literacy at 60 percent in 1760. New Hampshire city newspapers totaled ten by 1800.[32] Therefore, the fact that Albert's great-grandparents, Samuel and Louise Williams, were not literate, as evidenced by their X signatures on legal documents, points to lower socio-economic backgrounds for both. This lack of educational attainment would influence their priorities, as well as the lives of their descendants.

Several of Samuel Williams' children married into the neighboring Thomas White family, causing a large exodus when the majority of White and Williams families left Dublin sometime around 1808 for Cornish. Samuel's son Stephen Williams, Sr. [1782-1859], Albert's grandfather, became a county sheriff for fifteen years, and a stagecoach driver who died on his farm in Sullivan County in 1859 at 77 years old. Stephen Williams, Sr., and his wife Betsey White Williams [1781-1860] had eight children.[33]

Stephen Williams, Jr. [1812-1904], Albert's father, seemed to have been closest to his younger brother George [1823-1902], over other fraternal ties, perhaps because both worked in the gun manufacturing industry. George, who preferred to use his middle name Philander, married his first cousin Caroline White [1826-1909] and they lived much of their lives in Windsor, VT, across the river from Cornish, in New England's beautiful Connecticut Valley. As gunsmiths and machinists, both Stephen and Philander made significant contributions to American history and to Albert's letter collection.

This Connecticut Valley was home to the high-tech industry of the age: arms manufacturing and the development of machine tools. It was in these small factories that America enjoyed the beginnings of the Industrial Revolution. During the thirty years before the Civil War, twenty important arms manufacturing plants were established in the Valley and five in other parts of New England, some of which employed both Stephen and Philander.[34] The business of small arms manufacturing, insignificant to American industry as a whole, played a vital role in the development of machine tools and the precision measurement that made the tools possible.[35] The machine tool industry provided for the manufacture of machines that could create interchangeable parts with precision, and led the world in technological advancements in manufacturing that would eventually be recognized as the American system of manufacturing; a system of mass production.

The Windsor Armory, Windsor VT, in the 1860s. *Courtesy of American Precision Museum; Windsor VT*

The first machine tools were those that could manufacture identical, interchangeable parts for guns on a rapid, precision basis that significantly reduced the need for gunsmiths. These early machines could facilitate the creation of parts that far surpassed the handwork methods. Tended by a machinist, a table held a part to be cut that was mechanically fed into a multiple-toothed rotary cutter. The precision made the part interchangeable with others produced in the same manner.[36] Over time, machines proceeded along lines of refinement and machine tools became better able to reduce tolerances among parts.[37] The use of machine tools spread, becoming foundational for America's growth as a manufacturing powerhouse in the 19th century. Machine tools, factory organization, and the development of interchangeable parts resulted in the production of quality goods in abundance.[38] Modern Americans are surrounded by products essential to our daily lives that can be traced back to the innovations created by these antebellum machinists, and the subsequent spread of this technology.[39]

Arms making remained among the most highly skilled occupations in American industry at the time.[40] In making either rifles or revolvers, brothers Stephen and Philander would have stood at a similar lathe, in a hot and sweaty machine shop with other men their age. Wages were often paid according to piecework, and through time, skills became specialized.[41] As members of this industrial fervor, the two men were the coveted, well-paid, machinists of their day. One of their employment locations, the armory in Windsor, Vermont, established in 1843,[42] employed 100 men by 1851. A visiting Canadian charmingly found the young workmen "exceedingly ingenious and worked admirably." They manufactured rifles, manning machinery for planing, turning, drilling, and for constructing gun locks and stocks. "They were dressed with as much propriety as if they had been clerks in a dry goods store, and all that distinguished them as mechanics was the blouse or apron which they wore while at work." The Canadian was struck with the dignity of the New England laborer.[43] Stephen and Philander's many years in "the shop" argue for the probability that they worked on the manufacturer of guns, and as machinists, worked on the machine tools that produced interchangeable parts. Lathes, profiling and milling machines would have been at the heart of the Windsor tool manufacturing component of the location there.[44]

Work in factories provided a good living wage, but a contemporary from nearby Newport, New Hampshire was quick to report the harsh downside of factory work to his journal in 1847:

> This morning the direful peals of that factory bell were heard by me the first of anything. What a rich life it must be, to be constantly under the control of a bell, by the sound of whose chimes you must live, must get up by it, go to work by it, go to breakfast by it, go to dinner by it, go back to work by it, go to tea by it, go to work once more by it, leave off by it and go to bed by it. Lucas P. Bean used to call factories 'dens of misery' and the operative 'slaves.' Whether his expressions were too strong it matters not, some things are certain, that factories are unhealthy places; that their operatives are almost invariable rather ignorant; that they are subservient to the proprietors, being obliged in three-fourths of the establishments in New England to vote Whig ticket or be discharged.[45]

Cornish was home to at least two gunsmiths during the 1850s and 60s. Gunsmith David Hall Hilliard, Stephen's boss, celebrated the beginning shots of the Civil War with a generous gift to the government of his guns. The Hilliard weapons were known for cheap, quality rifles with an under-hammer firing mechanism. They featured a heavy telescope that would have been desirable for sharpshooters.[46] Hilliard tested every gun before it was sold and was credited as having had fifteen or fewer employees who made the unique guns. Stephen and likely his brother both worked for him in the 1850s.[47] Historians disagree on Hilliard's years of operation, but Stephen's letters shed new light on his earlier operation, as he had worked for Hilliard before 1857.[48] Stephen must be considered an expert workman in gunsmithing, although an undercurrent of discontent in his comments about Hilliard's family and business highlights issues of class identification.[49] Stephen may have felt a distinct class differentiation from the Hilliards.

Windsor, VT was the sight of the development of the machine tool industry beginning in 1829 with the National Hydraulic Company. No less than 30 related and associated notable engineering industries stemmed from Windsor's early prominence where some of the most important improvements in the mechanic arts emanated.[50] The brothers worked in gun manufacturing in Windsor, Vermont, just over the bridge from Cornish.[51] There the brothers produced guns which armed the North during the Civil War, and after the War, as verified by one of Stephen's letters, produced other machines at the plant. The Windsor machine shops were credited with directly influencing an estimated half of all weapons used by the North during the Civil War.[52] They not only produced rifles, but the companies in Windsor made the precise, state-of-the-art machinery that made possible interchangeable parts weapon production by numerous other New England concerns.[53] With the advent of the Civil War, coworker William Foster commented on the conditions: "Work continues to increase… the man I work for….makes us work every minute of the time. I never worked so steady as they do in his room… They keep one month's pay back."[54]

Many arms workers were not more than semi-skilled machine tenders, but some retained the skills of gunsmiths and remained among the most highly skilled and highly paid American workmen.[55] Stephen Williams, Jr. farmed for himself and worked for a farming neighbor, Newton Jackson, for at least four years, 1859-1863, while intermittently employed at the "shop". Based on this letter collection, it is known that Stephen worked for the Hilliard gun manufacturer, then Newton Jackson, and then in Windsor from November, 1862 until 1872.[56] Stephen's December 28, 1866 letter clarifies that he worked in painting at the Windsor shop and also worked on a drilling machine for stone quarries, as the manufacturing turned away from guns after the end of the Civil War.[57]

Stephen and Philander's letters to Albert are sprinkled with tidbits about the gun manufacturing industry of New England that began in the early 1800s and peaked locally with the Windsor armory. The history of gun manufacturing in Windsor is complex with a number of partnerships, buyouts, and changes in direction. In Windsor, N. Kendall and Company was the first of several small custom gun shops that are now celebrated in the American Precision Museum in original factory buildings built in 1846.[58] In 1843, Kendall had merged with Richard S. Lawrence producing guns that would be used in the Mexican American War. Kendall sold out in 1849 leaving Robbins and Lawrence in a partnership which spanned the transition in gun manufacturing from the older, moderate-sized plants which relied heavily on government contracts, and the newer moves to other products.[59] The Windsor Armory won a government contract in 1846 for 10,000 rifles, followed by a 15,000 gun contract.[60] Some of those guns found their way to the California gold fields, others to the Union ranks.[61] In all of their gun work, Robbins and Lawrence used the interchangeable parts system which greatly added to its use and development throughout the country.[62]

During the 1850s, the breech-loader Sharps carbine became one of the notable guns produced in Windsor and valued in the Civil War by sharpshooters.[63] After the War, the federal cavalry was armed exclusively with Sharps carbines.[64] Other contracts included a lucrative English rifle contract which ultimately overextended the Windsor plant and it split, allowing co-owner Lawrence to take the Sharps gun manufacturing to Hartford, Connecticut.[65] Remaining companies in Windsor included cotton mills, ones that created machine tools, saw mills, sewing and gun machine parts as well as specialty machinery.

Demand for guns grew through the last years of the 1850s and, not unsurprisingly, boomed during the Civil War years. Smaller gun shops began to fall away as the larger manufacturers grew to supply Westerners after the California Gold Rush, as well as addressing the generalized need for arms with new technological advancements.[66] By 1855 the Windsor armory employed 400 to 500 people.[67] In 1856, the Robbins and Lawrence company failed and the buildings sat idle for almost two years.[68] Then in late 1857, Lamson, Goodnow, and Yale purchased the building and reopened.[69] Philander's May 9, 1857 letter from Cornish says he is in the shop and it needs a new contract to continue, while his September 6, 1857 letter confirms the armory was not in operation, but "they think it will start soon."[70]

Philander Williams worked in three different locations, at a minimum: First in an unidentified shop, second in Windsor, VT, from 1857 onward, and for a short time in 1861 at Hartford, CT. Two of Philander's letters are dated in 1857 and he mentions employment in the shop and also frets about possible sales and buyouts of the business. One of Philander's letters dated June 1861 directs Albert to write to his Uncle in Hartford, Connecticut where he went to work on guns, noting that gun work was all that was available at the time. Hartford had two gun manufacturing centers at that time, the Sharps manufacturing company that had recently left Windsor, VT and the Colt Patent Firearms Manufacturing Company. The Sharps company started in Windsor, under Robbins and Lawrence, moving to Hartford, Ct. in 1855. The Windsor Armory workmen made all parts of rifles for a federal government contract, except the barrels which were made in Hartford, according to the local newspaper.[71] The Sharps company at Hartford, which likely employed

Philander in 1861, employed about 450 men during the Civil War and produced about 30,000 rifles annually, until its demise in 1871.[72] His employment in Hartford, Connecticut probably didn't last long, as by 1863 he was back home working at the local armory in Windsor. This armory employed 400 to 500 men including Philander and Stephen operating throughout the day and night during the Civil War.[73]

A Vermont draft listing of 1863 substantiates Philander's employment by the Windsor armory.[74] Of the 83 men listed for Windsor, 29 were employed by the armory, making it, by far, the largest employer in the town.[75] That employment did not necessarily keep men from being drafted for service during the war, but there are no records indicating Philander or Stephen served in the military. After the Civil War, the armory shifted to small arms production, as well as sewing machines, needles, saw milling equipment, drills, mining machinery and gun machine tools.[76]

The Williams brothers were probably well paid, as one historian estimated that the monthly average salary for small arms workers in 1860 in Connecticut was $37.50, or almost $9,700. in 2023 dollars, well above that of other industrial workers.[77] The Windsor armory maintained exacting standards,[78] leading to the conclusion that both Stephen and Philander attained elevated skill levels in arms production. Stephen's work in the Windsor armory no doubt funded his loans of significant sums of money to Albert for his purchase of Iowa farmland.

Scholars have noted the importance of the machinist in antebellum America, not only for supplying the Northern forces with guns, but for the spread of ideas and techniques that contributed to the machine tool industry that facilitated interchangeable parts, and eventually mass production.[79] And, although limited knowledge of the tasks and employment situations that Stephen and his brother Philander encountered is known, it can be assumed that their roles helped produce the guns, or the machines that made interchangeable parts for guns, that brought the North victory in the Civil War.[80] Albert's Uncle Philander and wife Caroline figured importantly in the family as they took care of Francis, Albert's youngest sister, for a time, and noted her loss when she moved away. Perhaps Albert had also lived with Philander and Caroline, subsequent to his parents' separation and divorce. Their only child, daughter Ella, was born in 1858 in Windsor.

Hall Family

There are myriad speculations for the origin of the surname Hall, which variously credit Vikings, salt miners and manor house architecture, among others. Whatever the many notions, it was among the most common surnames in England and subsequently Puritan America.[81] More than 40 Halls left England for America prior to 1650 during the Puritan Migration.[82]

The classic 1883 *Halls of New England* follows the family from its immigrant ancestor, Edward Hall, through to Albert's mother, Melinda, born October 13, 1817, the youngest of eleven children of Darius [1772-1850] and Betsey or Betty (Brown) Hall [1771-1844] of Croydon, NH.[83] Melinda's great-great-great-grandfather, the immigrant Edward Hall [1611-1670], appears in Massachusetts records as early as 1636 as a freeman. He lived in Rehoboth, where upon his death in 1670, his estate was valued at 84 pounds; roughly over three-hundred thousand dollars today.[84] Melinda [1817-1865] was descended from his youngest son Benjamin, [1668-1726].[85] Benjamin married Sarah Fisher [1668-1756] whose grandfather was also an English immigrant during the Great Puritan Migration.[86] From Benjamin, the line descends through two Edward Halls to Darius, Albert's grandfather. Both Edwards served the crown in mid to high levels and remained loyal to the King, while four of the youngest Edward's sons served in the Continental army during the Revolution.

The Revolution was significant to the family, as it sparked Edward [1727-1807] and Lydia Hall's [1730-1819] move to Croydon, NH with their ten children in tow.[87] Their youngest child, Darius, became a farmer and teamster on the road between Croydon and Boston, while supporting his own large cache of eleven children. Betsey (Brown) Hall had her first child in 1797 and her last, Albert's mother Melinda, at 46 years old giving her a life of constant and repetitive child rearing, as was typical for women of that era. At least nine of her children made it past childhood. Melinda obtained a fairly good education, as evidenced by her letters, but few stories about her survived as she died prior to the birth of

Albert's children. In contrast, her brothers Worthin and Nathan, who both pursued careers in the whaling industry shared their stories with Albert. He later captured the imaginations of his own grandsons with repeated tales of their rugged, manly pursuits in whaling.

Worthin Hall; about 1855

Mrs. Polly (Lovewell) Hall; about 1855

Mary Hall [Hubbard]. *All photos, unless otherwise identified, are courtesy of the author.*

Worthin Hall [1802-1886]

Melinda's most accomplished brother and one who figures importantly in the letters, as well as her children's and grandchildren's lives was always known as "Great Uncle Worthin," which would have been the proper terminology for Albert's son Worthin, named for the older man, and Albert's daughter Lavinia to use. A short biography in *Halls of New England* states Worthin was born in Croydon, NH July 11, 1802, making him fifteen years older than Melinda. Worthin:

> "went to sea in a whaling vessel in 1821 and followed that occupation for twenty eight years and for the last eighteen years of that time was commander of the ship; he has circumnavigated the earth twice, doubled Cape Horn six times, doubled the Cape of Good Hope six times, has killed 500 whales, and brought home 2,500 barrels of oil; he has obtained ample wealth, and has been a director of the bank of Newport, N. H. for many years; was representative of Newport 1866 and 1867; residence Newport, N. H., married Polly D. Lovewell" and had one child, Mary Elizabeth born in the Sandwich Islands, now Hawaii.[88]

The somewhat brisk history is at odds with the specific details of other sources, but a plethora of information exists related to the whaling industry in America, making it relatively easy to follow Worthin's adventures and successes as a whaling captain between 1837 and 1855 when he retired. Whaling provided Worthin wealth, and the chance at an early retirement from the sea with a subsequent shift to a career in banking, while he dabbled in politics.[89] Worthin served as state legislator from Sullivan County; an accomplished citizen who was credited with being "an earnest worker for public good."[90] He eventually purchased a second home in Grinnell, Iowa, presumably using it for extended vacations.

Stories of Worthin's successes are substantiated by his estimated worth in the 1870 federal census which would translate to over eight million dollars in 2023, a hefty sum. His wife, Polly (Lovewell) Hall [1806-1886] is mentioned in Albert's letter collection, and it appears that Albert's youngest sister Francis, only two years younger than their only daughter Mary [1849-1886], lived with the Worthin Hall's for a few months in 1861. At ten years old, they spirited Francis away to Iowa where she remained for the balance of her life.[91]

Albert's grandsons were captivated by the essence of Worthin's life, retelling tidbits of whaling adventures, as his rags-to-riches stories had been told to them by their grandfather. At 5' 10" with a light complexion and sandy hair, the earliest crew list available places Worthin in the crew of the *Falcon* in 1830. He continued for two voyages on the *Reaper,* working his way up through the ranks to eventually become a first mate on his 1835-36 voyage. These early voyages were ones in which Hall doubled the Cape of Good Hope, Africa, on voyages to the Indian Ocean. Extremely successful as first mate of the *Reaper*, he then mastered his own vessel, the *Izette,* for the first time in 1837, immediately after his marriage to Polly Lovewell.[92]

Whaling was a leading industry in the antebellum United States, driven by the need for many products obtained from whales. Whalers preferred to hunt sperm whale, which was considered the finest, although all other types were harvested. Whale oil, taken from boiling down the blubber, was used in lamps as a fuel, lubrication, and for making soap and candles. Spermaceti and ambergris, a substance found in the whale's intestines, were used in perfumes, candle making, ointments, cosmetics, and aphrodisiacs. Whale bone was transformed to women's corsets, umbrellas, buggy whips, yarn swifts, brushes, fertilizer, and other products.

Worthin Hall appears to have been of the middling world of whaling captains, disciplined, talented in managerial nuances, and lucky. Investing in whaling ships, as well as captaining them, allowed him to retire at 53 years old. The whale ship was a self-contained system, a "total institution" with the captain the master of the ship, credited with both the working conditions – good and bad – and the overall success of the voyage in monetary terms. Whalemen were condemned to cruise aimlessly, in a monotonous routine with little to do, until a whale was spotted. Men "before the mast" had little in rights and privileges, but it was America's first global industry. A very specific and peculiar institution, it maintained a finite beginning and end in American history.[93]

In 1847, the *Whalemen's Shipping List* newspaper published a long article that included observations about whaling masters. Whaleships were owned by "prudent and sagacious merchants" who had under investment between 20,000 and 50,000 dollars. Trips of two to four years or more were common as the ship visited distant ports and had to procure goods in remote and "savage" places. "What kind of a man would owners of common prudence and common sense be likely to select in whom to place so great a trust?" the paper opined. "They would select a man of sterling integrity, of nautical skill, of knowledge of that peculiar business, character and information to conduct such a voyage, to negotiate for supplies, and manage the important affairs of the ship at sea and on shore, and of such manners, habits, and character as to qualify him rightly to govern the crew, upon whose physical efforts and hearty good will depends the success of the enterprise." The paper acknowledged some "disgraceful exceptions" to the rule existed but surmised that most whaling captains were of the type they described. Masters had almost unlimited power on the vessel, only delegating some to the mates of the ship.[94]

Worthin captained ships during the apogee of American whaling. In 1846, more than 600 vessels sailed from New England ports; among them 400 from New Bedford. The industry's most profitable year was 1853.[95] Successes in whaling fueled an underlying belief in Manifest Destiny and in the settlement of the American west. New Englanders knew about the West from whalers and increasing interest in the Pacific Coast and the potential for trade with Asian countries became foundational for commercial access to the Pacific world.[96] Additionally, a high level of ethnic diversity within Worthin's whaling crews argues for the industry to have aided not only western interest and settlement, but the diverse nature and vitality of the region. Crew lists from 1848 found two men from England working alongside eight native Hawaiians and six Americans. Other crew lists identify men with black eyes and wooly hair, African Americans, as well as sailors with origins in Havana, Cuba and Dublin, Ireland.[97] Relationships more closely resembling equality were found on board whale ships, as whaling provided a rare measure of dignity to diverse sailors. Men knew their shipmates as individuals, largely judged on skills and abilities. The mutual cooperation needed for survival eclipsed prejudices.[98] An entire shipload of Worthin Hall's sailors deserted in San Francisco due to Gold Rush reports, and family lore also placed Nathan Hall among the early mining frenzy there.[99] Worthin's voyages lasted longer as time went by, as the supply of whales depreciated over time. The loss of whales and the discovery of fossil fuels – oil – in 1859 ultimately led to the end of commercial whale fishing.[100] Thus Worthin's career paid witness to and contributed to major changes in the country's history.

Mrs. Polly Hall also made contributions to American history through her role as whaling wife, but to fully understand her input takes a finer degree of detail. Whaling became a family venture for the Halls when Worthin included several family members on voyages. Worthin captained his first two trips without Polly on the *Izette*.[101] Polly Hall and Worthin's younger brother Nathan both sailed with him on the last three voyages he captained, as did nephew John Hall [1827-1855]: *Elizabeth*, (17 December 1844 to 15 May 1848), *Majestic* (1 November 1848 to 25 April 1851*)*, and *Natchez* (5 October 1851 to 22 April 1855). Logs for these voyages provide tidbits on Mrs. Hall's life and document Nathan moving up from green hand to boatsteerer, to first mate over the course of the three voyages.[102]

The captain's privilege in bringing his wife on voyages increased during the 1840s. There is a gap of time of roughly two- and one-half years from the return of the last voyage of the *Izette* in June, 1842 and the sailing of the *Elizabeth* in December 1844, which may mean that Worthin gave up on the whaling life because of Polly. Perhaps they settled on the idea of her accompanying him; a compromise.[103] Although no diary or journal of Polly's exists, it can be postulated that Polly's motivations included preserving domestic ties, following a sense of duty inherent in women's roles, the importance of companionship in marriage, and also expedience. A somewhat controversial practice was tolerated with reluctance, as the price to pay for a good captain. Whaling wives' lives mediated and maintained their husband's family and community identities, and studying American whaling provides a "compelling portrayal of the complexities, contradictions, pervasiveness, and significance of gender in Nineteenth-century America," according to one historian.[104] Women in the 19th century were supposed to be "demure, peaceable, poetic and pious…keep the home fires burning, … look after parents… farm and children, …. Budget and pay the bills and wait in dutiful patience for the lord and master to return."[105] Evidently, Polly lived a paradox; a Victorian women thrust into a life that required feminist skills. The distant location from America and the inherent challenges of being a whaling captain's wife served to isolate, reinforce, and magnify the need for independent thinking and skills.[106] Contemporary estimates placed one in six of all whaling captains as having been accompanied by their wives by 1853,[107] making Polly somewhat unusual.[108]

Credited with sailing on her husband's ships for ten years, Mrs. Hall likely chose, or was coerced by Worthin, to stay with the Hawaiian missionaries for extended periods of time.[109] Something of a trail blazer, Polly first set sail with Worthin in December 1844 on the *Elizabeth*,[110] while her second trip on the *Majestic* was significant for the birth of Mary, the couple's only child to have survived. Polly reportedly had "5 or 6 children" before Mary, a surprising number that may have included miscarriages.[111] Worthin dropped Polly off at Lahaina, Maui with the missionary Dwight Baldwin's [1798-1886] family and set sail for the whaling waters of the Arctic; Mary was born the next day, April 23, 1849. Worthin didn't know about his daughter's birth until June of that year when Captain Bartlett of the *Orozimbo* brought the news to him while sailing the Bering Sea.[112]

Mrs. Hall is not reported as having survived many harrowing circumstances, but she did witness her three-year-old Mary fall overboard, as her husband jumped in to save her and nearly drowned himself. It was a story frequently repeated. One historian wrote:

> While at sea, a most thrilling incident occurred: Mary, his darling and only daughter, while at play, fell overboard and in a moment would be swallowed up by the angry waves. In an instant, forgetting all personal danger, he plunged into the ocean after her. Bouyed up by her clothes, she rode upon the waves like a little fairy, and as her father approached, she raised her hands and imploringly toward him, exclaiming, "Father I am overboard!" And now who shall depict the terrible frenzy of that wife and mother as she sees them both sinking into a watery grave! She knew her husband was unaccustomed to swim; the ship under full headway, was fast leaving them behind; to her anxious heart it seemed the boat would never lower, and she felt that both must be lost. Twice they had already gone down. Once more, they shall never rise to bless her on earth. It is the last time. "Oh, my god! They are sinking!" Rushing forward with both arms extended as though she would fly to their relief, she exclaimed in the wildest despair, "They are lost! They are lost!" Overcome by her emotions she sank down in unconsciousness. As a good providence would have it, both were rescued alive. Nothing can be more touching than the pitying moan of that daughter, as she clung to the bedside of her father during the hours of her slow recovery from the death-grapple of the ocean.[113]

Logs of the *Natchez* provide less flamboyant memories of the events, as Nathan Hall's log notes that Worthin was "nearly exhausted" when recovered. Worthin must also have told the story to his nephew Albert with the caveat that he was dressed in his slippers, which were lost to the sea.

A partial log of the *Elizabeth*, kept by 20-year-old sailor John Melzard, provides a brief glimpse of the Halls through his contemporary observations. On September 15, 1845, off the coast of Baja California, a "boat took the Captain and his wife who rambled about on the shore while the boats were off fishing," making Mrs. Hall one of the first, if not THE first, whaling wife to walk the beaches of Baja California. The sailor resented the Captain and wife enjoying the beach and not actually working while the sailors were busily employed.[114] By November 2nd, the disgruntled sailor saw Mrs. Hall as a privileged and perhaps unnecessary member of the group. The *Elizabeth* landed on one of the islands off the Bay of Panama and Captain and hands found a Spanish house there inhabited by a woman. "The Captain's wife [Mrs. Polly Hall] paid a visit to the woman of the island and bestowed some of her New Hampshire politeness on her by shining up a log with notches cut in it to the house where she sat down on the only chair the house afforded which consisted of a dirty old hammock which serves for both chair, table, and bed."[115] He previously noted the island was a great place for whalers to stop when the captain didn't want to lose hands through desertion; much more likely if a ship docked in a coastal city's port where the sailors would have found many more opportunities for escape than those presented on an island.[116] Sailor Melzard's portion of the log ends within a few days, and by December Captain Hall reported the loss of six crew members and a whale boat. Melzard and five others had deserted to the island of Gorgona, seventeen miles off the coast of what is now Columbia.

Whalers figured prominently in the life of the missionaries on the Sandwich Islands, and conversely, the missionaries made life more bearable for the whaling crews. Doctor Dwight Baldwin, of Lahaina, Maui, spent a long and important mission to the Hawaiian Islands where Mrs. Hall and Mary stayed several seasons. There are numerous letters from the Baldwin family collection that provide context to the Halls' life.[117] Indeed, Mrs. Hall may have actually spent little time on board ship after the birth of Mary.[118] The history of the missionary efforts on the Hawaiian islands have been told in many other places.[119] Both whalemen and missionaries shared a common culture shaped by a common language, country, religion, and ethical beliefs. The two groups shared common disrespect for heathen or what they considered immoral pagan lifestyles.[120] Friendships developed between whalers who could take letters and transport missionaries from port to port in Hawaii, and the missionaries who provided supplies and sanctuary for the whaling crew. Whalers provided a constant market for products grown on Maui including hogs, goats, bananas, melons, ducks, fowl, beef, pumpkins, squash, onions, sweet potatoes, turkeys, and Irish potatoes, some of which were traded for whale oil, an important fuel.[121] By 1852, the visiting whalers were getting to be too intrusive, as missionary Baldwin reported that they had about 50 ships at Lahaina and many whaling Captains had wives and children with them: "Scarce a day but some of these families are with us."[122]

Mrs. Hall and Mary also stayed with Hawaiian missionaries, at Waimea, Kauai, which had a bay preferred by sailing captains, and, as the residence of the native Hawaiian king and chief of the island, attained supremacy as a better spot for obtaining supplies.[123] Waimea became the official port of entry for Kauai until about 1855, and the nucleus for the mission settlements on that island.[124] The Whitneys were the first missionaries there, soon followed by others.

George Berkeley Rowell [1815-1884], born in Cornish, NH was ordained as a Congregational minister in 1841, following his father's career path. Rowell married Malvina Jerusha Chapin [1816-1901] of Newport, NH.; both towns within the southwestern area of New Hampshire where the Halls lived substantial portions of their lives. Malvina extended an invitation to Mrs. Hall to stay with them as they shared a common friend.[125] The Rowell family was assigned to live in a house begun in 1829 originally for the Peter Gulick missionary family, currently under restoration as the Hale Puna house, one of the oldest in Hawaii.[126] Polly and Mary Hall stayed in that home with the Rowells from April 30, to September 4, 1850, then again from April to November, 1852.

Missionary George Rowell was delighted to welcome Mrs. Hall to his home in 1850 in a letter to Dwight Baldwin that preceded the birth of his son by only thirteen days.[127] On April 30, 1850, George Rowell again wrote to Dwight Baldwin: "Mrs. Rowell was confined four days ago with a son. Mother and babe are doing well... The ship *Majestic* is in the offing and Mrs. Hall is probably on the beach by this time or will be in a few minutes. She will be at our house soon. We are glad she has come and expect to enjoy her visit much, though we have never seen her as yet… I cannot wait for Mrs. Hall's arrival before I close this." Unquestionably, Polly would be a help to the newborn baby and recuperating mother.[128] Mrs. Malvina Rowell wrote in 1850 that: "Mrs. Hall left me on the 4th of Sept. on her return to Lahaina. I miss her company and lively little Mary, too."[129] Again in 1852, Mrs. Hall was greeted with the task of caring for the Rowell's newborn and Mrs. Rowell, herself, who was bedridden for four months after the birth of Ellen on March 1, 1852.[130]

Mrs. Mercy Whitney [1795-1872], lived on missionary row in Waimea in the 1850s, and kept detailed journals and letters that captured life on the island of Kauai. Mercy Whitney was among the first New England settlers who landed on April 4, 1820 and she mothered the first non-native baby born on the Hawaiian islands.[131] Befriending Mrs. Hall, on August 10, 1852, Mrs. Whitney recorded in her journal that "Mrs. Hall is desirous of visiting Waioli, as she is acquainted with some of Mrs. J's [Johnson's] friends in the States, and she promised Mrs. J's mother that she would try to visit her daughter if practicable, before she returned home. She is not accustomed to journeying on horseback but intends to go over there if able to ride so far, before he [Worthin] comes back again to Waimea."[132] Mrs. Hall could have employed nontraditional means, horseback riding, to achieve traditional ends, visiting with the Johnsons, but eventually choose not to try the ride with her three-year-old Mary in tow.

Religion incurred obligation to others, as Mrs. Hall imposed on her husband to facilitate her visit with missionary wife Mrs. Johnson. "Mrs. J" was Lois Hoyt Johnson [1809-1891], of Warner, New Hampshire, wife of missionary Edward Johnson and mother to his seven children. For fifty years beginning in 1837, they were located at Waioli, Kauai, the missionary outpost furthest north on Kauai island.[133] The Waioli mission was reached by landing at Hanalei Bay, considered to be a dangerous harbor and only visited by an occasional whaler.[134] Only two whalers attempted the challenging bay in 1845.[135] Nonetheless, Captain Hall picked up his wife and child at Waimea, Kauai, and made the stop in Hanalei harbor where he, Mrs. Hall and Mary stayed the night at Waioli, and visited with the Johnsons.[136] Perhaps Mrs. Hall was bringing information about Mrs. Johnson's mother who passed away in March, 1855, only a few months before the return of the *Natchez* to New England. Clearly, Polly Hall was deeply devoted to family, and felt her role as a conduit of information between Lois Johnson and her mother was more important than the loss of whaling time and inconvenience of the unplanned stop in Waioli. Her priorities took preference over her husband's, in this instance.

Polly's conspicuous kindness and aptitude in caring for the needs of the missionary wives was appreciated. Mercy Whitney noted: "I think we shall miss them very much having so little foreign Soc. [society] here. Mrs. H [Polly Hall] has been a great comfort to us all, particularly in the care she has taken of Sister R. [Rowell], and the babe, relieving me of a great burden. I felt when she first arrived, that the Lord had sent her as it was not her intention to stop at the island, but her H. [husband] thought he had better leave her, contrary to her expectations. The Lord go with and bless them all, is my sincere prayer."[137] A few days later Mrs. Whitney received mail addressed to Mrs. Hall. She opened and read Mrs. Hall's mail, the pamphlet "Advocate for Moral Reform."[138]

Mrs. Hall, returned to Maui where she boarded with another whaling captain's wife and assisted the Baldwin family.[139] Mrs. Charlotte Fowler Baldwin [1805-1873] attended the annual missionary general meeting held in Honolulu that Spring leaving Mrs. Polly Hall "to superintend housekeeping" of the Baldwin's home and mission at Lahaina for four to six weeks.[140] Polly Hall's letter to the Baldwin's at Honolulu is the only known example of her writing. On May 27, 1854, she wrote:

> Dear Mr. and Mrs. Baldwin
>
> We have this moment received your letter and hasten to answer it as there is a vessel going tonight, the first opportunity we have had except by the Marcia. Charles [the Baldwin's son] arrived Tuesday night about eleven o'clock. He seems quite well and much grown since I saw him last. He brought me news that my brother was in Honolulu. I wrote him immediately but probably the letter will go down with this, as doubtless it has been lying at the Post Office. We are getting along very well indeed. Do not give yourself any uneasiness about us. We have enough to eat and drink and things go on very pleasantly. Charles tells me he has written you. I was very glad to hear you were getting along well over your seasickness. Am much obliged for your trouble about the edgeings, and much pleased with them. With best regards from all we remain yours etc.
>
> Mrs. Hall and Louisa Woodbridge[141]

The *Natchez* was back in Lahaina, November 29, 1854 when the Hall family spent the Sabbath with the Baldwins.[142] Mrs. Hall had been there since June, occupying "her old house there," but this was to be the Hall's final visit with the Baldwins.[143] Mrs. Baldwin noted in a letter to her daughter Abigail, then at school in New England, that she hoped her daughter might want to visit with the Halls upon their return home.[144] Without doubt, Charlotte Baldwin and Polly Hall had forged a friendship and established a trusted relationship, helping to cement the ties between the whaling businessmen and the missionaries. Prior to leaving, Polly organized a tour of the *Natchez* ship for the Baldwin children, who were delighted to visit one of the whaling ships at anchor outside their home.[145] Mrs. Hall may be the best example yet known, of a woman who extended the community ties of New England with the Hawaiian missionaries through her role as a whaling captain's wife. She strengthened family and societal ties by living with the missionary families, helping out with tasks including child rearing, and bringing comforting news to those separated from family members by thousands of miles; all duties reinforced by their common Congregational religion, and a society that valued women's domestic role.[146] In the 19th century the spirit of capitalism was not divested of its religious motivations,[147] thus whaling wives provided a compassionate mediated intercession between both worlds.

It can ultimately be concluded that Polly's plucky attitude in sailing with her husband gave her an elevated level of respect within the family. Albert Williams's youngest sister Francis was sent to live with Mrs. Hall in 1861, and Francis' uncle Philander Williams, in one of the following letters, maintained it was for the better. It seems odd to modern readers that the family would not have believed that Francis should have been placed with her mother, not with an Uncle and Aunt, but men were given the right to their children after divorce, at this time, and Francis had been living with her father.[148] Perhaps the Worthin Hall's wealth and the possibility that they truly shared a strong loving relationship provided for stability that was factored into the decision. Polly had demonstrated proper homemaking and domesticity, as the Victorian world of the mid-1800s would have judged it. A fitting embodiment of the Victorian woman, Polly maintained a proper home on a whaling ship, a challenging location, but crucial to the success of the business her husband followed. Polly may have seen her primary duty to ensure domestic tranquility as homemaker, unchanged while at home in New England, while a visitor to the Hawaiian Islands, or as a partner at sea.[149] Her moral and family obligation was to make life easier and better for her husband, child, and all others with whom she came in contact. Polly had behaved in a respectable manner consistent with the Victorian view of women's behavior and spheres of influence.

Albert's mother Melinda, in contrast to her sister-in-law Polly Hall, was broke and unsuccessful. She had to work for a living, and she even had to turn to her brother Nathan for money for shoes.[150] Melinda was atypical for women of the 1850s, and to the citizens of that time period. Regardless of how compelling her complaints against her husband seem, Melinda would have been judged a failure; a woman who could not assiduously maintain a proper home for her husband and children, a bastion of proper morality and religious decorum.[151] Melinda's letters, moreover, tell us what was on her mind, and her relationships with people underscore her nightmares and her depression at a life she could not control.[152] Her work – that of performing domestic tasks in homes not her own – reinforced her loss. To some degree, Melinda had lost a familiar way of life and perhaps a safe emotional space by divorcing, and in so doing had lost the source of stability that having a home previously provided.[153] She saved herself through divorce, but she was excruciatingly aware of the painful reverberations that weighed upon her children for her decision. She saved herself, but her children paid the price.

Both Worthin and Nathan Hall retired from whaling in 1855. Nathan was no doubt traumatized by the early death of his only son James who accidentally shot himself while cleaning a gun, while Nathan was away at sea. Nathan moved to Williamstown, Vermont to pursue subsistence farming near his oldest brother Ariel, paying for the farm with his whaling earnings.[154] Ostensibly, Worthin left whaling because of the longing for a stable life with his wife and child. In the midst of the meticulous recordings of weather and navigation Worthin kept in his *Natchez* log, he uncharacteristically lamented: "Oh my dear wife, how I want to see you and the babe. What a fool a man must be to go and leave a wife and daughter for the sake of money that he cannot live a short time to enjoy at the most, but man will be fool enough to die a thousand times whilst alive just to try to get something to live upon. Just as he is a going to die but never mind my Dear somebody will be glad to have it and if they will wait patiently a short time they may have it so good by my dear wife and sweet little daughter."[155]

The Halls returned home to New Hampshire in 1855, where Polly and her husband attended church, visited relatives, and participated in local events.[156] More importantly, in 1861 they took over the care of Francis, Albert's younger sister, whose move to Iowa they facilitated in that year. Perhaps behind the scenes, the Hall family decided to circumvent Stephen Williams, Jr.'s parental rights and carve out a place for Francis, her mother and siblings, to live far from Stephen's ability to secure his lawful rights over them. In Iowa, Francis lived with her older siblings and her mother, Melinda.

The Halls returned to Iowa when Worthin Hall was so taken with the delights of Grinnell that he purchased a second home there,[157] perhaps during his long stay in 1878.[158] Worthin apparently asked Albert to change his last name to Hall, as Worthin was anxious about the lack of young men surnamed Hall in Albert's generation, and his own lack of a male heir.[159] Albert declined. A "temperance" master who ensured a ship devoid of alcohol, Worthin's obituary emphasized his whaling success noting he had "killed more than 500 whales and brought in more than 22,000 barrels."[160]

Albert's Early Life, Move to Iowa

Albert, born November 18, 1840 into these two prominent families, the Williams and the Halls, held deep roots in southwestern New Hampshire. Values bred into Albert from both sides of the family were tempered by a turbulent childhood. His parents had married on October 30, 1836, and their oldest child Annginette Hall Williams followed the succeeding year. Albert was sandwiched between this oldest sibling and younger sister Francis.[161] Little is known of Albert's childhood prior to July 20, 1852. On that date he witnessed a horrific argument between his parents which ultimately led to their divorce. Things had been simmering before that between the two. Melinda recounted several issues causing discord: a trip she had taken with her two older brothers bothered Stephen, an incident occurred in which she thought he had poisoned her tea, and her extended illness after the birth of Francis exacerbated their tensions.

They were living on their mortgaged farm in Newport, NH on that eventful day in July 1852 when the couple permanently separated. A small town of 2,020 people in 1850, Newport was situated in Sullivan County with less than 20,000 people in that year.[162] Melinda charged that she had been faithful to her marriage vows, but Stephen, as of January 1, 1848, had not. His harsh and cruel behavior between 1848 and 1852 had endangered her reason and injured her health, she avowed. On the day of their separation, he "willfully" and cruelly assaulted her, damaging her nose and locking her out, excluding her from his house, and refusing to allow her to return. Stephen and little Albert were playing with a gold coin when Melinda snatched the coin from Albert, as Stephen re-counted to a witness. Melinda testified that Albert had been present at an argument she and Stephen had which centered on a gold coin from California. Stephen used foul language, called her a whore, wished her dead, violently wrung her nose causing bruises, and accused her of entertaining other men. He told her he did not want to see her face again unless it was in her coffin. She left Albert with his father and went to live with her brother Ariel, taking Francis with her. When she subsequently returned for her clothes, Stephen was gone, and Albert had been locked out of the house by his father. She could not enter either as everything had been locked and closed against entry.[163] Later testimony alleged Stephen spit tobacco juice in her face and poisoned her tea, possibly with tobacco.[164]

New Hampshire passed statutes in the 1790s recognizing adultery, desertion, and cruelty, as well as other issues, as grounds for divorce.[165] Presumably, Melinda's charges fell within the accepted justifications for divorce; Stephen endangered her health and well-being. Somewhat uncommon, by 1860, only 1.2 out of 1,000 American marriages ended in divorce, signaling an upward trajectory in frequency that continued into the twentieth century.[166] Assuming that Melinda honestly felt her very life was threatened by Stephen, her action for divorce engenders compassion.

After separation, Melinda was forced to go to work to support herself, and she filed for divorce after three years, proudly avowing that she supported herself with her own labor. Depositions in the case supported Stephen's "cruelty and insults towards Mrs. Williams" as reported by a witness, Paul Wheeler. He quoted Stephen as calling his wife "a damned whore" and expected her to chase other men. Additionally, Stephen forbade Mr. Wheeler from trusting Melinda or providing credit because Stephen would refuse to pay for things she purchased at Wheeler's store.[167]

Albert was probably bound out from 1852 at about 11 ½ years old while also living intermittently with his father. In terms of labor, binding out fell on a continuum somewhere between slavery and being a hired hand.[168] The system was traumatic for the children involved.[169] Albert recalled eating scraps from the table of his hosts that led to food insecurity. Presumably he was not allowed to eat at the table at the same time as the host family, solidifying his lower status and lesser relationship to the host family.[170] His schooling was inconsistent. Overall, he was not treated as a full member of the host families.[171] It can be deduced from the letter collection that Albert lived with a minimum of two different families when bound out.

Albert's youngest sister Francis lived with uncles and aunts, residents who were not blood relations, as well as possibly being bound out with Albert. The 1860 census placed nine-year-old Francis Williams, in the home of John, a blacksmith, 61 years of age, and Lucy (Robinson) Fellows, 62 years old. They have no children in the census and accepting Francis into their home meant that she would be expected to cook, clean, wash, and otherwise help them with the trials of old age, as the 60s would have constituted an advanced age at that time.[172] Even without her mother's

Stephen Williams Jr.

Melinda (Hall) Williams

consistent presence, Francis learned the skills expected of a woman living at her time; domestic duties, care of others, as well as hay braiding, raising birds, and woodworking, as noted in one letter, all while paying particular attention to her schoolwork. Francis epitomized the cultural expectations of a young woman of nineteenth-century America, and her life's challenges expand our understanding of the richness of childhood experiences at that time.[173] Everything recorded in the letters about Francis' behavior relates to her work, rather than play, and the trauma of separation from her parents.[174] Francis, placed with the Worthin Hall family, eventually settled in Iowa in May 1861. She became one of the first students in Chester township, as a member of the 1862 class.[175] One poignant letter from Stephen to his daughter Francis after her move to Iowa reinforces the depth of separation engendered by the divorce. Its presence in Albert's letter collection raises questions as to why the letter was not received by Francis; possibly rejected by her to languish with her brother's stash?

Immediately following the celebration of his 16th birthday, Albert left the community of southwestern New Hampshire to follow his oldest sister Annginette [1837-1916] and her husband Luke Newton Sherman [1828-1889] to Iowa. A state since roughly ten years before Albert's journey westward, Iowa experienced its earliest settlements in 1833 and separated from Wisconsin territory in 1838. Iowa was considered part of the New West created from the Louisiana Purchase; by 1851 enjoying 50 counties.[176] Albert and his relatives settled in Iowa only through their connections to the Sherman family, the first permanent settlers of what became Chester Township, Poweshiek County.

William Sherman purchased land in Iowa in 1854,[177] hiring a local Grinnell man to plow the prairie and plant the first ten acres under cultivation in what would become Chester township, and also build the first habitation there.[178] William Sherman's sons, Luke and Jason Sherman, explored California during the Gold Rush, then settled in Iowa in 1855.[179] Jason W. Sherman, credited as the first settler in Chester township, Poweshiek County in September of 1856 by a standard County history, actually was accompanied by his wife and brother Luke and Annginette, according to her published memories.[180] Luke had returned to marry Annginette, Albert's oldest sister, who then left Croydon, New Hampshire on the day of their wedding, January 28, 1856 to permanently settle on September 3, just north of the rising town of Grinnell.[181] Because Iowa consisted primarily of farmland, family units with women and children were a major part of settlement.[182]

In later years, Annginette cheerfully recalled the significant "discomforts" of the pioneer life. Annginette had been educated at Claremont Academy, New Hampshire, and taught school prior to her marriage. Luke and Annginette came by rail to Clinton County, where she sent one letter to Albert from Lyons, Iowa. Then they secured a team and wagon arriving September 2, 1856, in Grinnell, then a town of about 200 inhabitants.[183] The following day, they settled in a claim shanty shack, only 12 by 16 feet, built by her husband's father, William Sherman's hired man. Lacking many necessities, they first hauled water from four miles away, then utilized a spring three-quarters of a mile from the home.[184] Snakes were an ever-present danger; hauling wood and securing a cow were major accomplishments. In the rainy season they erected umbrellas over their beds for protection from a leaky roof. They bought lumber and supplies in Iowa City and eventually built a substantial home. Luke Sherman successfully raised cattle, hogs, and sheep on a farm of over 800 acres.[185]

The plains, known for cruel weather and social isolation, imposed severe hardship on all settlers. The climate would forever be inhospitable,[186] nevertheless, resourceful and energetic people recreated the worlds they had left by making new homes in Iowa. Grinnell, the closest town to the Sherman and Williams' farms, was constructed on a New England pattern, giving the plains a reminder of home in visual aspects as well as ambiance. But the town was more than just family ties, it encompassed ideas and institutions that furthered a life familiar to the settlers.[187]

In 1854, Congregational minister Josiah Bushnell Grinnell dedicated the town named for him to "abolitionism, prohibitionism [sic], Congregationalism and education."[188] He expelled people who did not share his views. The sale of town lots funded the opening of a college, and the abolitionist John Brown spoke at Grinnell's church in February 1859. Collections were taken for fugitive slaves who passed through the village on the underground railroad.[189] Many early settlers came from New England expressing abolitionist beliefs, however few were as radical as Josiah Grinnell in his views of racial equality.[190] People of religious convictions needed to improve society and alleviate suffering, as a tenet of faith, and Grinnell became known as a safe haven for runaway slaves.[191]

Annginette's positive letters to Albert, which inspired his own move to Grinnell, glossed over the hardships in favor of the great potential of such rich farming opportunities. Presumably Annginette sympathized with Luke's workload and realized early on that her husband needed farm laborers.[192] Albert, a strapping teenager long accustomed to physical labor due to being bound out, became Luke's perfect assistant. For Annginette, it was a win-win. Luke and Annginette Sherman faced a terrible winter in 1856-7 when the temperatures in Iowa dropped to minus 30 below in degrees Fahrenheit,[193] although they were ultimately financially successful. Luke and Annginette Sherman had two daughters who died in childhood and an adopted son and daughter who survived them. A proponent of education, Luke Sherman was noted as a benefactor to Grinnell College giving small donations throughout his life and ultimately leaving the college a share of his significant estate after death.[194]

Although early histories of Poweshiek County erroneously place Albert Williams in Chester township in 1862 and not before,[195] Albert left New Hampshire in late 1856 on a hazardous journey to Iowa that required him to outwit would-be robbers and walk long distances.[196] People paid more to ride inside the stagecoach, while Albert paid less as he walked in accompaniment and shouldered a pole to help the stagecoach ford streams. A ten-dollar gold piece secreted in a shoe caused blisters. When Albert arrived at his sister's place in late 1856/early 1857 he hobbled around on bandaged feet, a consequence of his long walk, before going to work for his brother-in-law Luke Newton Sherman on his farm. Albert's labor was needed on the farm as young unmarried men were at a premium in Iowa, a problem that would soon be exacerbated by the Civil War.[197]

Spring arrived late in 1857, provisions were highly priced, much trade was carried on through barter, as the fecundity of the land itself beckoned. Iowa was challenging. Hence, Albert repeatedly requested money from his parents. The year 1857 signaled a financial Panic in America and the demand for agricultural products dropped when the Crimean War ended, and foreign wheat came into the American market. Stephen's letters to his son reflect in detail the problems of the Panic; little paper money, lack of financial stability, and increased prices. Farmers in the upper Mississippi Valley, including Iowa, were especially struck hard.[198] The Panic hit Iowa farmers when relatively little rail infrastructure existed, thus before they could establish a system of regional economic distribution, and as most towns totaled less than 5,000 people the situation worsened.[199]

Stephen's comments about the lack of money, wages dropping, and high unemployment all point to the effects of the Panic of 1857 on his region. The origin of the Panic revolved around the completion of western railroads and land speculation in Eastern financial markets. Speculative securities brokers, dealing in stocks and bonds, borrowed money from Eastern banks to fund western land purchases, then subsequently filed bankruptcies when their situations changed, draining bank reserves. As the value of western lands and speculative railroad securities fell throughout the year, the worst of the economic panic occurred during September and October 1857, nationwide.[200]

Underlying the economic realities were two larger factors: a bumper crop of wheat, coupled with a drop in demand that created a surplus and drop in value for farmers, moreover, the politics of the antebellum era created uncertainty in America's future. The pro-slavery Dred-Scott decision in March of 1857 cast uncertainty over the future of the western territories. Would slavery be extended at the expense of free soil? The western areas lost their attraction to Northerners, lessening settlement and interest in western railroads.[201] Additionally, a run on New York City banks in mid-October 1857 spread to smaller cities and specie became limited.[202] Of the commercial failures derived from the Panic, from January 1857 through March 1858, New Hampshire and Vermont were the hardest hit of the New England states.[203]

Even with national economic crisis at hand, Albert began purchasing land at five dollars an acre in 1857, according to the local newspaper.[204] The letter collection contains Albert's first deed for 80 acres, purchased from his brother-in-law Luke Sherman at considerably less, slightly more than one dollar an acre. However, the recorded memories in the Grinnell Old Settlers collection do substantiate Albert's need to work for roughly two years to be able to purchase the land. He quickly built his own one-room structure with wooden pegs instead of wasting precious dollars on metal nails.[205]

Through constant work in various pursuits, Albert was able to equal his uncle Worthin's rags-to-riches success in the eyes of local friends, if not in actual wealth. The President's opening address for the Grinnell Old Settlers Association in 1900 listed Albert Williams as the first "Poor Boy in Grinnell" success story. Albert worked four years for his first 80 acres of land, then worked a fifth year for a yoke of oxen, recalled the President somewhat inaccurately. Albert earned fencing for his farm by splitting rails on shares. He added to his acreage, soon quickly covered in waving harvests and loaded fruit trees.[206] The prairie blossomed under his touch, according to one old timer.[207] As a measure of his success, in 1900 he paid 140 dollars annually in taxes.[208]

By 1859, a community of about ninety houses with a population nearing 500 people constituted the settlement of Grinnell.[209] The entire state enjoyed only 89,000 farm families in 1860, and Albert was one of only 130,000 Hawkeye men between the ages of eighteen to forty-five.[210] Town lots set aside for Grinnell University became Iowa College when that institution moved from Davenport, Iowa to Grinnell. In 1859, only one professor, Leonard F. Parker, constituted the entire faculty. He rode out of town, for at least fifteen miles, in search of students.[211] He perhaps personally recruited Albert to a short-lived college career. He attended the earliest iteration of Grinnell College, as the Grinnell Old Settlers' Association recalled, and also a short-lived Lutheran College in Albion, Iowa for at least one semester in late 1860, as a letter attests.[212]

In 1860, Albert and his mother Melinda were recorded by the Federal census taker living with his sister Annginette, her husband, and their two-year-old daughter Clara. Melinda returned home before permanently settling with Albert sometime after Francis had been brought to Iowa in 1861, and after his purchase of land and permanent house construction.[213]

Moving to the Iowa frontier in the early 1860s was not based on male coercion, nor can we picture Melinda as a reluctant participant in "starting over" so far from her New Hampshire roots. She continued her autonomous life.[214] Work may have provided self-actualization for Melinda; it was a means to prove her worth to society and to herself and counter the societal tropes of women's dependency.[215] She left a community of numerous relatives who provided her some social support, to become a source of support to her children in an unsettled environment. She worked in Grinnell as a seamstress before passing away after a protracted illness, at 47 years old, on May 12, 1865, where she was interred in the Chester township cemetery. According to her daughter Annginette, she had joined the Universalist religion.[216]

Francis continued to live with relatives, attending school in Chester township until married to Civil War veteran William M. Hays [1839-1911], in 1868 at roughly 17 years old. William was the son of John, a blacksmith, and Sarah Hays who had settled in Chester township by at least 1858. The Hays family included several siblings who had migrated from Maryland.[217] William enlisted in 1861 in the Iowa 4th cavalry as a private, later enjoying promotion to corporal and sergeant, until finally mustered out in 1865.[218] Will and Francis had four children. Francis died at 48 years due to a "tumor of stomach," in March 1899.[219] Her obituary in local papers emphasized her religious devotion. Little is known of her adult life, but the letters in this collection provide insight into Francis' childhood, exemplary of the lives of children of this era.

Albert was 20 years old in 1860, a perfect age to have also served his new state in the great conflict with the Confederacy. Although the war was never fought on Iowa's soil, about 75,000 Iowans volunteered for the Civil War. Of those, 3,500 died from battle wounds and 8,500 from disease.[220] Historians have concluded that Iowa's dedication to unionism and a desire to end slavery made their contributions to the war effort germane to the defeat of the Confederacy, as Iowa filled her commitment to supply soldiers before a draft had to be instituted.[221] Was Albert unique for not serving his new state in the Civil War? Perhaps. However, at least two contemporaries remarked on how they did not serve. Some men hired substitutes and others felt the need for farm labor took precedence over their need to participate in military service.[222] Clearly, Albert felt a need to stay on the farm he was just establishing for his mother and younger sister. Although Albert did not serve in the Civil War, the letters in this collection reflect a keen interest in the event on Albert's part.[223]

Meanwhile, life in New England continued for Albert's father Stephen Williams. Jr. whose letters repeatedly detail the prices for commodities as the 1857 Panic and the Civil War brought rapid and severe changes to the economic lives of New England's citizens. Stephen remarried in 1864 after his painful divorce from Melinda Hall. Stephen and his youthful wife Rhoda Lamberton [1827-1914] had one child, Martha, nicknamed Mattie [1865-1917]. Tragically, both of Stephen's wives accused him of the same behavior: domestic abuse. Both received divorces; Rhoda's completed in 1879. Rhoda alleged several incidents of physical abuse in which Stephen kicked her with his heavy boots. She gained custody of Mattie.[224] Rhoda, awarded two thousand dollars in the divorce did not immediately collect it from Stephen. Counter to the normal demographic for the older New England men of his time, Stephen Williams, Jr., followed his children to Iowa. Arriving sometime between 1880 and 1882, he lived the remainder of his life with Albert.[225]

Rhoda prevailed in the collection case against Stephen in 1882 making her eligible to receive the $2000 dollar alimony judgement plus costs she had been awarded.[226] Stephen failed to pay, and she sued Stephen and Albert, arguing that Albert was a garnishee as a debtor of the defendant, Stephen. Albert owed his father money due to unpaid loans, and Rhoda believed that money could be hers when Albert repaid his father. Poweshiek County judge W. R. Lewis heard the case in August 1884, and ruled in favor of defendant, Albert Williams.[227] Albert asked that depositions from a number of relatives including Worthin Hall and both of Albert's sisters and their husbands not be considered.[228] Although duly summoned, Stephen did not attend the proceedings. The court found that Albert by 1875 owed Stephen a whopping $3448 dollars plus interest. Claiming that Stephen sent Albert a letter telling him to tear up the notes due him from Albert and both of his sisters, Albert argued that Stephen had canceled Albert's indebtedness. Stephen allegedly did this with the knowledge that his marriage had turned stressful and might dissipate. Stephen's subsequent gift of 200 dollars required that fifty be repaid, which Albert alleged he did in 1875. "The Court is unable to find from the testimony whether the gift to the garnishee [Albert] was for the purpose of putting his [Stephen's] property out of the reach of the plaintiff [Rhoda], in contemplation of separation, or only in good faith a gift to his son."[229] Albert received court costs of roughly two hundred dollars from Rhoda. Testimony from both Rhoda and Albert was submitted in writing to the court, and absent other testimony, questions linger as to Albert's veracity. The letter quoted by the court is not extant in the letter collection. The amount of money that Stephen reportedly contributed to Albert in gifts totals more than a third of the value of his farm, much more than the extant letters indicate was gifted to Albert. Finally, it is reasonable to assume that rifts between family members widened, as Albert's sister Annginette airbrushed both Albert and Stephen out of her published memories recorded in the 1890s.[230]

The various Williams family members who relocated to Iowa encouraged her vigorous growth to over one million people by 1870.[231] Stephen was rarely mentioned in the local Grinnell newspaper, although in 1883 they reported his six-week vacation in Vermont and New Hampshire.[232] In 1886, he returned from a six-month trip to Connecticut.[233] He moved to Campbell, California with Albert in 1893 and passed away in 1904 attaining almost 92 years. In the 1900 census, Stephen is listed as a widower, possibly an attempt to conceal the divorces and preserve a semblance of Victorian propriety.[234] Stephen's daughter Mattie taught school, married a doctor, had no children, and lived the majority of her adult life in Kansas near her mother.[235]

Jane Eliza Blair

Albert Gordon Williams, possibly afflicted with dyslexia, could not read until taught by his wife Jane Eliza Blair, according to family legend. A native of London, England, Eliza Blair is believed to be the daughter of William [1819-1860?], a shipwright and Ann Lewis Blair [1820-1852?]. Eliza's mother died when she was about 10 years old and William Blair quickly remarried Margaret Lewis, daughter of a mariner. Presumably William died after only a few years of marriage to Margaret, who, overwhelmed by William's children and three of her own, sent Eliza to America.[236] Reportedly, Eliza's aunt in America told Margaret to send her the oldest child. Family lore said a nametag was created and pinned on Eliza with her name and destination. Records indicate a 17-year-old female servant traveling alone named Eliza Blair sailed on the ship *Washington* to New York City in 1860, a passenger on the upper B Deck in steerage.[237]

A lengthy voyage in which the ship "becalmed" was blamed for Eliza's high-strung attitude and anxiety in later life. Surviving the journey, she arrived at the home of Henry [1831-1889] and Helen Lewis Rusco[e] [1828-1879] in Southeast, New York. Reportedly, Helen exclaimed upon seeing tiny Eliza, "Oh, you've sent me the youngest child, not the oldest!" This Aunt Helen was the younger sister of Ann Lewis; both the daughters of William and Annie (Finch) Lewis of St. Albans, Hertfordshire, England.[238] The marriage record for Margaret and William Blair said that Margaret's father was Thomas Lewis, perhaps making Margaret, Eliza's stepmother, a cousin of Helen and the deceased Ann Lewis

Blair. The tenuous tie between Helen Lewis Rusco and Eliza Blair ended early on when Eliza relocated to Fort Dodge, Iowa appearing there in the Federal census taken June 1, 1860.[239] Eliza was one of more than 100,000 immigrants to America in 1860. Of those, less than one percent settled in Iowa.[240]

Fort Dodge, located in central Iowa on the Des Moines river, became a hive of settlement activity in the late 1850s. Fort Dodge provided a substantive attraction – land – to the people of Putnam County, New York as two of Henry Rusco's brothers, Gilbert and George, as well as his sister Mary (Rusco) Thomas moved there in the 1850s. Fort Dodge, had been established as a garrison in 1850, in response to Native American threats.[241] Settlement soon followed. The registers and receivers of the federal land offices supervised the distribution of 76 percent of Iowa, Fort Dodge part of that process.[242] November 5, 1855 marked the opening of the Government Land Office in Fort Dodge where a thousand people impatiently waited for land, perhaps the Ruscos with them.[243] By Spring, 1859, three steamboats had made trips to the bustling new town.[244]

In Fort Dodge, Eliza Blair was soon surrounded by friends, distant relatives by marriage from the Rusco family, and acquaintances. The 1860 Federal Census recorded Eliza Blair as a servant in the Conklin H. Crosby household. The Crosby families of Fort Dodge were related to the Henry Crosby shoemakers of Southeast, New York, who had employed Henry and Helen Rusco as shoemakers, as noted in the 1850 census. Henry Crosby's brother Seth settled in Fort Dodge with his family including Conklin and Daniel, his sons. Brothers Conklin and Daniel, next door neighbors in the census, were both in the boot and shoe business following the family business started in New York.[245] Seth had a daughter Lavinia, who might have been the inspiration for the naming of Lavinia Williams, Eliza (Blair) Williams' only daughter.

The Ruscos and Crosbys settled in Fort Dodge between 1855 and 1860, when conditions bustled with enthusiasm, but remained somewhat rustic. Only one woman was recorded in the town in the summer of 1855, but by the fall of that year a least a dozen women were counted among a population that enjoyed dancing, card parties, candy pulling and sleigh rides.[246] By 1859 there were enough women to require a milliner as Mrs. C. H. "Conklin" Crosby announced on May 21, 1859, that she had come to Fort Dodge direct from New York with "a large and complete assortment of Millinery and Dress-Making Goods."[247] The 1860 census found 672 people residing in Fort Dodge, Iowa a land of exquisite natural beauty and opportunity. Eliza Blair remained in Iowa for the next thirty-three years of her life.

Although the exact details of Eliza's move to Iowa are irrecoverable, no doubt an opportunity to gain meaningful employment in Fort Dodge drove the spunky teenager to make the journey. Eliza's years in Iowa between her immigration in 1860 and marriage in 1866 include attendance at Iowa College, Grinnell in 1864-65, and subsequent school teaching in Chester Township.[248] Iowa College is now the nationally known Grinnell College, considered one of the best liberal arts colleges in the United States.[249] The letter collection contains a humble certificate allowing Eliza Blair to teach school in rural Iowa. Her authorization came from James Root, Jr., a superintendent of schools in Marengo, Iowa County for a six-month term of employment commencing on April 30, 1864, although no record of her teaching in Iowa County exists. Marengo had been incorporated in 1861 with a population of about 650. James Root Jr., the first principal of the first district, found his major responsibility at that time to ensure that statewide legal school requirements were met. Perhaps Eliza taught there, then moved on to Poweshiek County. Otherwise, the possibility exists that James Root, Jr. was such an accepted school administrator that his endorsement of a teacher held much influence and would have made Eliza acceptable in the adjacent county. Teachers were transitory on the Iowa frontier, and the subjects she taught were basic reading, writing, arithmetic, handwriting, grammar, and geography.

School teaching, an acceptable profession for respectable women, attracted almost 6,000 Iowa women by 1870.[250] A study of teachers in Iowa, Nebraska, and Kansas in the 1880s argued for an estimated 25 to 35 percent of all employed women as having been engaged in school teaching. Single women taught in high numbers and often found it an acceptable way to meet people, as well as to save for land purchases or to help family. Women also achieved self-realization from teaching, by helping to make a contribution to society, as well as gaining financial independence. Moreover, life in early Iowa encouraged both marriage and varied roles for women.[251]

Family lore maintains that Eliza taught school in Chester Township, Poweshiek County when she met Albert at church or while boarding with his family. Albert's youngest sister Francis was a pupil of Eliza's, and Eliza was also credited as teaching Albert to read. This memory creates ties to his childhood issues with being bound out, a situation offering poor formal education, and also to a potential for Albert to have suffered from some type of learning disorder. The letters offer tidbits about Albert's poor handwriting and spelling, both signs of learning challenges.

Grinnell enjoyed a population of 392 people in 1860 and had grown to over 1,400 by 1870, aided by its location on the main stage route from Iowa City to Des Moines.[252] Accordingly, roughly one thousand people lived in Grinnell when Eliza and Albert were married there on March 13, 1866. The couple had two children, Lavinia and Worthin Hall Williams, named for his father's uncle the whaling captain. The only letter in the collection to Eliza is from a cousin, 12- year-old Nettie Rusco, the daughter of Henry and Helen (Lewis) Rusco. It is dated only a month before the wedding and appears to be in response to a notification, or invitation, to the Rusco family in anticipation of the upcoming wedding.

Eliza's life as a farm wife would have centered on home, school, and church. Women's work, social responsibilities and identities were unequivocally based in the home.[253] She performed a number of monotonous tasks in support of the farm, and perhaps added to the family's wealth by selling home products. Eliza made her own clothes, and like the majority of farm owners, employed a hired female domestic servant for assistance.[254] Although lonely, perhaps homesick for London, Eliza was nevertheless not isolated, as she enjoyed the companionship of neighbors, children, and friendships with church-goers and extended relatives from Albert's associations.[255] Child care and food preparation and processing were constant daily responsibilities for farm women, including Eliza, keeping her tied to the farm with few opportunities to venture into Grinnell for shopping trips.[256] Economically, Eliza would have contributed essential tasks as a true partner of the farming venture; a team effort.[257] Women produced cash crops for local markets: chickens for egg sales, milk and butter, and bounteous gardens of vegetables.[258] Morally, Eliza would have created a home that conformed to standards of privacy and refinement.

The Iowa Farm

Albert Gordon Williams actively farmed in Chester Township, Grinnell from his arrival in 1856/7 until his departure for California in 1893. Like other farmers he was challenged to use his entrepreneurial skills to secure maximum output from his resources. He first acquired the farm then improved it while adapting to local conditions and regional peculiarities which required different strategies than those he had learned in New England.[259] Albert's specific innovations lay in the field of fruit tree horticulture. He pursued his passion as a nurseryman and established the Chester Nursery in 1866, located on his farm, six miles north and two miles east of downtown Grinnell.[260] The letter collection provides substantiation for Albert's trip to New England and return with tree saplings. An advertisement for the nursery lists standard apple trees at eight cents or five cents depending on size. The price circular lists other fruit trees, fruiting vines, and numerous flowering shrubs and evergreen trees, presumably supplying Grinnell and surrounding areas with trees for commercial and personal enjoyment. Generosity appeared a hallmark of the nursery's success as Albert offered a "substantial" full dinner to anyone venturing out to visit his farm, "even if they do not buy more than a currant bush or a grapevine."[261] Presumably Eliza and the hired girl cooked the substantial mid-day dinner for guests, adding value in sustaining the farm.

Financially successful with farming and with the nursery industry, an 1880 Federal agricultural census for Iowa gave Albert a total of 200 acres broken down as follows: 15 acres woodland or forest, 55 acres of orchards and 130 acres of tilled land that could be rotated in fallow, with 100 acres then planted in hay. The total farm value of $10,000 dollars enjoyed an overall production of $2,805 dollars. Chester township reported 104 farms total in 1880, with one, the richest, valued at $20,000 dollars. Williams and only eight other men had farms with values totaling $10,000 dollars each, the remainder valued at lesser amounts.[262] The availability of timber on the farm softened the adjustment from forested New England to the prairie.[263] Albert added to his land holdings until his final farm's size totaled 280 acres.[264]

Albert Wiliams - Wedding Photo; March 13, 1866

Jane Eliza (Blair) Williams; Wedding Photo

Albert learned about the challenges of Iowa farming from local newspapers, and from participation in agricultural events, organizations, and cooperatives. He successfully entered his "quality" apples in the local agricultural fair, sweeping first place prizes in 1888 and 1889 in categories including summer, fall, winter apples, and assorted specialty species.[265] In 1890 Albert was re-elected president of the Eastern Iowa Horticultural Association, serving for at least three years in that capacity and helping Poweshiek County attain prominence within Iowa for horticulture.[266] He also served on the board of the Poweshiek Central Agricultural Society being in charge of fruit, and consequently supporting historian Allan Bogue's assertion that: "The mid-west had more agricultural societies than any other section of the country in both 1858 and 1870."[267] In 1892, Albert pushed for rural daily mail service, arguing for the necessity of the mail, and the following year, Albert won first place in both apples and plums at the local fair.[268] The *Grinnell Herald* bragged that Albert read the newspaper every day and had been a consistent subscriber since its inception in 1868.[269] He continued to correspond with the paper and reported on local agriculture after moving to California.[270]

Like the other transplanted New Englanders, Albert valued education, although his own was lacking. He demonstrated his beliefs in the public sphere when in 1879, he served on the local school board. By 1881 he was president of the Chester Township school district.[271] In June 1891 his name was offered up by the newspaper for potential legislative representative. The paper was looking for "an intelligent farmer... an able earnest man" who could do good in the position.[272]

Religion was also central to the Williams' belief system.[273] As a Congregational, Albert eschewed liquor, becoming a delegate to the State temperance alliance meeting in Des Moines representing Poweshiek County.[274] The State struggled to find consensus on liquor control, which became the major political issue after 1870.[275] Eliza participated in the American Home Missionary Society, a joint Congregational and Presbyterian group which supported ministers in Iowa, as well as the Grinnell Association, which also forwarded Congregational values.[276]

Historians argue that the Midwest of the nineteenth century constituted the most advanced democratic society that the world had seen to date. People were decent, pragmatic, common-sense infused, modeled proper behavior, and espoused idealism.[277] The Midwest matters to American history as the democratic tradition tied together the American past and future with the pioneering ideals that Albert's life represents.[278] He was part of that mid-western normalcy; a hard-working, temperance advocate, church-going farmer and community leader. He said grace before every supper and believed in agrarianism; the superiority of rural life.[279] No doubt these characteristics were learned in New England and reinforced through these letters he received from relatives. These notions, passed down to his children, were continued in Campbell, California when he relocated there in the 1890s.

Ralph Grattan on the Williams Farm,
Grinnell IA; about 1920s

BLAINE & WILLIAMS   CAMPBELL, CAL.

Albert Gordon Williams, Campbell CA; about 1898

The Heartland Moves Westward, Children and the move to California

Albert's daughter Lavinia [1867-1961] recorded her early childhood memories of the Iowa farm and are included here as Appendix I, providing much detail on the Williams' farm life. Lavinia, nicknamed Vinnie, attended Iowa Agricultural College, now Iowa State University, Ames, Iowa from 1891 to 1893, as the late 19th century began to see large numbers of college-educated women.[280] Ames was founded in 1858 as a coeducational institution. One of her classmates was the esteemed botanist George Washington Carver who attended Ames from 1891 to 1894. The prominent scientist was the school's first African American student. She attended classes with him and reported to her descendants that he admired her strawberry blond hair which he said had the look of spun gold. It is doubtful that she knew Carver well, as she quickly settled on a fellow classmate, John Henry Grattan [1869-1952], as a likely beau.[281] The two were married in San Jose, California's First Congregational Church on February 8, 1894. The marriage license states that John Grattan, an Iowa native, was a resident of L County, Oklahoma Territory.[282]

John borrowed a race horse from his half-brother Marvin Trask Grattan and on a hot, dusty September 16, 1893, rode it in Oklahoma's Cherokee Strip Land Run staking out a quarter section homestead claim of 160 acres.[283] John built a one-room, sod-roofed log cabin where their three oldest boys were born. John became a prominent local banker, associated with banks in nearby Medford, Jefferson, and Pond Creek.[284] By 1895, John established the Grant County Bank in Medford and was on the executive committee of the Oklahoma Territory Bankers Association, organized in June 1897.[285]

The Old Chisholm trail passed by the homestead and Lavinia spent some harrowing moments when cattle drovers threatened her by driving cattle in a circle milling around the cabin. She told them to leave; her husband was inside sleeping. She lied, but they left.[286] On November 5th, 1896, Lavinia's father Albert Williams made a long trip to Oklahoma to bring his daughter and her two children back with him to his home in California for a visit. By May 1899 the John Grattan family had moved to San Jose, California where they appear in the 1900 census, John then a bank teller.[287] By 1902 the family moved to Colorado, eventually acquiring a cattle ranch in Broomfield.

Family lore says that Albert Williams and his family relocated to California for the mild weather in hopes it would improve his asthma. Undoubtedly, California's other lures may have included the ability to devote his full attention to his passion for horticulture in a less demanding environment. Albert, "A. G." Williams as he preferred in later life, was considered a leading horticulturalist of Iowa at the time of his move to California.[288] Albert had visited the town of Campbell in September, 1892,[289] allowing the *Mercury News* to report roughly a year later that Campbell could expect the permanent relocation of A. G. Williams and family who temporarily rented a house.[290] By January, 1894 Albert had purchased an acre of land on the corner of Grant and Harrison Streets and planned to build a large two-story home.[291] In February, 1894 they were welcomed as actual citizens of Campbell, hosting numerous friends and relatives from Iowa for the next twenty years.[292]

Campbell was a town of a few hundred people in 1893 when the Williams family moved west. Named for the first settlers, Benjamin and Mary Campbell, the farm they established, then five miles away from San Jose, is now part of the technology-rich Silicon Valley. The Campbells had migrated West before the Gold Rush. Arriving in 1846, they built the first sawmill in the valley.[293] Purchasing land in 1851, the Campbells quickly settled on their ranch in the downtown location of the current town named for them. Selling land to the railroad in 1877, the Campbells became the first postmasters of a tiny settlement of farmers and fruit growers.[294] Ruth Duncan Cutting and husband William of Riceville, Iowa, were credited as being part of the second family to settle in 1883 in what would become the new town.[295] Soon William Cutting's parents, siblings and other relatives joined them in becoming prominent members of the Congregational church.[296] The townsite was laid out in 1885, and among the first buildings were a YMCA and a blacksmith shop.[297] One of William Cutting's brothers, Frank Hurley Cutting, an early California impressionist artist, settled directly across the street from the Albert Williams' family on Harrison Avenue.

Aside from beautiful weather, the attractions of Campbell included its position as pioneer of the fruit industry, and a social milieu reminiscent of life in Iowa. Campbell's first shipment of five boxes of apricots in 1886 grew to 120 carloads the following year and the town developed around an 1887 subdivision in what is now the downtown. Benjamin

Campbell had a strong disobedience toward alcohol and town deeds prohibited the building of saloons; a clause he felt would help attract a better class of people to the settlement.[298] A "wholesome and attractive place to live," Campbell hosted numerous deciduous fruit orchards.[299] A quick review of the names and origins of Campbell's 1890s residents show a large number as having originated in Iowa. Almost 17% of the registered voters — all male, of course — in Campbell precinct in 1896 were born in Iowa, and like Albert, a fair number had been born in the New England states and had farmed in Iowa prior to the move to California. Albert was listed as one of 158 "orchardists" in Campbell, the most common occupation in the voting registry.[300] Campbell excelled in the fruit packing industry. The largest packer, J. C. Ainsley, had about 750 men on the pay roll who put out about 300,000 cases of canned fruit each year, by 1929. The industry was considered "the very life of the town." Every Spring season enjoyed limitless vistas of orchards — apricots, cherries, pears, prunes, plums — in bloom, no doubt helping give the Santa Clara valley its earliest alias as the "Valley of the Heart's Delight.[301]

For rural communities throughout the country the church was the key social institution. Life in both Grinnell and Campbell was a blending of family, church, and community activities. Two years before Albert settled in Campbell, the ties between the towns emerged when a meeting of Campbell Congregationalists at a private home included the showing of curios from the Grinnell cyclone of 1882.[302] The following year, a small but tidy Congregational church, organized by Rev. William Windsor of Iowa, was dedicated in Campbell at a cost of $2500. A room attached to the sanctuary served as a hall for lectures and socials, enhancing the communal aspects of the organization.[303] Perhaps a tribute to the many inhabitants with ties to the New England states, the Congregational Church hosted a traditional New England supper for members in 1907.[304] One local commented that: "our people hail with pleasure everything which tends to elevate the moral tone of the community and keep it on a high basis."[305] Without these early settlers from New England and the mid-west, Campbell would have been less prosperous, and perhaps less socially and politically conservative in establishing the institutions that framed society in the town. A sense of civic duty and a sense of community with others prevailed. New settlers recreated the life they had previously enjoyed upon moving to Campbell and continued in religious pursuits, temperance, and civic responsibilities that had been a hallmark of midwestern sensibilities.[306] The town boasted of 600 residents by 1904.[307]

Religion and religious sensibilities sustained both Albert and Eliza but was arguably more central to Eliza's life by bringing social advantages, as well as spiritual hope. In Campbell, Eliza Williams taught Sunday school at the Congregational church. For successive years she taught a large class of girls in Sunday school, watching them grow to maturity, and thus continued a commitment to youngsters that she had begun in Iowa.[308]

Eliza lived at a time when women's domestic sphere of influence moved into the larger political arena. Religious benevolent work expanded women's domestic traditions into the wider world and allowed women to challenge men's behavior without contesting gender roles.[309] Women were challenged to expand their moral authority and their duty to protect families and home. By joining women's clubs, local and national church associations, and the Women's Christian Temperance movement, suffrage came to the forefront of women's consciousness, and played a crucial role in the history of American women.[310] Eliza enjoyed prominent membership in her local Women's Christian Temperance Union, which offered a social attribute by hosting meetings at her home.[311] The organization was led by respectable, Protestant, and churchgoing women who also enjoyed economic prosperity.[312] Relying on a sense of women's moral superiority and moral outrage, the protest movement importantly came to critique American society.[313] Eliza also joined other clubs, and participated in events including a quilting bee.[314] In April 1895, she fell down a flight of stairs and although not seriously hurt, the item was newsworthy, and, noteworthy in that it substantiated Eliza's attainment of the feminine ideal of "lady," and underscored her prominence within the community.[315] In a somewhat tongue-in-cheek poem, herein reprinted as Appendix III, Albert related a disagreement with his wife about her dedication to women's causes.

Family obligations expanded with grandparenthood, and Eliza journeyed to Oklahoma Territory to visit with her daughter Lavinia after the birth of her children there, and both Eliza and Albert visited Lavinia and her family in Barr, Colorado in 1904, subsequent to the birth of her youngest son.[316] If the Williams' had expected a quiet retirement in Campbell, it was not to be. Albert and Eliza returned to their farm in Chester township almost annually for many summer vacations.[317]

Perhaps from a religious sense of duty to community, Albert expressed his authority through memberships and political pursuits. He was chosen for a committee to review the railroad park issue, and he ran for town council in 1896.[318] Appointed to the position of Justice of the Peace in that year, he then ran for the post two years later.[319] His speech at a Republican meeting emphasized the judgeship as being simply dependent upon the peoples' wishes.[320] He received 730 votes and came in third.[321] Shortly after the losing outcome, C. L. Williams filed a petition in Superior Court for A. G. Williams of Campbell, arguing that a number of votes were miscounted in favor of Irving Herrington, the winner. They alleged these votes should have been credited to Albert.[322] It was not the only election result contested, however the ruling remained.[323] The title of judge stuck with Albert for the remainder of his life in Campbell, although he did not serve again.

Inspired by the little town's potential, A. G. invested in the Bank of Campbell which had incorporated in 1896,[324] and in 1904 he was elected president of the Campbell Republican Club.[325] In 1913, Albert made front page news with the purchase of a new four-passenger Ford car.[326] Albert attended meetings of the Campbell improvement club, the Odd Fellows and the farmer's institute. The Odd Fellows met at the Congregational church and dedicated their chapter, the Morning Light Lodge number 42, to friendship, love, and truth; again, reiterating the cultural expectations of American society at the time.[327]

Albert and Eliza's only son, Worthin Hall Williams, born May 30, 1870, in Grinnell and obviously named for his great-uncle the whaling master, was the first in the family tradition of naming men Worthin after their uncle. Born with a congenital heart problem, Worthin did not enjoy good health, although like his parents, he joined numerous organizations. He played the French horn in a Campbell musical group and also sang in a vocal quartette for the local Cambrian literary and social club.[328] In 1896, as part of a YMCA literary entertainment, Worthin gave a speech in favor of giving women the right to vote.[329]

On May 16, 1896, Worthin Williams partnered with Frank Blaine to become a printer and editor of the Campbell newspaper, as well as a partner in a photography studio.[330] Both Worthin Williams and Frank Blaine listed their occupation as printer in the 1896 voting register; presumably both shared duties as editor/photographer in the businesses. Short-lived, the Blaine - Williams photography studio lasted until Blaine's death on December 26, 1897,[331] forcing Worthin into other pursuits.[332]

"Well known and liked by those who knew him," Worthin Williams changed occupations and lived several years in Southern California beginning in 1901, subsequent to his marriage to Margaret Morgan. Worthin worked in Los Angeles as an electrician, but by 1910 was considered a horticulturalist following in his father's footsteps. The move to southern California probably reflected a desire to be close to Margaret's family. The two did not have children and returned to Campbell in 1918, after his mother's death, perhaps to aid in the care of his father and his wife's father, Bennett Morgan, a Civil War veteran then living in Campbell who died in 1919.[333] Margaret survived Worthin when he died at 50 years old on October 30, 1920.

Albert Williams figured prominently in the lives of his grandsons partly due to the deterioration of his daughter Lavinia's marriage. John Grattan had left the Broomfield ranch for a move to Denver in 1910, presumably to pursue a political career.[334] John's September 22, 1910 letter to the *Avalanche Echo* newspaper, from Denver, confirms his move and appointment by the Colorado State Farmer's Union to a position as State Inspector for produce.[335] Their oldest son Worthin, named for his uncle, Worthin Hall Williams, recalled the hired ranch hands would not take direction from his mother, nor from him at fifteen years old, after his father's departure. By February, 1912, Worthin Grattan, a high school sophomore, was living with his grandparents in Campbell, California where in April he listened to distress signals of the sinking ship Titanic on a crystal radio he had made.[336] The second son, Henry, also lived intermittently with his grandparents who gave him the nickname Chick; Henry was corrupted to hen and chickens, and the nickname evolved.[337] Lavinia's third son, Leland Grattan, born in Oklahoma Territory in 1899 also lived in Campbell with his grandparents for his high school years when noted in the local newspaper as returning to Colorado for the summer of 1917 between school years.[338] In 1918, his WWI draft registration indicated he worked in a Campbell cannery. In 1919, Leland and his grandfather journeyed to the farm in Grinnell, which Leland eventually acquired, living there for most of his life.[339]

Albert Williams (standing) and Eliza Williams (seated in Ford Model T) in 1913; in front of their home on Grant and Harrison Streets, Campbell CA

Interior of the Williams Home in Campbell CA. *Courtesy of Sourisseau Academy for State and Local History, San Jose State University*

Lavinia and John divorced in October 1918, as Lavinia alleged "extreme and repeated acts of cruelty." John countered that Lavinia treated him with "cold indifference" and that she had left the children with him in 1912 for an extended trip to Iowa and a three-month stay with her father. In 1913 she abandoned her home and went to live with her father, taking only her youngest child, Ralph. John continued that Lavinia had always treated him "as a failure," holding up her father "as an example of success and as one to be imitated," thus influencing his children against him.[340] As historian Glenda Riley noted, the American West had and has the highest divorce rate. Divorce "fit well with widely expounded ideas regarding western democracy, individualism, change, and reform." Divorce gave people options to pursue happiness, and democratic ideals justified the rationale for divorce.[341]

Albert's niece, Myrtle Hays [1881-1918] daughter of his youngest sister Francis, and her father visited Campbell in 1900, and then she also stayed in 1908, possibly for a year.[342] Myrtle Hays married William B. Nutting, and they had three children. Tragically Myrtle died as a result of the last childbirth, when her youngest baby was only three days old. Albert's will gifted money to Myrtle's brother, and to her three children.[343]

Albert and Eliza celebrated their 50th wedding anniversary in March 1916, but their happiness was cut short. Within two and a half months, Eliza passed away after a month's painful illness.[344] The newspaper noted her "beautiful Christian character and exceptionally winning personality." At 75 years of age her death was considered a large loss to the whole community.[345]

Albert also died in Campbell on November 12, 1922,[346] having overcome the adversity of childhood trauma and food insecurity when bound out and having suffered the uncertainties of Iowa's early pioneer years. Newspaper accounts indicate something akin to pneumonia took him, and avowed he was a regular attendee of Campbell's Congregational church. Albert made thirty trips across the country to visit his Iowa farm. The last one, which occurred in October, had left him tired and susceptible to disease.[347] A Campbell paper expressed personal loss as local pioneers passed on, "the makers of the early history of our town; upright, trustworthy citizens."[348] Lavinia, born in January, 1867 in the home at Chester township that her father had built, also died in the same home on January 12, 1961, two days past her 94th birthday.

This letter collection provides elegiac observations of daily happenings, foregrounding personal lives, and delivering both a micro level analysis of the effect of these occurrences on the writers, while also confirming their place within a larger picture of historic events. Moreover, the letters document the dynamic forces crafting the experiences of families suffering dissolution due to divorce. The letters enable analysis of affective bonds, which for Albert, reinforced constants in his life; family ties and cultural parameters. Albert, a product of his time, practiced composure and self-control, demonstrating the discipline needed for a virtuous, principled life.[349] The letters assisted his inner growth and helped prevent his becoming brutalized by a problematic childhood.

For scholars, the letters provide an avenue to interrogate power structures of the 19th century, men's power over women, as well as the power of the wealthy over the middle class. The divorced Stephen Williams, Jr. bested his ex-wife in holding their children near to him; behavior upheld legally. Melinda's heartfelt loss of her daily contact with her children is palpable in her heart-wrenching letters to her son. Ultimately her wealthy brother, Worthin Hall, and his wife facilitated Melinda's ability to live again with her children on the Iowa frontier, eschewing the rights of their father, and providing a window on the agency of women when driven by extraordinary circumstances.

Drawn to Iowa by his sister, Albert then enabled the chain migration of other relatives to the State. Scholars may find a new narrative of Middle West settlement financed by comparatively prosperous New England parents, in turn supporting women's historians in establishing the agency of women in settlement practices. Establishing and then finding success in farming was only facilitated by generous loans or gifts of money from his parents, and support from a caring wife. The success of Albert's business, the Chester Nursery, lies directly in the unique midday dinner offerings to nursery customers; meals cooked by his wife. Albert's Iowa residence was arguably emblematic of the lesser forces of individualism in favor of familial support which in turn engendered reciprocal responses. Familial ties took precedent. His lack of compassion for stepmother Rhoda, while demonstrating sympathy and reciprocity with other family members, establishes Albert's empathy for his father, while arguing for his ability to capitalize on an overall lesser status for women. His behavior also confirmed a belief in a sense of community, a larger group, prompting responsibilities toward others exemplified in public service. In a similar disposition as his Puritan ancestors, Albert combined his theology with a vision for a better society, and felt a personal service to its advancement, both in Iowa and later in California, while also reaping financial success and respect from the society in which he lived.[350]

---

[1] Old Settlers' Association President, *Annual Meeting of Old Settlers' Association of Grinnell, Iowa,* 1900, President's Opening Address, 36.

[2] Ben Lafferty, *American Intelligence: small-town news and political culture in Federalist New Hampshire,* (Amherst: University of Massachusetts Press, 2019), 12; for general histories of New Hampshire see George Barlow, *The History of New Hampshire,* (Concord, NH: published by J.S. Boyd, June 4, 1842), Hobart Pillsbury, *New Hampshire, Resources, Attractions, and Its People, A History,* Five volumes, (New York: The Lewis Historical Publishing Company, 1927); J. Duane Squires, T*he Granite State of the United States; a history of New Hampshire from 1623 to the present,* (New York: American Historical Company, 1956).

[3] Lafferty, *American Intelligence,* 18-19, By 1800 the State reached 183,858 people.

[4] William H. Child, *History of the Town of Cornish New Hampshire with genealogical record, 1763-1910,* 2 vols, (Concord, NH.: The Rumford Press, 1910), Vol I, 110; see also Hugh Mason Wade, *A Brief History of Cornish, 1763-1974,* (Hanover, NH: University Press of New England, 1976). By 1775 Cornish boasted 309 people. The population almost doubled by 1786, nearing 1000 by 1790.

[5] Child, *History of Cornish,* Vol. I, 188-9 for population stats; 191, for 1840 population.

[6] For brief histories of these towns see D. Hamilton Hurd, *History of Cheshire and Sullivan Counties, N.H.,* (J. W. Lewis: Philadelphia, Pa., 1886).

[7] On the Puritan Migration see: Robert Charles Anderson, *The Great Migration Begins: Immigrants to New England, 1620-1633, Volumes 1-3 ,* (Boston: New England Historical and Genealogical Society, 1995*);* Robert Charles Anderson, *The Great Migration, Immigrants to New England,* 1634-1635, Seven volumes, (Boston: Great Migration Study Project, New England Historic Genealogic Society, 2007); Scott McDermott, *The Puritan Ideology of Mobility: Corporatism, the politics of place and the founding of New England towns before 1650,* (London: Anthem Press, 2022); Allen French, *Charles I and the Puritan upheaval: a study of the causes of the great migration,* (Boston: Houghton Mifflin Company, 1955); Alison Games, *Migration and the Origins of the English Atlantic World,* (Cambridge, Mass.: Harvard University Press, 2001).

[8] Wendy Warren, *New England Bound, Slavery and Colonization in Early America,* (New York: Liveright Publishing Corp., 2016), 50; 23-24; 20,000 people came, 24.

[9] McDermott, *Puritan Ideology,* 1-4; 24, 26, for middle sort of people, not rich nor poor; see also T. H. Breen and Stephen Foster, "Moving to the New World: The Character of Early Massachusetts Immigration," *The William and Mary Quarterly,* Vol. 30, no. 2, (April 1973): 189-222.

[10] French, *Charles I and the Puritan Upheaval,* 346 lists reasons for migration including service to the church to carry the gospel to other locations, England was overcrowded with a high cost of living, common sense in looking for a better life; research based on Winthrop's papers; Games, *Migration,* 15-16 31-32, 72-73, 83-85, 132-137 found a huge range of variables between unique settlers as to reasons for immigration; McDermott, *Puritan Ideology,* 3, found Puritan ideology encompassed numerous factors, religious, economic, intellectual and social, that drove people to the new world. Religious ideology as the basis.

[11] Stephen West Williams, *Genealogy and History of the Family of Williams in America,* (Greenfield, Mass.: Merriam & Mirick, 1847) chronicles the extensive family.

[12] George Chandler, *The Chandler Family; The Descendants of William and Annis Chandler who settled in Roxbury in 1637,* (Worcester, MA.: Charles Hamilton Press, 1883), 244 the original author of the book on the Chandler line picked up the death date of our Samuel's great-grandfather Samuel Williams and mistakenly believed that our Samuel {1751-1799] had died in infancy. Williams, *Genealogy and History,* 37, The similarities with Samuel Williams and his younger brother, John Chandler Williams, were numerous. Both fought in the Revolution. Both were illiterate, but John was able to attain an impressive education and become a lawyer. Both removed to sparsely settled areas of New England.

[13] Williams, *Genealogy and History,* 25, for English location of origin; Harrison Williams, *Life and Ancestors of Robert Williams of Roxbury, 1607-1693,* (W. F. Roberts, Co. Press of Washington Company: 1934), 25 for ships *Rose* and *John and Dorothy*; See also: Frederick Adams Virkus, *Immigrant Ancestors, A List of 2,500 Immigrants to America before 1750,* (Baltimore: Genealogical Publishing Company, 1963), 74; *Colonial Families of the United States,* 597 on Ancestry.com for *John and Dorothy.*

[14] Breen and Foster, "Moving to the New World," 199-200.

[15] Williams, *Genealogy and History,* 29.

[16] Anderson, *The Great Migration Begins: Immigrants to New England, 1620-1633,* Vol III, 1386.

[17] The complicated story of Sylvanus Warro is recounted by Wendy Warren in *New England Bound,* 172-175. Warro impregnated a white servant girl of Park's, Elizabeth Parker, as well as stealing money from Park. He was whipped and forced to pay for the child's support. The son was indentured for 30 years.

[18] Warren, *New England Bound,* 266, n22, for 1700 population numbers, 250; Antonio Bly, "A Prince Among Pretending Free Men, Runaway Slaves in Colonial New England Revisited," *Massachusetts Historical Review,* Vol 14, (2012): 97; during the 1760s Massachusetts had a population of 4,566 slaves.

[19] Lafferty, *American Intelligence,* 19; Amherst, NH had a population of 2,369 in 1790 making it one of the larger cities in the state after Portsmouth, Gilmantown, and Rochester.

[20] Child, *History of Cornish,* Vol I, 58-59.

[21] Isaac W. Hammond, ed., *State of New Hampshire, Rolls of the Soldiers of the Revolutionary War, 1775 to May 1777, with a appendix embracing the diaries of Lt. Jonathan Burton,* (Concord: P.G. Cogswell, 1885), 41.

[22] Daniel F. Secomb, *History of the Town of Amherst, Hillsborough, NH Hillsborough County, New Hampshire (first known as Narragansett Township Number Three, and subsequently as Souhegan West)*, (Concord, NH: Evans, Sleeper & Woodbury, 1883), 368-9, 370, Samuel received a coat as part of his allocation. Captain Josiah Crosby's Company in Col. Reed's regiment was one of the thirteen companies in the first New Hampshire regiment, also later called Stark's regiment.

[23] Hammond, *State of New Hampshire, Rolls*, 103.

[24] Secomb, *History of the Town of Amherst*, 371.

[25] Hammond, *State of New Hampshire, Rolls*, 207, Samuel signed with an X; Samuel Williams as part of Josiah Crosby's Company in October 12, 1775; 235, Samuel Williams listed as a private under Lt. John Hill returning from Seavey's Island on Nov. 5th, 1775.

[26] Samuel Carroll Derby, *Early Dublin: A List of Revolutionary Soldiers of Dublin, New Hampshire*, (Columbus, Ohio: Press of Spahr and Glann, 1901), 18, places Samuel Williams, a private, under Captain John Mellen's company in Col. Enoch Hale's regiment. They marched to reinforce the garrison at Ticonderoga where Williams served from June 28 through July 2, 1777.

[27] Lois K. Stabler, *Very Poor and of Low Make; the Journal of Abner Sanger*, (Portsmouth, NH: Historical Society of Cheshire County, 1986), 467, population; Hurd, *History of Cheshire and Sullivan Counties*, 185, 310; Levi Leonard and Josiah Seward, *The History of Dublin, NH*, (Dublin, NH: Published by the town of Dublin, 1920), 172, 195-196; Secomb, *History of Amherst*, 373; Albert Stillman Batchellor, *Revolutionary Documents of New Hampshire*, Vol 30, State Papers Series, (Manchester, NH Printed for the State, 1910), 45 Samuel Williams soldier from Dublin, NH. Samuel was not listed as part of a regiment from Amherst in December of 1775.

[28] Stabler, *Very Poor and of Low Make*, 467 for 900 residents in Dublin in 1790; 522, Williams fetched the doctor.

[29] Stabler, *Very Poor and of Low Make*, 456 to 542 covers December 3, 1791 to December 11, 1794 mentioning Samuel Williams several times.

[30] *Dublin Town Records 1768-1830*, Microfilm, LDS Family History Center, Salt Lake City.

[31] Leonard and Seward, *History of Dublin, NH*, 947, gives her first name as Lois, and records only five children.

[32] Lafferty, *American Intelligence*, 11, 108, 214, ten newspapers by 1800.

[33] Child, *History of Cornish*, Vol. I, 420; Anonymous, *Portrait, and Biographical Record of Johnson, Poweshiek, and Iowa Counties, Iowa* (Chicago: Chapman Bros., 1893), 483, for high sheriff; Edmund Wheeler, *History of Newport, New Hampshire: from 1766 to 1878, with a genealogical register*, (Concord, NH: Republican Press Association, 1879), 88 Stephen Williams a driver on the Lebanon route. This collaborates Henry Grattan's belief that Stephen Williams was a stage driver who got the job because of his driving abilities. He could drive close to the curb without hitting it.

[34] Felicia Johnson Deyrup, *Arms Making in the Connecticut Valley; A Regional Study of the Economic Development of the Small Arms Industry, 1798-1870*, (York, Pennsylvania: George Shumway, pub., 1970), 121.

[35] Deyrup, *Arms Making in the Connecticut Valley*, 215; Geoffrey S. Stewart, *Arming the World, American Gun-Makers in the Gilded Age*, (Essex, Ct.: Lyons Press, 2024), 14, simplifies the mechanization of arms-making as dependent upon three things: almost obsessive reliance upon gauges to measure parts, use of specialized machine tools to make the part identical, and strict quality control.

[36] Merritt Roe Smith, "John H. Hall, Simeon North, and the Milling Machine: The Nature of Innovation Among Antebellum Arms Makers," *Technology and Culture*, Vol 14, No 4, (October 1973): 547.

[37] Deyrup, *Arms Making in the Connecticut Valley*, 11.

[38] American Society of Mechanical Engineering, *Landmarks in Mechanical Engineering*, (West Lafayette, Indiana: Purdue University Press, 1997), 143.

[39] See David R. Meyer, *Networked Machinists, High-Technology Industries in Antebellum America*, (Baltimore: John Hopkins University Press, 2006); see also Robert A. Howard, "Interchangeable Parts Reexamined: The Private Sector of the American Arms Industry on the Eve of the Civil War," *Technology and Culture*, Vol 19., no 4, (Oct. 1978): 633-649, argued for the failures of interchangeability leading to the continued use of gunsmiths by private factories.

[40] Deyrup, *Arms Making in the Connecticut Valley*, 100, other highly skilled occupations are engraving and printing.

[41] Ibid., 34, 100, for skills.

[42] Meyer, *Networked Machinists*, found the beginnings in Windsor with the partnership of Richard Lawrence and Nicanor Kendall in a small gun shop in Windsor. Samuel Robbins joined them the following year and they began bidding on government contracts, 250.

[43] *Vermont Journal*, October 31, 1851, 2.

[44] Deyrup, *Arms Making in the Connecticut Valley*, 153 milling machines used irregularly shaped cutters which acted as formers of the work, or of the part being finished. Cutters ran at high speed (driven by steam power) and shaved particles off the work reducing hand work by a gunsmith; 155, the turret lathe was the most important in small arms manufacture. In lathes, the work piece revolved rapidly as the piece was fed into the lathe.

[45] Jayna Hooper, ed., *Jacob Wheeler's Journal of Matter and Things in General, 1847*, (Newport, NH.: Newport Historical Society, 2016), 12.

[46] Guy Hubbard, "Development of Machine Tools in New England," *American Machinist*, Vol 59, Issue 16, (October 18, 1923): 581; Robert E. Gardner, *Small Arms Makers, A Directory of fabricators of firearms, edged weapons, crossbows and polearms*, (New York: Bonanza Books, 1963), 92, believed that David Hall Hilliard began in Cornish, NH in 1842, then when he died in 1877 was succeeded by his brother George E. Hilliard. George E. was actually his son according to Child, *History of Cornish*, Vol. I, 204, every piece tested for accuracy, 181.

[47] Guy Hubbard, *Industrial History*, (Windsor, VT: Windsor Town School District, 1922), 61, Hilliard employed fifteen men "who learned their trade so thoroughly under Hilliard that many of them later filled very responsible positions in the large armories of the country." Child, *History of Cornish*, 183, for testing each gun.

[48] Deyrup, *Arms Making in the Connecticut Valley*, 223, gave Hilliard's operating years as 1860-1880.

[49] Child, *History of Cornish*, Vol. 1, 183, Hilliard employed several expert workmen.

[50] Guy Hubbard, "Leadership of Early Windsor Industries in the Mechanic Arts," A Paper Read Before the Vermont Historical Society at Windsor, September 4, 1922, Proceedings of the Vermont Historical Society, 1921, 22, 23, (Montpelier: Capital City Press, 1924), 169.

[51] See Harold Fisher Wilson, "The Roads of Windsor," *Geographical Review*, 21, (1931): 381, which maintains that the first bridge linking Cornish and Windsor over the Connecticut River was built in 1796.

[52] Mark Rondeau, "Vermont Gunmakers Armed the Union," *Bennington Banner*, June 13, 2012, https://www.benningtonbanner.com/stories/vermont-gunmakers-armed-the-union,178994.

[53] Carrie Brown, *Arming the Union, Gunmakers in Windsor, Vermont*, (Windsor, VT.: Vermont Historical Society, American Precision Museum, 2012), 37; Carrie Brown, "Guns for Billy Yank: The Armory in Windsor Meets the Challenge of Civil War," *Vermont History*, Vol 79, no 2 (Summer/Fall 2011) Vermont Historical Society publication: 141-161.

[54] William Hale Foster to Maria Foster, 21 August 1861, Foster Private Letter Collection, referring to the Windsor, VT manufacturing center.

[55] Deyrup, *Arms Making in the Connecticut Valley*, 4, 9.

[56] Ibid., 221, notes E. B. Alden gun manufacturer in Claremont, NH from 1863-1868, 223, Carlos Clark, gun manufacturer in Windsor from 1856-1868; Gardner, *Small Arms Makers*, 38, puts Carlos Clark in Windsor from 1832-46. The later years found Stephen employed by the Lamson, Goodnow and Yale, E. G. Lamson and Company, and Windsor Manufacturing Company (Windsor Armory), and for the Jones and Lamson Machine company of Windsor, Vermont, and successors.

[57] In the 1850 census, Stephen Williams, Jr. had real estate valued at $1800 dollars, roughly $70,000 today.

[58] See AMSE, *Landmarks*, 153-155; www.americanprecision.org; Merritt Roe Smith, "The American Precision Museum, Windsor, VT," *Technology and Culture*, Vol. 15, no. 3, (July 1974): 413-437.

[59] Deyrup, *Arms Making in the Connecticut Valley*, 122-3.

[60] Brown, *Arming the Union*, 7.

[61] Deyrup, *Arms Making in the Connecticut Valley*, 123, Gold fields.

[62] Joseph Wickham Roe, *English and American Tool Builders*, (New Haven: Yale University Press, 1916), 191.

[63] Guy Hubbard, "Leadership of Early Windsor Industries in the Mechanic Arts," A Paper Read Before the Vermont Historical Society at Windsor, September 4, 1922, Proceedings of the Vermont Historical Society, 1921, 22, 23, (Montpelier: Capital City Press, 1924), 174.

[64] Deyrup, *Arms Making in the Connecticut Valley*, 209, 1869 source.

[65] Deyrup, *Arms Making in the Connecticut Valley*, 123; Roe, *English and American Tool Builders*, 192. What became the English Enfield rifle not only supplied guns to British troops but were also sold to the Confederacy. Thus, troops on both sides of the Civil War used arms that emanated from the innovations of Windsor, VT.

[66] Deyrup, *Arms Making in the Connecticut Valley*, 129; larger manufacturers included Colt and Kendall, Robbins and Lawrence.

[67] *Vermont Journal*, July 20, 1866, 2.

[68] *Vermont Journal*, December 4, 1880, 8.

[69] *Vermont Journal*, October 30, 1857, 2 for late 1857, and for under the direction of Col H. D. Smith; *Vermont Journal*, December 4, 1880, 8, named company; Brown, *Arming the Nation*, 8; Deyrup, *Arms Making in the Connecticut Valley*, 194, Robbins and Lawrence became Lamson, Goodnow, and Yale in 1859, and later the E. G. Lamson company of Windsor, which supplied the machine tools that were used at the Springfield, Mass. government armory to produce guns, as well as supplying rifling machines, drill presses, milling machines and gun sights to other New England gun manufacturers, 224, lists the businesses in Windsor as N. Kendall and Company from 1835-1843; Robbins, Kendall & Lawrence, 1844-1847; Robbins and Lawrence, 1847-1855; Lamson, Goodnow & Yale, 1855-1864; E. G. Lamson and Company, 1864-1867; Roe, *English and American Tool Builders*, 187, lists the Robbins and Lawrence company selling off several branches, but by 1859 becoming Lamson, Goodnow and Yale; George Philander's two letters written in 1857 would have been in reference to employment by Robbins and Lawrence according to the time line in Roe, which seems most consistent with Philander's letters. Deyrup's list of company changes does not pick up the sale in 1857 mentioned in Philander's letter of September 6, 1857. Stephen worked for Lamson under another business collaboration. See also Gardner, *Small Arms Makers*, 111, for E. G. Lamson and Company years of operation in Windsor as 1850-1867, producing Palmer and Ball's carbines during the Civil War; page 213 for Windsor Manufacturing Company established in 1864 as a successor to E. G. Lamson; Guy Hubbard, "Leadership pf Early Windsor Industries in the Mechanic Arts, A Paper Read Before the Vermont Historical Society at Windsor, September 4, 1922," *Essays in the Social and Economic History of Vermont*, (Montpelier, Vermont Historical Society, 1943), 259, found the Lamson & Goodnow Manufacturing Company of the Shelburne Falls, Massachusetts purchased the Windsor Armory in 1858 and began manufacturing of Windsor Sewing Machines in 1858, 260, the White sewing machine is a lineal descendant of these machines. During the Civil War the armory operated under the names Lamson, Goodnow and Yale, and E. G. Lamson, and the Windsor Manufacturing Company, and manufactured 50,000 Springfield rifles, 1,000 Palmer Breech Loading Rifles, and 1,000 Ball Repeating Carbines for the Union, as well as hundreds of machine tools for the government and private armories, 260.

[70] Between 1857 and 1858 Philander and family moved from Cornish, NH to Windsor, VT, presumably following his employment in the Windsor armory.

[71] *Vermont Journal*, July 20, 1866, 2.

[72] Deyrup, *Arms Making in the Connecticut Valley*, 183; 213, for end in 1871, Sharps move to Connecticut, 124, 182, for numbers. Colt had incorporated in Hartford in 1854 and became the largest private armory in the world for its time, producing about 850,000 revolvers from 1840 to 1865. See Winston O. Smith, *The Sharps Rifle, its history, development and operation*, (New York: W. Morrow and Company, 1943).

[73] Deyrup, *Arms Making in the Connecticut Valley*, 183, for men employed; and Hubbard, *Leadership of Early Windsor*, 178, nearly 500 men.

[74] Vermont Provost Marshall General, Record of the Provost Marshall General, State of Vermont, Consolidated List Class II, Second District Vermont, Records of the Provost Marshall General's Bureau, Civil War, Vol. II, 1863-65, 273, referring to the E.G. Lamson company, in Windsor. The listing does not contain Stephen Williams' name, possibly because he would have been considered too old to draft.

[75] Ibid; *Vermont Journal*, December 4, 1880, 8, During the Civil War, the Windsor armory produced Springfield rifles on contract from the Government.

[76] Deyrup, *Arms Making in the Connecticut Valley,* 213, 226, Windsor Manufacturing Company lasting from 1867-68; Roe, *English and American Tool Builders,* 187, by 1869 the Jones, Lamson and company operated the machine shop in Windsor; *Vermont Journal,* December 4, 1880, 8, originally manufacturing sewing machines, the Windsor armory then switched to the production of Springfield rifles during the Civil War years.

[77] Deyrup, *Arms Making in the Connecticut Valley,* 249, 8, 9, the average annual wage of small arms workers was well above that of other industrial workers from 1850 through 1940.

[78] Brown, *Arming the Union,* 20.

[79] Merritt Roe Smith, "John H. Hall, Simeon North, and the Milling Machine: The Nature of Innovation among Antebellum Arms Makers," *Technology and Culture,* Vol. 14, No. 4 (Oct. 1973): 591; Meyer, *Networked Machinists.*

[80] By 1870, the armory in Windsor had been recommissioned as a cotton mill, although Philander is listed as a gunsmith in the 1870 census; the 1880 census shows Philander as a farmer; *Vermont Journal,* December 4, 1880, 8; *Vermont Journal,* February 22, 1902, 8, Philander's obituary.

[81] Charles S. Hall, *Hall Ancestry, A Series of Sketches of the lineal ancestors of the children of Samuel Holden Parsons Hall,* (New York and London: G. Putnam, 1896), 79, found the name Hall to be of Saxon origin and some genealogists have traced the name to Frederick De Halle in Tyrol and the son of Austrian King Albert; David B. Hall, *The Halls of New England, Genealogical and Biographical,* (Albany, N.Y.: Private Publishing, Printed for the author by J. Munsell's Sons, 1883), vi-vii, intro, ties the name to the Norwegian term for flint, which might suggest Viking origins; or from medieval English manor houses which had physical halls as part of the architecture; or the Welsh word for salt and subsequent naming of the men who worked in salt works.

[82] Hall, *Hall Ancestry,* 80.

[83] Hall, *Halls of New England,* 541.

[84] Ibid., 527.

[85] Ibid., 528-9.

[86] Virkus, *Immigrant Ancestors,* 30, Anthony Fisher Born in Syleham, England in 1591 and emigrated in the *Rose* in 1637 to Dedham, Mass.; See also Philip A. Fisher, *The Fisher Genealogy, Record of the Descendants of Joshua, Anthony and Cornelius Fisher of Dedham, Mass, 1636-1640,* (Everett, Mass: Massachusetts Publishing Company, 1898).

[87] Croydon, a small town settled in 1763, had 801 people at the 2020 census; It's peak of population was in 1820 when there were 1,060 people. See also: Mary Lou McGuire, Croydon, New *Hampshire, Two Villages Under the Mountain: Four Corners and East Village,* (Croydon, NH: Croydon Historical Society, 2022).

[88] Hall, *Halls of New England,* 556; see also Edmund Wheeler, *History of Croydon, New Hampshire,* (Claremont, NH: Printed by the Claremont Manufacturing Company, 1867), 110-111, short biography of Worthin Hall; See Hurd, *History of Cheshire and Sullivan Counties, New Hampshire,* 162 short biography of Worthin Hall, 157, for Justice of the Peace, 154, as representative of Croydon for 1866 and 1867, 165, membership on committee of arrangements for the 1866 centennial. There are significant inconsistencies with the spelling of Worthin between records and with various generations. The spelling has been standardized to Worthin.

[89] See Wheeler, *History of Newport,* 68; Edmund Wheeler, *Croydon, NH 1866, Proceedings at the Centennial Celebration on Wednesday June 13, 1866,* (Claremont, NH: Printed by Claremont Manufacturing Company, 1867), 167, for Justice.

[90] *New Hampshire Sentinel,* March 21, 1867, 2, State Legislature; *New Hampshire Argus and Spectator,* December 17, 1886, obituary, quote.

[91] From the context of one of Melinda Hall Williams' letters it also seems likely that Albert's oldest sister, Annginette, also boarded with Worthin and Polly Hall prior to her marriage and move to Iowa.

[92] *Reaper* log, Whaling Journal, 1835-1837, Log # 378, Peabody Essex Museum; For contemporary views of the whaling life see J. Ross Browne, *Etchings of a Whaling Cruise: With Notes of a Sojourn on the Island of Zanzibar* (New York: Harper, 1846); Francis Allyn Olstead , *Incidents of a Whaling Voyage,* (New York: Appleton and Company, 1841); Prentice Mulford, *Prentice Mulford's Story,* (Oakland, CA: California Relations #35, reprint, bio books, 1953). Lovewell is often spelled as Lovell.

[93] For general histories of whaling see Eric Jay Dolin, *Leviathan, The History of Whaling in America,* (NY and London: WW Norton and Company, 2007); Briton Cooper Busch, *"Whaling will Never Do For Me," The American Whaleman in the Nineteenth Century,* (Lexington: University of Kentucky Press, 1994), 172, before the mast; and Elmo P. Hohman, *The American Whaleman,* (New York: Longmans Green, 1928); Alexander Starbuck, *History of the American Whale Fishery,* reprint (Secaucus, NJ: Castle Books, 1989).

[94] *Whalemen's Shipping List and Merchant's Transcript (hereafter WSL),* June 8, 1847, 4; See also Margaret S. Creighton, *Rites and Passages, The Experiences of American Whaling, 1830-1870,* (Cambridge, Mass.: Cambridge University Press, 1995), Chapter 4, "The 'Old Man', The Sea Captain's Split Personality," 85-115; Daniel Vickers with Vince Walsh, *Young Men and The Sea, Yankee Seafarers in the Age of Sail,* (New Haven and London: Yale University Press, 2005), Chapter Seven on ship mastery, 214-247, in a study that focuses attention on Salem, Massachusetts.

[95] *WSL,* January 13, 1852, 1; Dolin, *Leviathan,* 206, total of 735 American whaling ships in 1846, 1853 most profitable; Lisa Norling, "Ahab's Wife, Women and the American Whaling Industry, 1820-1870," IN *Iron Men, Wooden Women, Gender and Seafaring in the Atlantic World, 1700-1920,* ed. Margaret Creighton and Lisa Norling, (Baltimore and London: John Hopkins University Press, 1996), 72; Edouard A. Stackpole, *The Sea-Hunters, The New England Whalemen During Two Centuries, 1635-1835,* (Philadelphia and New York: J.B. Lippincott Company, 1953), 473, believed: "The peak of American Whaling came in 1846 when six hundred and seventy-eight ships and barks, thirty-five brigs, and twenty-two schooners, composed the fleet"; world's whaling fleet comprised over 900 vessels.

[96] Elliott West, *Continental Reckoning, The American West in the Age of Expansion,* (Lincoln: University of Nebraska Press, 2023), xxviii, 30, 114, xxvi. "All of these impulses drew on and reinforced each other," that West calls "the gloss of confidence summed up in the term 'manifest destiny,' that the United States was bound to dominate the lands between its current border and the Pacific."

[97] Salem and Beverly, Massachusetts US, Crew Lists and Shipping Articles, 1797-1934, Crew lists on Ancestry.com.

[98] Brian Rouleau, "Maritime Destiny as Manifest Destiny, American Commercial Expansion and the Idea of the Indian," *Journal of the Early Republic*, 30, Fall 2010: 391, 394 notes a cosmopolitan work force did not ensure cosmopolitan ideas; Busch, *Whaling Will Never Do For Me*, 33-41.

[99] West, *Continental Reckoning*, 8, found early settlers in 1848, subsequent to the gold discovery, established one of the West's prime characteristics. From that time on "the region would be the most culturally and ethnically mixed part of the nation."

[100] See Busch, *Whaling Will Never Do*, 195n11; In 1840/1 a whaling voyage could expect to last 34 months, but by 1857/8 it lasted 45 months.

[101] *Columbian Centinel, Boston,* August 9, 1837, n.p. for August 1, 1837 marriage in Nashua, NH; Wheeler, *History of Croydon*, 110-111; The *Izette,* left Salem in October of 1837, made a two-year successful voyage to the Indian Ocean, Frances Diane Robotti, *Whaling and Old Salem*, (New York: Bonanza Books, 1962), 79-80; returned December 20, 1839 with 250 barrels of sperm oil and 2,050 barrels of other whale oil. Hall then captained the second voyage of the *Izette* leaving Salem from May 2, 1840 to June 19, 1842.

[102] See Judith Navas Lund, *Whaling Masters and Whaling Voyages Sailing From American Ports, A Compilation of Sources*, (New Bedford: Ten Pound Island Book Co., New Bedford Whaling Museum, 2001,); For general studies of whaling wives see Joan Druett, *Petticoat Whalers. Whaling Wives at Sea, 1820-1920*, (Auckland, New Zealand: Collins Pub., New Zealand, 1991); Emma Mayhew Whiting and Henry Beetle Hough, *Whaling Wives*, (Boston: Houghton Mifflin Company, 1953); Norling, Lisa, "Ahab's Wife, Women and the American Whaling Industry, 1820-1870," IN *Iron Men, Wooden Women, Gender and Seafaring in the Atlantic World, 1700-1920*, ed. Margaret Creighton and Lisa Norling, (Baltimore and London: John Hopkins University Press, 1996), 70-91; For specific journals of whaling wives see: Joan Druett, ed., *"She Was A Sister Sailor," Mary Brewster's Whaling Journals*, (Mystic, Ct.: Mystic Seaport Museum, 1992; Anne MacKay, ed. *She Went A-Whaling, the Journal of Martha Smith Brewer Brown from Orient, Long Island, New York, Around the World on the Whaling Ship Lucy Ann, 1847-1849*, (New York: Oysterponds Historical Society, 1993); Stanton Garner, ed. *The Captain's Best Mate, The Journal of Mary Chipman Lawrence on the Whaler Addison, 1856-1860*, (Hanover and London: University Press of New England, 1966). Nephew Worthin Hall Ames also sailed on the *Natchez*.

[103] Norling, "Ahab's Wife," 71. Historian Lisa Norling has postulated that captain's wives were pulled to sea by feelings of the era that placed women's most important function to be by their husband's sides. She argued that gendered spheres structured the whaling industry through a particular set of female images, crafted by Victorian notions of the time period, and the substance of women's work, generally tied to the home.

[104] Norling, "Ahab's Wife," 70-91 compelling, 85, maintain husband's family and community identities; 89, for "was generally restricted to the most favored, the most successful, or perhaps the most persuasive captains." See also Joan Druett, *Petticoat Whalers*, Chapter 2, "To Preserve Unbroken The Ties of Domestic Life," women's reasons for accompanying their husbands on whalers; duty to be with husbands, 18-19; wifely devotion, 22.

[105] Druett, *Petticoat Whalers*, 19; See also Nancy F. Cott, *The Bonds of Womanhood, "Women's Sphere" in New England, 1780-1835*, (New Haven and London: Yale University Press, 1977), Chap. 2, 63-100, on domesticity; and Glenda Riley, *Inventing the American Woman, A Perspective on Women's History*, (Arlington Heights: Harlan Davidson, 1987), Chap. 3, 63-87, on the proper sphere of women in establishing the home.

[106] Patricia Grimshaw, "'Christian Woman, Pious Wife, Faithful Mother, Devoted Missionary,' Conflicts in Roles of American Missionary Women in Nineteenth-Century Hawaii," *Feminist Studies*, 9, no. 3, (Fall 1983): 513, for the same concept with regard to missionary wives.

[107] "Lady Whalers," *WSL*, Vol XI, no 48, February 1, 1853, 2.

[108] Druett, "She was a Sister Sailor," 417 who lists 443 women, primarily whaling captains' wives as having gone to sea during the period of 1820-1920; 415, Mrs. Worthin Hall is credited with her *Natchez* voyage, but erroneously not the earlier sailings.

[109] Wheeler, *History of Newport,* 68, credits her with 10 years of sailing.

[110] Joan Druett, "Whaling Wives, Sister Sailors," *Sea History* Magazine, 74, (Summer 1995): 20-22 credits whaling wife Mrs. Gray as "trailblazing" when she set sail with her husband in June 1844. By Druett's standards, Polly was a trailblazer; First mate, Martin Arey's log of the *Elizabeth* (Peabody Essex Museum Log #546) noted that Mrs. Hall and husband stayed in San Francisco during a stop in late August through September 17, 1846, when the population was less than 500 people. On May 29, 1847, "Mrs. Hall very sick," one of two entries about Mrs. Hall's health may indicate a miscarriage.

[111] Mercy Whitney, *Journal* 1, 1848-1852, Hawaiian Mission Children's Society Museum and Library, Honolulu, (hereafter HMCSML), 83.

[112] *Majestic* and *Natchez* log, 1848-1855, Nathan Hall, log keeper, Log #1741, Peabody Essex Museum, 44, 45, 57; Hall, *Halls of New England*, 556; Mary's birth date. For biographies of Dwight Baldwin and family see David W. Forbes, Ralph Thomas Kam, Thomas A. Woods, *Partners in Change, A Biographical Encyclopedia of American Protestant Missionaries in Hawaii and their Hawaiian and Tahitian Colleagues, 1820-1900*, (Honolulu: Hawaiian Mission Children's Society, 2018), 91-96; Mary Charlotte Alexander, *Dr. Baldwin of Lahaina*, (Berkeley: Stanford University Press, 1953), a biography written by Baldwin's granddaughter, 135, notes the population of Maui at 112 nonnatives in 1846; see Chapter 12, The Whaling Fleets at Lahaina; Francis John Halford, *Nine Doctors and God*, (Honolulu: University of Hawaii Press, 1954), chapter VIII, Dwight Baldwin, Doctor-Dominie, 119-131.

[113] Wheeler, *Croydon, NH 1866, Proceedings,* 110-111.

[114] *Elizabeth, Majestic, Natchez*, 1844-1855, Nathan Hall, log keeper, Log #1490, Peabody Essex Museum, first 14 pages appear to have been written by John Melzard; the remainder of the volume by Nathan Hall; Ancestry.com for *Elizabeth* crew list provides age; See Druett, *Petticoat Whalers*, 139, who credits Mrs. Mary Brewster as "breaking new ground" when she accompanied her husband on a whaling cruise to Lower California in November, 1846; the boat refers to the 28 to 30 foot whaling boats attached to the sides of every whaling ship.

[115] *Elizabeth, Majestic, Natchez*, Melzard section November 2, 1845, n.p.; this was probably Isla Del Rey, one of the Pearl Island group in the Bay of Panama, based on latitude and longitude recorded in the log.

[116] Ibid.

[117] Alexander, *Dr. Baldwin of Lahaina*, 200, 213; 251, for several seasons; See HMCSML Digital Archive, Baldwin letter collection online at hmha.missionhouses.org.

[118] *WSL* February 28, 1854, 2, noted the fastest voyage to Hawaii from New Bedford at 79 days or 2 ½ months; Whiting and Hough, *Whaling Wives*, 54 for fastest passage between Honolulu and New Bedford at 95 days. The journey by whaleship from New Bedford to Lahaina, Maui was between three to six months on average, giving Mrs. Hall only a few months on board, traveling to and from the islands.

[119] Forbes, et al., *Partners in Change*; Rufus Anderson, *History of the Sandwich Island Mission*, (Boston: Congregational Publishing Company, 1870); William R. Hutchison, *Errand to the World: American Protestant Thought and Foreign Missions* (Chicago: University of Chicago Press, 1987), 62-63, Hawaii as a triumphant success; 86-89, problems of success.

[120] Busch, *Whaling will Never Do*, 106-7.

[121] Cummins E. Speakman, Jr., *Mowee, An Informal History of the Hawaiian Island*, (Salem, Mass.: Peabody Museum of Salem, 1978), 99, recalling 1843 options.

[122] Druett, *Petticoat Whalers*, 155, quoting a Dwight Baldwin letter of October 22, 1852.

[123] Ethel M. Damon, *Koamalu; a story of pioneers on Kauai, and of what they built in that island garden,* Vol 1, (Honolulu: Private pub., 1931), 400.

[124] Edward Joesting, *Kauai, The Separate Kingdom*, (Kauai: University of Hawaii Press and Kauai Museum Association, 1984), 162.

[125] Mercy Whitney, *Journal I*, HMCSML, n.p.

[126] Damon, *Koamalu*, 300; 302, for a sketch of Waimea in 1853, 474, photo. George Rowell is credited with building a sandstone or coral stone church at Waimea, 86 by 42 feet which still stands. Mrs. Hall's later stay on Kauai overlapped with the church construction credited to George Rowell; www.halepuna.org; National Register Nomination Gulick-Rowell House credits the Peter Gulick family with early construction beginning in 1829, National Historic Places Register Reference Number is 78001027.

[127] George Rowell – Missionary Letters – 1848-1850 - to Dwight Baldwin: Dated Waimea, April 13, 1850; 1, 2. *Hawaiian Mission Houses Digital Archive*, accessed March 8, 2023; hmha.missionhouses.org/files/original/8aa301dceabb3ca7ae232e0ade521bbc.pdf.

[128] George Rowell, - Missionary Letters - 1848-1850 - to Baldwin, Dwight, *Hawaiian Mission Houses Digital Archive*, accessed March 8, 2023, http://hmha.missionhouses.org/items/show/726.

[129] Lucy E. (Hart) Wilcox, - Letters to Lucy Eliza Hart Wilcox at Waioli - Rowell, Malvina J. (Waimea) ~ August 29, 1850," *Hawaiian Mission Houses Digital Archive*, accessed March 8, 2023, http://hmha.missionhouses.org/items/show/2572. Later date, September 23, 1850, is incorporated into letter to Mrs. Wilcox.

[130] Samuel Whitney, Missionary Letters - 1819-1870 - from Whitney, Mercy, *Hawaiian Mission Houses Digital Archive*, July 6, 1852; accessed Sept. 19, 2023 https://hmha.missionhouses.org/items/browse?collection=163; Forbes, et al., *Partners in Change*, 539.

[131] Forbes, et al., *Partners in Change,* 1; Joesting, *Kauai*, 124, for mothered.

[132] Whitney, *Journal II*, HMCSML, 15, August 10, 1852; see Halford, *Nine Doctors*, chapter XII, 179-194, 222; Forbes, et al., *Partners in Change*, 558-564, for biography of James Smith, missionary.

[133] See Lois S. Hoyt Johnson, - Journal - 1836-1838, *Hawaiian Mission Houses Digital Archive*, accessed February 8, 2022, http://hmha.missionhouses.org/items/show/81; Ethel M. Damon, editor, *Letters from the Life of Abner and Lucy Wilcox*, 1836-1869, (Honolulu: Privately Printed Honolulu, 1950), 243-246; Forbes, et al., *Partners in Change*, 359-360.

[134] Joesting, *Kauai*, 141.

[135] Lois Johnson letter, November 1845 says they have been visited by only 2 whalers this fall, one French and one American ("seemed temperate and moral") who recruited two Native Hawaiians for work, Lois Johnson to Sister Lyons, November 3, 1845, 3, online at http://hmha.missionhouses.org/files/original/95ba7270af58ebad27bf9180904e433d.pdf

[136] Nathan Hall, logs of Majestic/Natchez, PEM, log #1741, n.p.

[137] Whitney, *Journal II*, HMCSML, 24 at top.

[138] Whitney, *Journal II,* HMCSML, 28, Pamphlet dated February 16, 1852. Nineteenth-century women were allowed authority in the sphere of love and nurturance, thus pamphlets of this nature reinforced societal expectations for women. Women's domestic work was an extension of women's inherent nature; see Jeanne Boydston, *Home and Work, Housework, Wages, and the Ideology of Labor in the Early Republic*, (New York: Oxford University Press, 1990); Richard Shiels, "The Feminization of American Congregationalism, 1730-1835," *American Quarterly*, Vol.33, no.1, (Spring 1981): 46-62, the Congregational religion glorified motherhood and sanctified the home.

[139] Nathan Hall, Majestic/Natchez, PEM, log #1741, n.p.; She returned to Maui by April 6th, 1853 when she started rooming with Mrs. Anne (Newman) Edwards, wife of Captain Pardon Edwards of the *George Washington*.

[140] Letters and Papers of Alexander and Baldwin Families in Hawaii, HMCSML, Charlotte Fowler Baldwin to daughter Abigail, Folder 155, letters dated March 26, 1854 and April 10, 1854, HMCSML; Sereno Edwards Bishop, *Reminiscences of Old Hawaii, with a brief biography by Lorrin A. Thurston*, (Honolulu: Hawaiian Gazette Company Limited, 1916), 56 the general meetings for missionaries were held annually in Honolulu and lasted from 4 to 6 weeks.

[141] "Baldwin, Dwight - Missionary Letters - by writer - G-K - mostly non-missionary," *Hawaiian Mission Houses Digital Archive*, accessed March 8, 2023, http://hmha.missionhouses.org/items/show/218; Louisa Woodbridge, wife of whaling captain Ebeneezer Hawes Woodbridge, were both from Dartmouth, Mass. Captain Woodbridge captained the ship *Metacom* from 1853 to 1857, but no known log for this voyage exists. Woodbridge captained four ships during his career including the *Fortune* from 1847-1850. A James Lovell, possibly Polly's brother James as the spelling of the last name is inconsistent between records, is listed on the crew list of the *Fortune*. He may have again shipped out with Woodbridge on the *Metacom*. Mrs. Hall and Mrs. Woodbridge had a long relationship having been on Maui together prior to 1851.

[142] Letters and Papers of Alexander and Baldwin Families in Hawaii, Charlotte Fowler Baldwin to Dwight Baldwin, Folder 154, HMCSML, foundation notes, original letter in the Van Dyke collection, "Capt. Hall and his family will spend the Sabbath with us."

[143] Letters and Papers of Alexander and Baldwin Families in Hawaii, Emily Baldwin to her sister Abigail, June 27, 1854, Folder 433, HMCSML.

[144] Letters and Papers of Alexander and Baldwin Families in Hawaii, Charlotte Baldwin to Abigail Baldwin, Letter dated November 30, 1854, Folder 155, HMCSML.

[145] Letters and Papers of Alexander and Baldwin Families in Hawaii, Emily Baldwin to Dwight Baldwin, December. 6, 1854, Folder 433, Lahaina Restoration Foundation notes, original letter in Van Dyke collection, HMCSML library; Emily notes that Captain Hall regretted having to leave without being able to personally say goodbye to Dwight Baldwin; See also Bishop, *Reminiscences of Old Hawaii,* 59.

[146] Nancy F. Cott, *The Bonds of Womanhood,* Chapter 5, 160-196, on a sense of sisterhood between Antebellum era women, 168, the identification of women with feeling rather than reflection implied that they would find truly reciprocal interpersonal relationships only with other women; Lori D. Ginzberg, *Women and the Work of Benevolence: Morality, Politics, and Class in the Nineteenth-Century United States,* (New Haven and London: Yale University Press, 1990), 6, the identification of women with morality had a powerful hold on society, conservative benevolent women were likely to be members of wealthy, locally influential family and community networks as reflected by class; Ernest Beaglehole, *Social Change in the South Pacific, Roatonga and Aitutaki,* (New York: McMillan Company, 1957), 28, on Congregationalism.

[147] R. Richard Wohl, edited by Moses Rischin, "The Country Boy Myth and Its Place in American Urban Culture, The Nineteenth-Century Contribution," *Perspectives in American History,* Vol. III, (1969): 77-156, 80

[148] See Woloch, *Women and the American Experience,* 21-22.

[149] Many women's historians have discussed the dominant themes of respectable women's lives as tied to domesticity. See Barbara Welter, "The Cult of True Womanhood, 1820-1860," *American Quarterly,* Vol. 18, no. 2, Part I, (Summer, 1966): 151-174, discussed the four traits of ideal womanhood as piety, purity, submissiveness, and domesticity. Creating and maintaining a home dominated women's lives. Nancy F. Cott, *The Bonds of Womanhood,* 158, found ministers used the concept of "women's sphere" to esteem female importance while containing it; Amy Kaplan, "Manifest Domesticity," *American Literature* 70, no. 3 (September 1998): 581-606; Jeanne Boydston, *Home and Work, Housework, Wages, and the Ideology of Labor in the Early Republic,* (New York: Oxford University Press, 1990), 144,159, argued for the pastoralization of housework, labor was gender-driven, housework eventually became culturally invisible; Glenda Riley, *Female Frontier, A Comparative View of Women on the Prairie and Plains,* (Lawrence: University Press of Kansas, 1988); Barbara Leslie Epstein, *The Politics of Domesticity: Women, Evangelism, and Temperance in Nineteenth-Century America,* (Middletown, CT: Wesleyan University Press, 1981), 2-4, argued for class as shaping domesticity and Protestant evangelism of middling class women of New England and the mid-west; Amy G. Richter, *At Home in the Nineteenth-Century America, A Documentary History,* (New York: New York University Press, 2015), 4, "many Americans sought to re-create or approximate the ideals of refined and respectable domesticity in new settings," 5, people used the values of domesticity to interpret and change their lives.

[150] Nathan Hall, *Majestic/Natchez,* PEM, log #1741, n.p.

[151] See Amy G. Richter, *At Home in the Nineteenth-Century America,* for a discussion of the importance of the home to nineteenth-century Americans; middle class white women were deeply rooted in the home which embodied the power and tested the limits of American values.

[152] See Elizabeth Hampsten, *Read This Only to Yourself; The Private Writings of Midwestern Women, 1880-1910,* (Bloomington: Indiana University Press, 1982), 40, observed that "women describe where they are in relation to other people more than according to a spot not the map," 68, men wrote about themselves, events, and specific distinctions, while women saw patterns in life.

[153] See Faye E. Dudden, *Serving Women: Household Service in Nineteenth-Century America,* (Middletown, CT.: Wesleyan University Press, 1983), 5, defined household help as different from domestic service. Under Dudden's definition, hired help might have been hired for spring cleaning, harvest, etc. for short periods of time. This definition fits best with the hired people noted in the census; Woloch, *Women and the American Experience,* 118, and especially Chapter Six, Promoting Woman's Sphere, 1800-1860.

[154] For a contemporary view of Vermont subsistence farming see Collamer M. Abbott, "'Gramp' Abbott's Life, Farming in Central Vermont, 1865-1913," *Vermont History* 39, (1971): 31-42; Williamstown Historical Society, *Williamstown My Own, The History of Williamstown, Vermont, 1781-2012,* (Williamstown: Williamstown Historical Society, 2012), 208, on Wesley Seaver, Nathan's son-in-law; Nathan Hall, *Elizabeth, Majestic, Natchez,* 1844-1855, Log #1490, Peabody Essex Museum, n.p.

[155] Worthin Hall, *Natchez* log # 827, New Bedford Whaling Museum, 50.

[156] Wheeler, *Proceedings at the Centennial Celebration,* 71. In 1866, Mrs. Polly Hall joined other ladies to celebrate the centennial of Croydon by serving on the Committee of Ladies; see also Nathan Hall, *Elizabeth, Majestic, Natchez,* 1844-1855, Log #1490, Peabody Essex Museum, n.p.

[157] *New Hampshire Argus and Spectator,* July 21, 1882, 2, Luke and Annginette Sherman visit NH; *New Hampshire Argus and Spectator,* August 30, 1878, 2; *Grinnell Herald,* July 2, 1878, 3, Captain, wife, and Mary visited for several weeks; *Grinnell Herald,* October 8, 1880, 3, says Capt. Worthin Hall and Capt. Daniel Hall of Williamstown, Vermont were visiting.

[158] Poweshiek County, Iowa, *U.S. Probate, School and Court Records, 1850-1954,* General Index Vol 4, 1887-1902, on Ancestry.com; Sherman guardianship of Mary (Hall) Hubbard's sons.

[159] See Dean Crawford Smith and Melinde Lutz Sanborn, *Vital Records of Croydon NH to the End of the Year 1900,* (New England Historical Genealogical Society Boston, 1999), Polly oldest sibling with three brothers, David, Noah, James; Polly b. Dec 8, 1806 and d. March 1, 1886. Worthin d. Sept 13, 1886.

[160] *Vermont Phoenix,* December 31, 1886, 1, died in Croydon at 84. Albert's grandsons recalled a story that Worthin Hall suffered from inner ear balance issues that may have stemmed from his many years at sea. He could not stand without swaying back and forth as if on a ship at sea. He had to hold the handrailing of Albert's porch in order to not be cast overboard into the Iowa farmland.

[161] Annginette b. October 23, 1837; Frances b. February 21, 1851. Worthin F. Grattan always referred to his great-Aunt, as Annginette Hall, as if both names constituted her true given name.

[162] Jayna Huot Hooper, *Celebrating Community Newport, New Hampshire, 1761-2011, 250 Years and Beyond,* (Newport, NH: Newport Historical Society, 2011), 82.

[163] Melinda H. Williams v. Stephen Williams, Jr. Divorce Decided July, 1856, Sullivan County Superior Court Records, New Hampshire State Archives, Concord, NH., 1-19. Jayna Hooper and Larry Cote, *The Diary of Charles Emerson,* (Newport, NH: Newport Historical Society, 2021), x, says that there were a dozen men from Newport, New Hampshire who participated in the California Gold Rush, among them ship master Shubael Hawes, page 11, who appears in the 1850 Federal census in the home immediately preceding Stephen Williams' home.

[164] Ibid., 35.

[165] Norma Basch, *Framing American Divorce, From the Revolutionary Generation to the Victorians*, (Berkeley: University of California Press, 1999,) 47.

[166] Glenda Riley, *Divorce, An American Tradition*, (New York and Oxford: Oxford University Press, 1991), 78-79; see also Nancy Cott, *Public Vows: A History of Marriage and the Nation*, (Cambridge and London: Harvard University Press, 2000), for marriage as a function of society and public policy; Martin Schultz, "Divorce in Early America: Origins and Trends in Three North Central States," *Sociological Quarterly*, 25, 4, (Autumn 1984), 523, the increase in American divorce rates reflects a steady, prolonged process by which more and more spouses have sought a legal remedy for their marital problems.

[167] Melinda H. Williams v. Stephen Williams, Jr. Divorce, 20; See Amy Richter, *At Home in the Nineteenth-Century*, 52, noted that women who worked for wages were morally suspect. Stephen's testimony appears to rely on this notion.

[168] Ruth Wallis Herndon and John E. Murray, *Children Bound to Labor, The Pauper Apprentice System in Early America*, (Ithica and London: Cornell University Press, 2009), 38, 40 binding out waned during the nineteenth century with the heaviest activity from 1750 to 1800.

[169] Riley, *Divorce*, 7, notes modern studies which indicate the negative impact of divorce on children was greater than ever previously suspected.

[170] Dudden, *Serving Women*, 37 argued that eating together is one of the most fundamental ways to form and maintain relationships.

[171] Albert and Francis were together, either bound out or living with their father from this date in 1852 until he left for Iowa in late 1856/early 1857. It is difficult to determine if and to what extent Albert may have suffered child abuse. Late in life, Albert recalled his childhood to his grandsons, and then his grandsons retold the memories to later generations. For an historical discussion of violence within the family setting see Linda Gordon, *Heroes of Their Own Lives, The Politics and History of Family Violence, Boston 1880-1960*, (New York: Viking, Penguin Books, 1988), who based her book on social work agency case studies.

[172] Child, *History of Cornish*, 153-4.

[173] See Elliott West, *Growing Up With the Country, Children on the Far Western Frontier*, (Albuquerque: University of New Mexico Press, 1998) for a general exploration of the lives of 19th century children.

[174] Elliott West, "Child's Play: Tradition and Adaptation on the Frontier," *Montana, The Magazine of Western History*, Vol 38, no. 1, Winter 1988, 2-15, argued that children turned work into play, and that play was critical to childhood in the mid-1800s.

[175] Francis was taught by her sister-in-law, Eliza Blair Williams presumably from 1864 until Eliza's marriage in 1866.

[176] Thomas R. Baker, *The Sacred Cause of Union, Iowa in the Civil War*, (Iowa City: University of Iowa Press, 2016), 2, "The new west in 1860 included Missouri, Arkansas, Louisiana, Iowa, Kansas, Minnesota, and the territories of Oklahoma and Nebraska." Bob Brown, *Echoes from Middle Iowa's Historic Past*, (Fort Dodge, Iowa: Messenger Printing, 2002), 28, for 50 counties; For general histories of Iowa see Leland L. Sage, *A History of Iowa*, (Ames: Iowa State University Press, 1987); Dorothy Schwieder, *Iowa, The Middle Land*, (Ames: Iowa State University Press, 1996), and Allan Bogue, *From Prairie to Corn Belt*, (Chicago and London: University of Chicago Press: 1963); The Iowa frontier period included this beginning date up to 1870.

[177] G. H. White, *Historical Sketch of Chester Township*, read at the quarter centennial, July 4, 1881, (Grinnell: Cravath and Shaw Steam Printers, 1881), 4-5, for purchase of 1800 acres. The Shermans, New England Congregationalists, were counted among the first settlers of Croydon, New Hampshire in 1763.

[178] Ibid, ten acres planted in corn.

[179] Anonymous, *Portrait, and Biographical Record of Johnson, Poweshiek, and Iowa Counties, Iowa* (Chicago: Chapman Bros., 1893), 483.

[180] Leonard Fletcher Parker, *History of Poweshiek County, Iowa; A History of Settlement, Organization, Progress, and Achievement*, (Chicago: S. J. Clarke Publishing company, 1911), 324 on Chester township, 326 on Jason W. Sherman; Old Settlers Association, *Proceedings of the Old Settlers' Association of Grinnell*, "March 19, 1895, The Shermans by Mrs. A. H. Sherman," *Proceedings of the Annual Meeting of the Old Settlers of Grinnell*, (Grinnell, Iowa: Signal Printing, 1895), 14-17, William Sherman bought a farm first in Poweshiek County, Iowa, while living in Lyons, Iowa. Jason Sherman and wife Anginette (Blanchard) Sherman, of Croydon, NH married only one month before Luke and Annginette Sherman in Claremont, NH. Both of the Sherman brothers returned to NH to marry, then both couples, Jason and wife and Luke and wife Annginette Hall Williams, settled in Chester Township in September 1856.

[181] Old Settlers Association, "March 19, 1895, The Shermans by Mrs. A. H. Sherman," 14-17, for Sept. 2, 1856, as first night in Grinnell and next day in what would become Chester Township. The 1856 Iowa State census lists 70 dwelling houses with 70 families in Grinnell, Poweshiek County; State of Iowa, *Census Returns of the different Counties of the State of Iowa for 1856, Printed by the Authority of the Census Board*, (Iowa City: Crum and Boye Printers, 1856), 335. See also Glenda Riley, *Building and Breaking Families in the American West*, (Albuquerque: University of New Mexico Press, 1996), 14, who found another example of a man residing in Poweshiek County in 1854 who returned to New Hampshire to marry a woman he had begun to court before he left for the West.

[182] Glenda Riley, *Frontierswomen, The Iowa Experience*, (Ames: Iowa State University Press, 1994), xiii, critiques the stereotypes of pioneer women.

[183] Old Settlers Association, "March 19, 1895, The Shermans by Mrs. A. H. Sherman," 14-17, for date of settlement in Grinnell; Parker, *History of Poweshiek County*, 10, population of Grinnell in September 1856.

[184] Ibid., 15, size of shack, hauled water.

[185] A lengthy biography of Annginette is in the book *Portrait, and Biographical Record of Johnson, Poweshiek, and Iowa Counties, Iowa* (Chicago: Chapman Bros., 1893), 482-484; 483, says she and Luke were the first settlers; Old Settlers Association, *Proceedings of the Old Settlers' Association of Grinnell, Second and Third Annual Meetings*, March 19, 1895, "The Shermans by Mrs. A. H. Sherman," 14-17 for snakes, wood, cow; See Brown, *Echoes from Middle Iowa's Historic Past*, 27, for pioneer problems including wild animals, hostile Indians, and prairie fires; See Glenda Riley, *Female Frontier, A Comparative View of Women on the Prairie and Plains*, (Lawrence: University Press of Kansas, 1988) for frontier women's lives as bounded by traditional domesticity. A short obituary for Annginette Hall Sherman appeared in the *Long Beach Press-Telegram*, February 10, 1916, 2. Her obituary also reflects a reluctance on her part to use Williams as a maiden name, perhaps she took her mother's side during her parent's divorce and emphasized her descendance from the Hall side of the family.

[186] See David B. Danbom, *Sod Busting, How Families Made Farms on the 19th - Century Plains*, (Baltimore: John Hopkins University Press, 2014), 2, 8.

[187] See Susan E. Gray, *The Yankee West, Community Life on the Michigan Frontier*, (Chapel Hill: University of North Carolina Press, 1996), for the continuation of New England values in the Midwest, and the continuation of New England folkways in the Midwest among strong market participation, 48, Midwest farmers used a strategy of diversified commodity production, 172, key Yankee institutions were local government, church, and school; See also Frank L. Herriott, "Seventy Years in Iowa," *Annals of Iowa* 27 (1945): 97-118, for the memories of early Grinnell settler, Joanna Harris Haines.

[188] Thomas A. Lucas, "Men Were Too Fiery for Much Talk, The Grinnell Anti-Abolitionist Riot of 1860," *Palimpsest*, Vol 68, no 1, (1987): 14.

[189] For a history of the Underground Railway in Iowa see: Lowell J. Soike, *Necessary Courage, Iowa's Underground Railroad in the Struggle Against Slavery*, (Iowa City: University of Iowa Press, 2013).

[190] Lucas, "Men Were Too Fiery," 14; Soike, *Necessary Courage*, 10, Congregationalists were among the most active anti-slavery religious groups.

[191] Soike, *Necessary Courage*, 10, 148.

[192] The idea of sympathetic understanding of husband's work in the Iowa frontier is explored by Glenda Riley *Frontierswomen, The Iowa Experience*, (Ames: Iowa State University Press, 1994); Annginette may have also believed that Iowa offered Albert his best opportunity for advancement.

[193] Nettie Sanford, "History of Marshall County, Iowa, Chapter IV," *Annals of Iowa*, Vol. 9, no. 2, (April 1871): 544.

[194] Josiah Bushnell Grinnell, *Men and Events of Forty Years, Autobiographical Reminiscences of an Active Career from 1850 to 1890*, (Boston: D. Lothrop Co., 1891), 347; See also Anonymous, *The History of Poweshiek County, Iowa*, (Des Moines: Union History Company, 1880), 924 for short bio of Luke; Luke Sherman's will is on Ancestry.com at *Poweshiek County, Iowa, U.S., Probate, School, and Court Records, 1850-1954*.

[195] Parker, *History of Poweshiek County*, 326; White, *Historical Sketch of Chester Township*, 7.

[196] He left after December 7, 1856, based on a letter written to Albert in Cornish, and arrived before an April 28, 1857 letter written to him in Grinnell.

[197] See Baker, *Sacred Cause*, 69; Memories of the journey are captured in his daughter's thoughts in Appendix I.

[198] James L. Huston, "Western Grains and the Panic of 1857," *Agricultural History*, 57, 1, (January 1983): 14-32, 15; Charles W. Calomiris and Larry Schweikart, "The Panic of 1857: Origins, Transmission and Containment," *The Journal of Economic History*, Vol 51, no. 4, (Dec 1991): 814, New Hampshire and Vermont were the hardest hit of New England states.

[199] Thomas R. Baker, *The Sacred Cause of Union, Iowa in the Civil War*, (Iowa City: University of Iowa Press, 2016), 15, 16.

[200] Calomiris and Schweikart, "The Panic of 1857", 809, 811, 819.

[201] Ibid., 815-816.

[202] Ibid., 821-824.

[203] Ibid., 814.

[204] *Grinnell Herald*, Sept 28, 1917, 4.

[205] Old Settlers' Association President, Annual Meeting of Old Settlers' Association of Grinnell, Iowa, 1900, President's Opening Address, *Proceedings of the Annual Meeting of the Old Settlers of Grinnell*, (Grinnell, Iowa: Signal Printing); Old Settlers' Association President, Annual Meeting of Old Settlers' Association of Grinnell, Iowa, 1902, *Proceedings of the Annual Meeting of the Old Settlers of Grinnell*, (Grinnell, Iowa: Signal Printing).

[206] Old Settlers Association, *Proceedings of the Old Settlers' Association of Grinnell*, Proceedings of the Seventh Annual meeting, 1900, 30-31; Historian Allan Bogue described the split rail fences that surrounded pioneer fields in *From Prairie to Corn Belt*, 73-74, 74 Some farmers hauled rails as far as twelve miles; Schweider, *Iowa The Middle Land*, 134, adequate fencing was a major difficulty prior to the Civil War.

[207] Old Settlers Association, *Proceedings of the Old Settlers' Association of Grinnell*, Proceedings of the Ninth Meeting, 1902, President's Address, 5.

[208] Old Settlers Association, *Proceedings 1900*, 31, $140 is equal to between 5,000 and 12,000 in 2023 dollars.

[209] Soike, *Underground Railroad*, 148.

[210] Baker, *The Sacred Cause of Union*, 17, 69, for 130,000.

[211] Katharine Macy Noyes, *Jesse Macy: An Autobiography*, (Springfield, Ill and Baltimore, Maryland: Charles C. Thomas 1933) 149.

[212] Noyes, *Jesse Macy*, 6-7, 149, 163, notes the attendance of a classmate, Jesse Macy, at the first Grinnell University and Iowa College in December 1859 when Albert would have also attended. Unfortunately, there is no list of classmates from this time.

[213] *Grinnell Herald*, March 31, 1899, 2; Francis (Williams) Hays came to Grinnell in 1861; one of the first students in the Chester Township school in 1862, White, *Historical Sketch of Chester*, 9.

[214] Sara Zeigler, "Wifely Duties: Marriage, Labor and the Common Law in Nineteenth-Century America," *Social Science History*, Vol. 20. no. 1, (Spring 1996), 72, found labor obligations associated with marriage sharply curtailed the autonomy of married women; See Alice Kessler-Harris, *Out to Work, A History of Wage-Earning Women in the United States*, (Oxford: Oxford University Press, 2003), the classic study of working women; Lee Virginia Chambers-Schiller, *Liberty, A Better Husband, Single Women in America: The Generations of 1780-1840*, (New Haven and London: Yale University Press, 1984), 8, 218n29, notes the contradictory nature of research on women's lives in the West; Margaret Jacobs, "Western History: What's Gender Got to do With It?" *Western Historical Quarterly*, Vol. 42, no. 3 (Autumn 2011), 303, "gender is fundamental to the ordering of society, and the creation of individual and collective identities."

[215] Nancy F. Cott, *The Bonds of Womanhood*, 20, women's work was considered adjunct and secondary to men's work.

[216] Kessler-Harris, *Out to Work*, 48, found women seamstresses a rather common occupation, 65, in New York about twice as many women desired work as seamstresses as jobs available; Dudden, *Serving Women*, 130, the usual work of seamstresses was done for women who did not sew and who wanted custom work; *National Eagle*, June 10, 1865, 3; Anonymous, *Portraits, and Biographical Record of Johnson, Poweshiek, and Iowa Counties, Iowa*, 483.

[217] White, *Historical Sketch of Chester*, 7.

[218] *Roster and record of Iowa soldiers during the War of Rebellion*, on Ancestry.com.

[219] Died March 28, 1899.

[220] Robert Cook, "A War for Principle? Shifting Memories of the Union Cause, 1865-1916," *Annals of Iowa*, 74, 3, (Summer 2015): 225, quoting from Leland Sage, *History of Iowa*, (Ames: 1974) 153-4; See Dorothy Schwieder, *Iowa, The Middle Land*, (Ames: Iowa State University Press, 1996), Chapter Five, Iowans and the Civil War Era, 67-82; See also Ginette Aley and J. L. Anderson, editors, *Union Heartland, The Midwestern Home Front During the Civil War*, (Carbondale: Southern Illinois University Press, 2013).

[221] Baker, *Sacred Cause*, 145, 164-5.

[222] Emery Bartlett, "Letter to Grinnell: Emery S. Bartlett to his children and grandchildren," *Annals of Iowa*, Vol 44, no 6, (Fall 1978): 419-440; Herriott, "Seventy Years in Iowa," 97-118, Ms. Harris said her brother Will was needed at home and Emory Bartlett also did not serve, commenting on substitutes hired to take their places.

[223] Bogue, *From Prairie to Corn Belt*, 182, argued that the depletion of farm laborers to the Civil War increased the use of farm machinery.

[224] Rhoda M. Williams V. Stephen Williams, September 2, 1879; Sullivan County record of divorce, 37, State of New Hampshire State Archives, Concord, NH.

[225] See Hal S. Barron, *Those Who Stayed Behind, Rural Society in Nineteenth-century New England*, (Cambridge: Cambridge University Press, 1984), 82, only 5.2% of older men from Stephen's age cohort left New England, 87, 92, social connections and family ties were factors in out migration. Stephen left Cornish, New Hampshire after the 1880 census placed him, a laborer, at 67 years old in the household of George Sargent.

[226] Rhoda Williams V. Stephen Williams and Albert Williams, Poweshiek County. Circuit Court, December 1883, Box 745, December 18, 1882. Poweshiek County Clerk of Court, compensation of $2028.66 plus interest.

[227] Poweshiek County, Iowa, No. 5, Circuit Court, Poweshiek County Appearance Docket, Judgment Docket, Execution Docket and Fee Book, Box 745, Book 3, 41. No additional information on this judgment was available from the Poweshiek County Clerk. See Poweshiek County Circuit Court Record, Vol. 2, 1882-1886, Case 683, 221-225, *Poweshiek County, Iowa, U.S., Probate, School, and Court Records, 1850-1954* on Ancestry.com.

[228] Poweshiek County Appearance Docket Judgement Docket, Execution Docket and Fee Book, Box 745, book 3, 41.

[229] Poweshiek County, Circuit Court Case 683, 223.

[230] See Old Settlers Association, *Proceedings of the Old Settlers' Association of Grinnell, Second and Third Annual Meetings*, March 19, 1895, "The Shermans by Mrs. A. H. Sherman," 14-17.

[231] Schwieder, *Iowa, Middle Land*, 35 for 1870 population of 1,194,020.

[232] *Grinnell Herald*, September 4, 1883, 3.

[233] *Grinnell Herald*, April 30, 1886, 2.

[234] *Campbell Interurban Press*, September 22, 1904, 7, obituary for Stephen, at 91 years, 10 months, and 15 days old.

[235] Stephen and Rhoda had one child, daughter Martha E. Williams (1865-1917), nicknamed Mattie, born October 24, 1865, in Cornish. The 1880 census shows Rhoda, divorced, and Mattie, 13 years old, living in Cornish in a dwelling by themselves. Mattie grew up to become a school teacher, and she and her mother eventually relocated to Kansas. Mattie married a doctor, John Chambers, in 1894 in Brown, Kansas, and soon the couple moved to a small farming community in the northern part of the state where John was credited as being the city physician. Rhoda joined her daughter in Hanover, Washington, Kansas in 1897 where she developed a close-knit group of friends. By 1900 the three lived in one household. The marriage produced no children, and Mattie devoted her life to lodge and society endeavors. Rhoda died suddenly in 1914 and Mattie lingered with an unstated illness for several years finally succumbing in 1917; *Hanover Herald*, February 13, 1914, 1; *Hanover Herald* January 26, 1917, 1. John Chambers remarried in 1919 to Emma Artemesia "Artie" Hobbs of Cheyenne Wyoming, a childhood sweetheart. They remained in Hanover, until retiring to Sulphur Springs, Arkansas where John Chambers died in 1934; *Hanover Herald* August 22, 1919, 1.

[236] Wedding and birth records from England have been unavailable. An 1851 census places William and Ann in greater London with son Edward, ten years old, and daughters Eliza, Ann, and Louisa.

[237] Passenger list online on Family Search.org, the ship sailed from Liverpool to New York City, then on to Boston; *New York Herald*, July 17, 1860, 8, forty-four days from Liverpool to NY. The forty-four-day trip was longer than comparable sailing ships listed by the paper, thus supporting the family story that the ship was becalmed.

[238] Helen Ruscoe is buried in the Methodist Cemetery in Southeast, New York. Her tombstone carries the information that Helen was the daughter of William and Annie Lewis of St. Albans, Hertfordshire, England; see http://putnamgraveyards.com/southeast/methodist/roscoe.html#roscoe_helen; See also Letter 37 from Eliza's cousin when the family then lived in Patterson, New York, near Southeast.

[239] The 1860 Federal census of Fort Dodge was taken over seven days beginning on June 1st. The date conflicts with the passenger record of the ship *Washington* which landed in New York in July according to the *New York Herald*, July 17, 1860, 8. The 1900 Federal census indicates Janie (Blair) Williams came to America in 1860. Possibly there was an arrangement for Eliza to work for the Crosby family and they reported to the census taker that Eliza was expected, thus she was included in the census.

[240] Marcus L. Hansen, "Official Encouragement of Emigration to Iowa," *Iowa Journal of History and Politics*, Vol. XIX, 1, (1921): 170.

[241] Benjamin Gue, *History of Iowa From its Earliest Times to the Beginning of the Twentieth Century*, Vol I, (New York City: Century History Company, 1903): xiv; 257-267.

[242] Bogue, *From Prairie to Corn Belt*, 29.

[243] W. Oakley Ruggles, "Early Reflections of Fort Dodge," *Iowa Journal of History*, 49, (April 1951): 173; *Fort Dodge Republican*, August 30, 1862, 3, for Gilbert Rusco acquiring 80 acres by 1862 in Douglas township, Webster County

[244] Folmer, ed., *This State of Wonders*, 38.

[245] *Iowa Northwest*, July 15, 1869, 4, Daniel M. Crosby advertised a shoe store in Fort Dodge; there were only three male Crosbys in the 1860 census, Daniel, Conklin and father Seth.

[246] Ruggles, "Early Reflections of Fort Dodge", 169-170, 183.

[247] *Fort Dodge Sentinel* May 21, 1859, 2.

[248] Iowa College, *Catalogue of Iowa College, 1864-65, Grinnell Iowa,* (Montezuma, Iowa: Printed at the Republican Office, 1864), 8, 10. She would have attended with Jesse Macy whose biography notes he attended Iowa College in 1864-5; Noyes, *Jesse Macy,* 164, "Like many other students he taught school during the long winter vacations."

[249] Christopher Jones, Grinnell College Special Collections, personal communication with author; Schwieder, *Iowa the Middle Land,* 126- 127 Iowa College, originally a Congregational school, was first established in Davenport in 1848 and known as the Harvard of the West.

[250] Glenda Riley, *The Female Frontier,* 104, estimated 5, 663 female Iowa teachers in 1870.

[251] Andrea Radke-Moss, "Willing Challengers; Women's Experiences in the Northern Plains, 1862-1930," in *Women on The North American Plains* ed by Renee M. Laegreid and Sandra K. Mathews, (Lubbock: Texas Tech University Press, 2011), 48-67; Mary Hurlburt Cordier, *Schoolwomen of the Prairies and Plains* (Albuquerque: University of New Mexico Press, 1992), 13, 21, 26, 46; Glenda Riley, *The Female Frontier,* 103-4; Polly Welts Kaufman, *Women Teachers on the Frontier,* (New Haven and London: Yale University Press, 1984), xxii, in 1848 only 23 of 124 Iowa teachers were women, by 1865, 65% of Iowa teachers were women.

[252] Parker, *History of Poweshiek County,* 113 for Grinnell population in 1860; Soike, *Necessary Courage,* 253 n 23, credits Grinnell with 600 people in 1859.

[253] Christine Stansell, "Women on the Great Plains, 1865-1890," *Women's Studies,* 4, (1976): 90. See also, Susan Strasser, *Never Done: A History of American Housework,* (New York: Pantheon Books, 1982), a classic study of American housework including the cultural perceptions about women and housework.

[254] Amy Richter, *At Home in Nineteenth-Century America,* 52, argued that domestic labor, a component of a moral home, ultimately served as a marker of class and racial difference.

[255] See Schwieder, *Iowa, the Middle Land,* 50-51, on farm women's life, 51 on distinction between isolation and loneliness; The 1870 federal census lists Albert and Eliza with one child, Jennie (Lavinia) and two employees, a farm laborer, Myron Mayo born in Ohio, 21 years old, and Z. C. Cadwellader, a female domestic servant born in Ohio; Bogue, *From Prairie to Corn Belt,* 184, found that in 1869 in Poweshiek County there were 1,634 farm owners. Of those, 932 employed farm laborers.

[256] See Lavinia's memories, Appendix I, and Schwieder, *Iowa, Middle Land,* 141, for generalized comments on farm life for women, 142, for children filling an emotional void after leaving kin; Riley, *Frontierswomen,* 136, arguing that the very conditions of the Iowa frontier fostered characteristics that led to strong-mindedness or her own opinions; Deborah Fink, *Open Country Iowa, Rural Women, Tradition and Change,* (Albany: State University of New York Press, 1986), 2-3 argued that women's farm work was significant, women struggled to make a living and create links with each other to have control over their world, 36, farm women rarely crossed into the male sphere to work in the fields; Glenda Riley, "Not Gainfully Employed: Women on the Iowa Frontier, 1833-1870," *Pacific Historical Review,* Vol 49, no. 2, (May 1980): 237-264, for an expansion on the farm tasks typical of Iowa women of the 19th century.

[257] *Grinnell Herald,* February 5, 1892, 3. One of her closest neighbors, Mrs. Mary Fisher, appears to have been her best, non-relative, friendship.

[258] Fink, *Open Country, Iowa,* 36, describes a dual economy system on Iowa farms with the wife's making home products like cloth, candles, soap, etc for cash kept separate from the husband's income from farming; Glenda Riley, "'Not Gainfully Employed,' Women on the Iowa Frontier, 1833-1870," Pacific Historical Review, 49, no. 2, (May 1980): 237-64, for the essential role of women in agrarian households; See James Savage, ed., "Times Hard but Grit Good, Lydia Moxley's 1877 Diary," *Annals of Iowa,* 47, (1984): 270-290, for a contemporary Grinnell farm wife diary.

[259] See Bogue, *From Prairie to Corn Belt,* Chapter Ten, Some are Innovators, 193-215, 236, farmers from New England were more likely to try fruit and stock raising. Albert did both.

[260] *Grinnell Herald,* February 5, 1873, 3, Ad; date 1866 comes from family detail on the back of a photo.

[261] *Grinnell Herald,* May 2, 1882, 2; *Grinnell Herald* February 13, 1891, 3, A.G. issued an "Annual Circular" of nursery offerings, see Appendix II.

[262] *Manuscript Federal Agricultural Census,* Iowa 1880, Ancestry.com, other values include 10 horses, total livestock, wages paid to help, farming implements and machinery 450 dollars.

[263] Schwieder, *Iowa, the Middle Land,* 52; *Grinnell Herald,* March 18, 1881, 3, he sold cattle.

[264] *Campbell Interurban Press,* November 17, 1922, 2, Albert's obituary; Bouge, *From Prairie to Corn Belt,* Chapter Seven, Crops in the Field, 123 -147, notes specialization in crops came about as part of a market economy; today the farm is devoted to corn and soybeans, but during the mid-1800s, fruit and hay were important.

[265] *Grinnell Herald,* September 13, 1889, 2; *Grinnell Herald* September 14, 1888, 3 Poweshiek County central agricultural society exhibition has Albert with quality in apple collection.

[266] *Grinnell Herald,* December 5, 1890, 3; Albert was elected president in 1887 and presented a paper on winter protection per *Grinnell Herald,* December 18, 1887, 3.

[267] Bogue, *From Prairie to Corn Belt,* 204; *Grinnell Herald,* January 20, 1888, 3.

[268] *Grinnell Herald,* January 26, 1892, 3.

[269] *Grinnell Herald,* September 28, 1917, 4; Schwieder, *Iowa, The Middle Land,* 120 reported Iowa was the state with the highest literacy rate in 1870.

[270] *Grinnell Herald,* March 29, 1898, 3.

[271] *Grinnell Herald,* April 8, 1879, 3 school board; *Grinnell Herald,* August 16, 1881, 2; *Grinnell Signal,* April 21, 1883, 4, part of school board.

[272] *Grinnell Herald,* June 5, 1891, 2.

[273] See Nancy F. Cott, *The Bonds of Womanhood,* Chapter 4, 126-160, for the centrality of religion to women's lives.

[274] *Grinnell Signal* January 23, 1886, 1; *Grinnell Herald,* September 15, 1893, 2.

[275] Schwieder, *Iowa Middle Land,* 211-217.

[276] Schwieder, *Iowa, Middle Land*, 110, 115; *Grinnell Herald*, September 30, 1887, 2; Grinnell Association; *Grinnell Herald* April 29, 1881, 3, group was an association of Congregational churches and ministers in Iowa that served in towns located for 100 miles across Iowa at the location of the railroad. They met annually.

[277] Jon K. Lauck, *The Good Country, A History of the American Midwest, 1800-1900*, (Norman: University of Oklahoma Press, 2022), 3, most advanced, 4-5 idealistic, decent, democratic.

[278] Jon K. Lauck, *The Lost Region, Toward a Revival of Midwestern History*, (Iowa City: University of Iowa Press, 2013), 82; see also Bouge, *From Prairie to Corn Belt*.

[279] See Schwieder, *Iowa, Middle Land*, 172 on agrarianism: "Throughout the 19th century, Iowa's population remained overwhelmingly rural, Iowans espoused agrarianism, the belief in the superiority of rural life. Accordingly, individuals raised on farms were superior both physically and morally. Farms produced stable, hardworking, independent people who therefore constituted the nation's best citizens." Epstein, *The Politics of Domesticity*, 6, found temperance based in the church, committed to the defense of religion and a conservative morality.

[280] The 1885 Iowa State census lists 17-year-old Lavinia as a college student. Perhaps she attended Grinnell College prior to Cedar Falls, then Iowa Agricultural College. See Appendix I.

[281] John Henry Grattan was born December 17, 1869, in Ludlow, Allamakee, Iowa near Waukon, to Henry Guyant and Roseanna M (Bryant) Russell Grattan.

[282] Marriage certificate, State of California, County of Santa Clara, marriage date February 8, 1894, Book K, 578, of Marriage Certificates; *San Jose Mercury News*, February 9, 1894, 4 church located at Third and San Antonio Streets, San Jose.

[283] See Mrs. Tom "Lou" Boyd, et. al., "A Diary of the Cherokee Strip," *Journal of the Cherokee Strip*, 16, no. 9, (1974): 1-20, for settlers' memories of the day; Bureau of Land Management Government Land Office Records, certificate 385 states: The Northwest Quarter of Section twenty-five in township twenty-eight North of Range four West of Indian Meridian in Oklahoma Territory containing one-hundred and sixty acres was allotted to John H. Grattan February 26, 1896, at www.glorecords.blm.gov.

[284] See Jim Fulbright, *Trails to Old Pond Creek, The Early Days of Trade and Travel in Northwestern Oklahoma*, (Mid-South, Goodlettsville, Tenn., 2005) for a history of Pond Creek, Oklahoma and environs, 158, C. Q. Chandler from Iowa presided over the Bank of Pond Creek, 216, two banks in Medford by 1896, 1895 Grant County Bank and First National in 1896.

[285] Michael J. Hightower, *Banking in Oklahoma before Statehood*, (Norman: University of Oklahoma Press, 2013), 212.

[286] See Wayne Gard, *The Chisholm Trail*, (Norman: University of Oklahoma Press, 1954), vii, 81, for a discussion of the specific route of the trail through Oklahoma territory.

[287] *San Jose Mercury News* (hereafter *Mercury News*), May 8, 1899, 5.

[288] *Mercury News*, January 26, 1895, 7.

[289] *Grinnell Herald*, September 30, 1892, 3.

[290] *Mercury News*, November 20, 1893, 5, rented from Mrs. Harrison.

[291] *Mercury News* January 4, 1894, 3.

[292] *Grinnell Herald* December 21, 1894, 2, James Tomson went to Campbell to visit the Williams' family; *Mercury News* December 6, 1894, 6, Mrs. Fisher of Chester Township to spend winter with her friend Mrs. A. G. Williams; *Mercury News* June 27, 1897, 7.

[293] T. A. Cutting, *Historical Sketch of Campbell*, (Campbell: R. H. Knappen, Press, 1929), 3.

[294] Ibid.

[295] *Mercury News*, November 1, 1917, 7 obituary for Ruth Cutting; T. A. Cutting, *Cutting Kin*, (Campbell, CA: Private Publishing, 1939), 42, William went to Campbell and met Ruth who already had 10 acres and had settled with her family in 1883; Jeanette Watson, *Campbell, the Orchard City*, (Campbell, CA: Campbell Historical Museum, 1989), 150, Duncans settled in 1885.

[296] Cutting, *Cutting Kin*, 29, C. D. Cutting had five sons in Campbell.

[297] Cutting, *Sketch of Campbell*, 9.

[298] Watson, *Campbell, the Orchard City*, 47-50; *Campbell Weekly Visitor*, March 5, 1904, 1, first lots laid out in 1887.

[299] Cutting, *Sketch of Campbell*, 9.

[300] Santa Clara County Great Register of Voters, 1896, Campbell Precinct, California State Library, on Ancestry.com.

[301] Cutting, *Sketch of Campbell*, 12; See also, Warren Tufts, et. al., "The Rich Pattern of California Crops," IN *California Agriculture*, Claude B. Hutchinson, editor, (Berkeley and Los Angeles: University of California Press, 1946), 113-238, found in the early 1890s California's Fruit crops were still in their infancy with only a few hundred thousand tons produced per year, 151.

[302] *San Jose Herald*, March 24, 1891, 3.

[303] *San Jose Herald*, March 14, 1892, 3; *Hanford Sentinel* September 17, 1908, 8, Rev. Windsor; Watson, *Campbell, the Orchard City*, 55 Congregational Church in 1895; Cutting, *Sketch of Campbell*, 6, Rev. Windsor purchased his farm in Campbell in 1888.

[304] *Mercury News*, October 30, 1907, 9.

[305] *Mercury News*, January 26, 1895, 7.

[306] *Campbell Interurban Press*, 8 March 1912, 1, Albert on a building committee for the Congregational church; See Jon K. Lauck, *The Lost Region*, for a discussion of mid-western history that supports community and civic engagement as key concepts.

[307] *Campbell Weekly Visitor*, March 5, 1904, 1.

[308] *Campbell Interurban Press*, June 9, 1916, 3.

[309] See Nancy F. Cott, *The Bonds of Womanhood*, Chapter 4, 126-159, for a fuller discussion of the meaning of religion in the lives of Victorian-era respectable women, 147, "no other public institution spoke to women and cultivated their loyalty so assiduously as the churches did."

[310] Joan Marie Johnson, *The Woman Suffrage Movement in the United States*, (London and New York: Routledge, 2022), 47, many California suffragists emerged from the WCTU and the women's club movement, 61.

[311] *Mercury News,* October 11, 1902, 7; *Mercury News* March 28, 1903, 5, *Mercury News* May 6, 1901, 3, Mercury News September 17, 1900, 7, Mrs. Williams a Treasurer and committee chair. She had also been on the WCTU committee in Iowa, *Grinnell Herald*, February 14, 1882, 3; *Grinnell Herald*, June 19, 1891, 3, Eliza coordinated a children's day at the church; Epstein, *Politics of Domesticity*, 4, found: "Both religious activity and women's temperance were motivated to a large degree by women's anger over their subordinate status, and for much of the late nineteenth century the woman's temperance movement supported the feminist goals of woman suffrage and of woman's equality in the public arena," See Chapter Five, 115-146, "The Women's Christian Temperance Union and the Transition to Feminism." See Ginzberg, *Women and the Work of Benevolence*, 202-206, who found the WCTU arguing that only through the protection of women and the home could society's virtue be saved, women's moral superiority could control male intemperate behavior; Johnson, *Woman Suffrage Movement*, 50, found the WCTU had 150,000 members at its height.

[312] Epstein, *Politics of Domesticity*, 116-117.

[313] Paula Baker, "The Domestication of Politics, Women and American Political Society, 1780-1920," *The American Historical Review*, Vol 89, no. 3, (June 1984): 637.

[314] *Mercury News*, February 5, 1905, 2, for quilt; *Mercury News* November 9, 1901, 7, Mrs. Williams a member of the Book Club.

[315] *Mercury News*, April 5, 1895, 2.

[316] *Mercury News*, September 25, 1898, 6, for Oklahoma; *Campbell Interurban Press*, November 10, 1904, 7.

[317] *Grinnell Herald*, November 4, 1904, 5, at the farm for the summer and returning in November. As early as 1904, they were spending considerable time in Chester Township; *Mercury News*, May 20, 1894, 6, *Mercury News* December 6, 1894, 6, noted Mrs. Fisher of Chester, Iowa visited Mrs. Williams; *Mercury News*, January 26, 1895, 7; Mr. and Mrs. Patton of Iowa guests; *Mercury News*, May 6, 1900, 6, Will Hays, husband of Francis, Albert's youngest sister, and his daughter Myrtle Hays visited; *Mercury News* June 3, 1900, A. G., John Grattan and Will Hays on a camping trip; *Mercury News*, July 25, 1897, 5, Shermans. The Williams' hired a farm manager who ran the farm in Iowa after their move to Campbell. It has remained in the family for over 150 years.

[318] *Campbell Weekly Visitor*, January 4, 1896, 4 for committee; *Grinnell Herald*, September 15, 1896, 3 reported A. G. was in Grinnell for a two-month visit.

[319] *Mercury News*, December 9, 1896, 7; see *Mercury News* July 15, 1898, 3 on a trial under Williams that made news. In 1898 small criminal matters of the city or township, and criminal cases not heard before the Superior Court, came up before Justices of the Peace. Municipal court has now taken the place of Justice of the Peace courts; *Mercury News* October 5, 1898, 4.

[320] *Mercury News*, November 4, 1898, 5.

[321] *San Jose Herald*, November 10, 1898, 5, for 730 votes.

[322] *Mercury News,* December 11, 1898, 3; Herrington received 782.

[323] *Mercury News*, December 30, 1898, 5.

[324] Cutting, *Sketch of Campbell*, 10, A. G. Williams was an early justice of the peace, and one of the first stockholders.

[325] *Campbell Weekly Visitor*, May 4, 1904, 1.

[326] *Campbell Interurban Press* January 17, 1913, 1.

[327] *Mercury News*, May 10, 1907, 13.

[328] *Campbell Weekly Visitor*, April 25, 1896, 1.

[329] *Campbell Weekly Visitor*, March 7, 1896, 2.

[330] *Campbell Weekly Visitor*, May 16, 1896, 4 has the first use of the Blaine - Williams logo in the masthead of the newspaper; May 23, 1896, 2, establishment of the partnership in the newspaper and photography business.

[331] Cutting, *Sketch of Campbell*, 7, the Blaine family arrived in the 1880s; Watson, *Campbell, The Orchard City*, 263 for death.

[332] Worthin Williams reported his occupation as laborer in the 1900 census.

[333] *Grinnell Herald*, November 16, 1920, 1, obituary; married on April 2, 1901.

[334] *Colorado Transcript*, October 29, 1914, 6, 13, discussed John's potential as a progressive candidate from Jefferson County who would be able to draw votes from both Republican and Democratic political parties. He ran as a Progressive in 1914; John again ran for a seat as a representative to the Colorado Assembly in 1916 on the same ticket as Charles Evans Hughes for president and suffered the same fate.

[335] *Avalanche Echo*, September 22, 1910, 1.

[336] *Campbell Interurban Press*, February 9, 1912, 1; *Mercury News*, February 12, 1912, 9 for arrival in Campbell.

[337] *Campbell Interurban Press*, 14 May 1915, 1.

[338] *Campbell Interurban Press*, June 15, 1917, 1.

[339] *Grinnell Herald,* February 28, 1919, 1.

[340] Lavinia Williams Grattan V. John Grattan, State of Colorado, County of Jefferson, District Court, No 2026, Filed June 2, 1917, Separate Maintenance; The five sons were: Worthin Felowskiamoy, b. Jan 18, 1895 in Medford, Oklahoma; Henry, b. June 26, 1896 in Medford; Leland Gordon Grattan, b. April 26, 1899 in Medford; Eugene Blair Grattan, b. April 18, 1902 in Barr, Colorado; Ralph b. May 2, 1904 in Brighton, Colorado, per family bible; Worthin's strange middle name came from Lavinia's sorority sisters who placed their initials in a hat and drew out the initials to form a name that the first born child of the women would receive.

[341] Riley, *Building and Breaking Families*, 5, 113, 145.

[342] *Campbell Interurban Press*, October 18, 1912, 1, for a year; *Grinnell Herald*, September 22, 1908, 2.

[343] A. G. Williams, probate records, District Court of Iowa in and for Poweshiek County, Iowa Judicial Branch 2, A.G. Williams estate, Probate number 4454, Poweshiek, County, farm in Iowa valued at $49,000 in will; nephew Frank Hays, children: Donald Nutting, Mildred Nutting, and Paul Albert Nutting, possibly given a middle name in honor of his great Uncle.

[344] *Campbell Interurban Press,* June 9, 1916, 3, Eliza's death May 31, 1916; Albert issued a card of thanks; *Grinnell Herald*, June 6, 1916, 3 she suffered for four weeks.

[345] *Grinnell Herald*, June 20, 1916, 4 reprinting the *Campbell Interurban*; *Grinnell Herald*, August 11, 1916, 3, Albert and son Worthin were in Grinnell.

,

[346] His death certificate lists his cause of death as chronic interstitial nephritis, the same cause listed on his wife's death certificate, a condition related to kidney failure.

[347] *Campbell Interurban Press,* November 17, 1922, 2; *Grinnell Herald*, November 14, 1922, 1 obituary.

[348] *Campbell Interurban Press*, November 24, 1922, 4.

[349] See R. Richard Wohl, edited by Moses Rischin, "The Country Boy Myth and Its Place in American Urban Culture, The Nineteenth-Century Contribution," *Perspectives in American History*, Vol. III, (1969): 103, who found the middle-class Victorians of the 19th century "stressed ambition, the virtues of sustained application, and the uncomfortable but necessary discipline of principle inhibition. Composure and control were their watchwords."

[350] McDermitt, *Puritan Ideology of Mobility*, xix, quoted historian Abram van Engen on John Winthrop as trying to convey "a principle of sympathy that forms good communities through the reciprocity of fellow feelings." Abram C. van Engen, *Sympathetic Puritans: Calvinist Fellow Feeling in Early New England* (Oxford: Oxford University Press, 2015), 56.

Letter 1

To Albert Williams, Cornish, NH
From Annginette Hall Williams

Envelope: Croydon Flat, N. H. [Apr]
[3 or 4 letters under return address]
1 to Albert G. Williams Cornish, N. H.

Croydon Flat [NH] Feb 20, 1853
Dear Brother,

I take my pen to inform you how I am and how mother is.[1] I am very well but feel rather sad because school left off last Friday. We all felt very bad when the last day came. I should think that about half of the school were in tears part of the time. I could not help thinking how different it was from the last day down to Newport[2] last winter. Mother has been living to [*sic*] Mr. Perkins[3] since I wrote you last until today she has gone to Newport to stay a week. She is well I think But she thinks a great deal about you and Frances.[4] She wants to see both of you very much, but it does not seem as though she could want to see you more than I do. I have not seen you or Fanny[5] for an Age, it seems to me. I don't wonder that you miss your home very much, but take courage and look for better times. Try and learn as much as you can and you will soon be old enough to seek a home for yourself. I miss my home some but not as much as you do. I presume because I have got a good home now and mother is where I can see her quite often all most all the trouble I have is I cannot see you and Fanny as often as I want to. Mother wishes that you were where she could see to your clothes and comfort and advise you. I feel bad when I think what a happy place our home might have been what a little Paradise I might have said. But when I think what it was I think the best has been done that could be. We must try to think all is for the best so keep up good courage and be a good boy and you will gain friends where ever you go. I hope it will be so you can go to school this spring and if you do, try to learn a great deal. Freeman Dodg[e][6] came down here to school the last part of this term and he inquired about you and sent his love to you. Write to me as often as you can perhaps you can learn something by writing to me. You will learn to write better if nothing more. You know that the more you write the better you can write. I see you wrote that letter that you wrote to me better than you did the one you wrote to Mother and I presume you will gain on the next one that you write, so I hope you will write to me as often as you can. I will answer as many letters as you will write to me and I hope that you will answer all that I write to you. Now you remember and write to me all about Frances and yourself and all the folks that you can think of. I was very pleased on receiving your other letter and hope to receive another as good but I don't know but I have wrote as much as you will want to pick out at once. Give my love to all inquiring friends and tell them I should like to see them.
But good bye for now. I hope that I see you err long. From your ever loving sister.
Annginette H. Williams,
Croydon Flat, N. H.

---

[1] Melinda Hall Williams. This is a sad and poignant letter reflecting the torn status of the family and the hardship that the breakup of the parents' marriage inflicted upon the children. Albert would have been 12 at the time, and from the context of the letter he and Francis were living together, possibly with their father. Annginette lived near her mother, Melinda.
[2] The family was living in Newport, NH in 1852 at the time of Stephen and Melinda's separation.
[3] Mr. Perkins could be a reference to James Perkins from Croydon. In the 1850 census he was 64 and lived only two doors away from Ariel Hall, Melinda's brother. In the 1850 census for Croydon he is living with what appears to be his wife Anna, 58, and a young man, Marshall Perkins, 27, who is listed as a physician.
[4] Francis Williams [Hays], [1851-1899] Albert's younger sister.
[5] Nickname for Francis Williams.
[6] Freeman Dodge [1838-1907], the son of William [1811-1880] and Lucinda Stockwell Dodge [1815-1871] of Croydon. Freeman was only two years older than Albert, and presumably a schoolmate. William Dodge, a shoemaker, had several other children. Freeman was a 22-year-old teamster in the 1860 census and his father was listed as deputy sheriff in the town of Claremont, N. H.

Letter 2

To Albert Williams, Cornish, NH
From Annginette Hall Williams

Address on outside of folded letter paper:
Albert G. Williams
Cornish. N. H.

Croydon Flat, [NH]
March 20, 1853
Dear Brother,

With much pleasure I seat myself to write you a few lines to let you know how we all are over here. I am quite well and have been all the since you was over hear [*sic*]. Mother was well the last time I saw her. She has been gone to Newport[1] the last week. She thinks of staying two or three weeks. She is sewing for Mrs. Harvy [*sic*] the printer's wife.[2] I thought I should get over there before this time when you was over here but it has not been so that I could. I thought perhaps I could go over with Mrs. Taylor,[3] but she went before I knew anything about it. It has got to be such bad sleighing and the snow is so near gone that it is not likely I shall get over there until it gets to be wheeling. I never wanted to see anybody so much as I do little Fanny[4] but I have got to wait patiently I suppose until there is an opportunity, but it seems as though I could not.
Augusta Ames[5] is at the point of death. She has been sick seven or eight months with the Consumption. The doctor told her a day or two ago that she could not live but a few days more. Van Buren Perry[6] is sick with the Brain Fever. They are afraid that he will not get any better. All the rest of the Folks are well around here I believe. Now you write to me just as soon as you receive this and tell me how Francis is. Be sure and write the day you get this. Good by from your sister
Annginette H. Williams

---

[1] New Hampshire.

[2] Experience Crosmon Harvey [1819-1860] was the wife of printer Matthew Harvey [1815-1885], of Newport, N.H. They had a one-year-old child in the 1850 census.

[3] Hannah Taylor [1787-1867] and her husband Nathan [1787-1869] lived right next to the Stephen Williams family in the Newport, N. H. 1850 census, so that is probably the person Annginette refers to in this letter.

[4] Little Fanny a nickname for Annginette's youngest sibling, sister Francis Williams, then two years old and presumably either bound out with Albert, or living with their father.

[5] Augusta Ames [1829-1853], a first cousin, is listed in the 1850 Newport, N. H. census as the 20-year-old daughter of Sarah Ames, 43, in a female headed household. Augusta's father, Jacob Ames died in 1849. Sarah Hall Ames [1806-1879] was Melinda's sister. Augusta died 10 days after this letter was written. One member of the household was Worthen Hall Ames, named for his uncle, who sailed on the whale ship *Natchez* with him.

[6] Van Buren Perry died of brain fever on April 30, 1853 at seven years old. In the 1850 census the Perry family lives within a few houses of the Nathan Hall [1813-1900] family in Croydon, Melinda's brother and Annginette's uncle.

Letter 3

To Albert Williams, Cornish, NH
From Melinda Hall Williams

On outside of folded letter:
Postal stamp Nov 7 Newport NH Paid 3
Albert G. Williams
Cornish N. H.
In the care of Daniel Bryant esq[1]
[blob of sealing wax][2]

Newport [NH] November the 6th 1853
My Dear Son,

I take this opportunity of writing to you. I have been intending to write to you for this long time but something has occurred to prevent. I have thought a great deal about you since I was over there and of many things that I wished that I had said to you and there is no day that passes without thinking of you and little Frances and I should have written many times before now if I could have known that you would have received my letters without comments. But I have felt so lonely and sad this day that I thought that I must write. This day Fanny Hawes' remains were laid in the silent tomb.[3] I went to the funeral it seemed very hard for her to be taken from Friends that loved her so well. Grandpa Kibbey died today.[4] The Old and the young both die we know not whose turn it may be mine. But if we live as we should we need not fear. The best way to prepare for death is to live good lives. Have nothing to do with evil in whatever shape it appears. And have a firm trust in a God that does all <u>things well</u>. You are young my dear son, but not too young to know that there is a great many troubles in this world. I think you can realize the better than I could when I was many years older. Seventeen years one week ago[5] since I left My own Dear Parents and if anyone had foretold the trials that I should pass through I should have said <u>never I should die first.</u> But I still live and still hope for happier hours. I hope to enjoy many happy days with my dear Children yet. I hope to see you a <u>good</u> and <u>useful man.</u> I hope to see you watch over Frances with a Brother's love and <u>almost</u> a <u>Mother's</u> care. When you are twenty she will not be ten. And your influence will be great over her, and it is now I hope you will never laugh at anything she does <u>wrong</u> if it does look cunning but always speak to her as you think your Mother would were she present. Give her a few kisses for me the first time you see her and I will pay you with interest when I see you. I may come over there again this fall as Annginette wants to come very much. I have not seen her for two weeks as I have been down here to the village that time.
Now Albert I want you to write to me Now the same day and the same hour that you get this. Direct to Croydon Flatt. I want you to write about your affairs every little thing will be interesting from you and then I will write again and write more cheerfull [*sic*] but I did not feel very happy to day and October has been a very sad month. Some of the saddest events of my life have happened in that month.[6] But I will write no more now.
Remember what you promised me about writing. So good bye
From your affectionate Mother
M H Williams[7]

---

[1] The original letter is on blue stationary folded over several times with the address printed on the outside. A broken lump of sealing wax used to hold the fold together. Melinda was separated from all three of her children. Albert and Francis were presumably bound out together to the Daniel Bryant family. Her pain and concern at the inability to see her children or take care of them weighed heavily on her mind. She carefully underlined each letter with a small hatch mark on the words she wanted to emphasize, herein fully underlined. Albert was presumably bound out to Daniel Bryant [1803-1864], a farmer, and wife Chloe (Hildreth) Bryant [1800-1890] at the time of the writing of this letter. They had a daughter Charlotte who was the same age as Albert, as well as a son Edward four years older. See Letter 35 which mentions Edward as an adult.
[2] By about 1860 the use of sealing wax ended; *William Merrill Deker, Epistolary Practices, Letter Writing in America before Telecommunication,* (Chapel Hill and London: University of North Carolina Press, 1998), 59.
[3] Fanny Hawes was probably the 17-year-old Frances Hawes [1832-1853] whose family was right next door to the Stephen Williams family in the 1850 census in Newport, NH. Her parents were Shubael, previously a whaling captain, and Nancy Hawes. She married Frederick Crocker in 1851 and died on a European trip on June 27, 1853, resulting in a delay in interment. She was buried in the Newport, NH, Maple Street Cemetery.

---

[4] Grandpa Kibbey was probably Phillip W. Kibbey [1761-1853] who died on November 5, 1853 in Newport, NH. He was an 89-year-old resident farmer of Newport in the census of 1850, living with presumed children and grandchildren. He appears on the page following the Stephen Williams, Jr., family in the 1850 census, so they were located geographically close to one another in Newport. Kibbey served in the American Revolution and lived in Claremont, NH in 1790, thus a long-time resident of the same part of New Hampshire where Melinda lived. There is no information indicating a consanguineal relationship, although Philip's daughter Lucy was married to Fisher Dudley who gave testimony in Melinda's divorce. There is one letter in the collection from George Dudley, the son of Fisher and Lucy who were neighbors of the Williams family in Newport, NH.

[5] Melinda and Stephen were married on October 30, 1836.

[6] Stephen Williams, Jr.'s birthday was October 18, and Melinda was married to him on October 30, 1836. Anginette was born October 23, 1837. Perhaps these dates in October are the ones to which Melinda refers.

[7] Melinda (Hall) Williams, Albert's mother.

Letter 4

To Albert G. Williams, Cornish, NH
From Melinda Hall Williams

Newport [NH] Nov 11 [1854][1]
My Dear Son

I am thinking you would like to hear from me by this time. I am very well now. I have been down here four weeks. I make my home at Mr. Higbees.[2] I have not had one day to myself since I was at Cornish. I have as many as five weeks work engaged now. I was very glad to hear from you. I went to Croydon two weeks ago yesterday to Poor James[3] funeral and I received your letter then. I suppose you have heard of his death. You have no idea how much he suffered. He thought he should die as soon as he was shot. He was anxious to live to see his Father.[4] The last words he said were: When my Father comes and asks for me tell him to go to the graveyard. Oh Albert how thankful I feel to my Heavenly Father for the life and health of my children.
I do worry a great deal about you. I fear some accident will befall you, but I hope that James sudden and accidental death will be a warning to you to be careful in the use of fire arms. <u>Do promise me you will be very careful will you</u>. I hope that you will go to school all that you can this Winter and try and learn. I want to see you very much. There is not a day passes without my thinking of you. I begin to count the weeks that must pass before you will come over again. We will have a nice time when you do won't we. I wish you lived where I could see you once in a month.[5] I believe it would do you a great deal of good. Annginette[6] is getting along finely with her school.[7] Don't you feel proud of her[?] <u>I do</u> and you must <u>try</u> to do as well as she does you know. I have had the whole care of her and her Father thought she would never be anything. I sincerely hope you can if little Fanny[8] will both be better than she is if you are not people will say they have needed <u>their</u> Mother.
Good by
M. H. Williams
At the top of the first page written upside down is:
Write soon direct to Newport N. H. Kiss My little One.[9] I wish I could kiss you both. Good by. May God bless you. M. H. W.

---

[1] Letter appears to have been written in 1854, based on content.

[2] The 1850 census shows a John Higbee family in Newport, NH. He was listed as a trader, possibly shop owner. He and his wife Adeline had three small children. John Higbee was mentioned in the local newspaper in 1852; *Whip and Spur*, September 18, 1852, 2. Presumably they still resided in Newport in 1854 when Melinda worked for them as possibly a domestic, or as a store clerk. There is a different Higbee family in Claremont, NH in the 1860 census.

[3] James Hall [1842-1854], the only son of Nathan and Martha Hall, died November 2, 1854 at 12 years old, from an accidental gunshot when he was cleaning a gun. He is buried in the Croydon Cemetery. Nathan was Melinda's brother, making James a first cousin to Albert.

[4] Nathan Hall was the first mate of the *Natchez* whaling ship at this time, and away at sea at the time of James' death.

[5] Albert is bound out or living with his father at this time and Melinda appears consumed by the loss of her daily interactions with her son. Her raw emotion is highlighted by her underlining certain sentences to give them prominence.

[6] Annginette Hall Williams [Sherman], Albert's oldest sister.

[7] Possibly a reference to her teaching school.

[8] Albert's youngest sister Francis.

[9] Melinda is asking Albert to kiss his little sister Francis in their mother's absence, leading to the conclusion that Albert and Francis were at this time bound out together to a local family or they were living with their father. Francis would only have been 3 ½ years old; quite young to have been away from her mother.

Luke Newton Sherman and wife Annginette Hall (Williams) on their wedding day, January 28, 1856

Letter 5

To Albert G. Williams, Cornish, NH [?]
From Melinda Hall Williams

Croydon [NH] Jan 28 [1856][1]
My dear Son

I seat myself to write you a few lines as I know not what to do with myself. This has been a sad, sad day for me. I can not work and I cannot read and if I go to bed I cannot sleep. I did not know but I should feel better to write you than anything else. Annginette[2] has gone and left me alone. Yes it seems as tho [sic] <u>alone, alone</u> would ring in my ears forever. She was married this morning at eight o'clock and started for the west immediately. They were married here by the Methodist Minister. There was no one here excepting Newton's brother[3] and wife beside ourself.[4] You never went to a funeral that was more solemn. It seemed as though we were taking our last look of her and perhaps we have, but she has gone with one who has lived in town from childhood until three years past and he has always been respected. His brain has never been heated by liquor nor his mouth defiled by tobacco and he is now to [sic] old to commence. I hope he has wealth too which is desirable with other good things although a curse when that is all one has to depend on for happiness. I think she will be happy but O[H] Albert do you know how lonely your poor mother will be without her. If you was only with me I could endure it better but I am <u>alone alone</u>. You must write often and not forget me. Sometimes I almost wish that I never had tried to make anything of her and let her been [sic] hateful then no one would have wanted her. She stopped at Claremont[5] and [took] hers and Newtons Daguerreotypes for you. They thought she could not leave any present that you would prize more. When you come over you can have them. How did you get home that day? Did Fanny[6] most freeze? When are you coming over? How do you get along with your school?
Annginette said that she should write to you in a week after that she got there. You must answer it soon. You can get some better writer to direct it.[7] Now write to me soon and let me know that I have one child left that thinks of me.
So good by for the present
Melinda H. Williams[8]

P.S. Direct your letter as I shall go back this week. Newton presented Annginette a beautiful gold watch and chain as a bridal gift.
M. H. Williams

---

[1] Year is determined from content of letter.
[2] Annginette Hall Williams [Sherman} [1837-1916], Melinda's oldest child.
[3] Luke Newton Sherman [1828-1889] was Annginette's husband.
[4] This is probably a reference to Luke's brother Jason W. Sherman and wife Anginette (Blanchard) who local historians place in Chester Township, Grinnell, Iowa at the same time as Luke and Annginette; September 1856. Jason and Anginette were married December 20, 1855 in Claremont, NH, and presumably all four of the newlyweds left together on January 28th for Iowa.
[5] New Hampshire.
[6] Fanny was a nickname for Albert's youngest sister, Francis Williams [Hays].
[7] Her concern with Albert's ability to write is consistent with family lore regarding Albert's possible dyslexia.
[8] Albert's mother.

Letter 6

To Albert Williams, Cornish, NH
From Annginette Hall (Williams) Sherman

Lyons [Iowa][1]
Apr. 14 1856
Dear Brother

I received your letter this week I now commence to answer which I may not finish for several days. I was very pleased to receive so pretty a letter & one so well written & composed. I think you have improved very much in both respects since I had a letter before from you. I hope you will still strive then to do write to mother & myself very often & each time try to write better than before. & spelling need[s] to be study[ed] hard. But that you must not think but you can learn to spell without out use of the spelling book. Each word before you write it think how to spell it and if you are not very certain ask some one that does know, or go to a dictionary & hunt the word up. If you have not such a book get one. You can for a small amount of money, fifty cents at most. & you will desire more benefit than that from it in a month if you use it.[2]

You speak of your inclination to come out here at some future day. I hope that inclination will continue & I trust father will Yield to you if he considers your good he certainly would wish you to come. Could you see the ground here you could imagine what could be raised on it. It is as black as any dirt you ever saw in any place. To give you a[n] idea of the richness of the soil by telling you of the size of a pig weed that was pulled up out of a field of corn it was seventeen feet high & grew in a hill of corn that was ten feet high. So you see it must be good ground. The people raise a great deal of wheat here on this place. They have sowed 56 acres of wheat all in one piece. Just think how that field will look. You never saw so much ground in one field and that ground without one stone or stick or stump on it. The ground is so entirely free from gravel that a sled will run on the dirt without grating a mite.[3] You speak of the one you look to for direction not being as good as you wish. You can look for direction to a far better one than the one you speak of yes! You can look to one above for direction. He it is to whome [sic] we all should look for protection in all times of need in all times of trial. He it is! Christ is the one that set us a perfect example and if we follow in his path we shall not so much need the protecting care of any human arm. When you are in trouble or in want of direction go to the Bible that book of all books & there you are sure to find that consolation which you need when your [sic] separated from friends, mother & sisters and it may be a father, remember there is a father for all men whose watchful care is ever over us & who will not suffer any of his creatures to be really alone. But I must draw my letter to a close by requesting you to write immediately. Please give my love to father, grandfather & mother,[4] and all the rest of the inquiring friends. Kiss little Frances for me. Tell her of her sister that she may not forget me. Remember my dear brother that though I am far away still my heart is with you, my prayers are for you, & God's blessing is on you. From your sister, A. H. S.[5] [additional letters on opposite side of letter] A. [unintelligible]. H.

---

[1] This letter from Annginette Hall (Williams) Sherman came from Lyons, Iowa where her husband's family had lived intermittently. Her father-in-law, William Sherman, and family settled in Lyons, Iowa in 1854. In 1855, William purchased a total of 1800 acres in Chester Township, hired a man from Grinnell to plow the prairie and plant ten acres in corn, and construct a "shanty" home there. The home, finished by 1856, was occupied by Annginette and Luke Sherman in September, 1856. Presumably Annginette and husband Luke Sherman stayed in Lyons from the time of this letter in April until September, 1856 when they moved to Chester Township, Grinnell with Luke's brother Jason and his wife. On September 1, 1856, Jason Sherman settled in Grinnell, almost directly west of Lyons, according to G. H. White, *Historical Sketch of Chester Township,* read at the quarter centennial, July 4, 1881, (Grinnell: Cravath and Shaw Steam Printers, 1881), 4-5.
Eastern Iowa along the Mississippi river had been settled by the 1830s. Lyons, within Clinton county was settled by 1835 in an area that would become North Clinton, Iowa. An advantageous place to establish a ferry across the river, the Lyons' ferry boat system was crucial for emigrants between 1840 and 1848, as the boats were large enough to carry wagons across the Mississippi. Railroad lines reached Lyons in 1856. The railroad bridge at Lyons which later merged with Clinton was begun in January 1859 over the Mississippi. Lyons experienced a rapid growth from 1853 to 57 and was a town of fine residences and significant population at the time Annginette and Luke Sherman passed through;

P. B. Wolfe, *Wolfe's History of Clinton, County, Iowa,* Vol. I, (Indianapolis, Indiana: B.F. Bowen and Comp., 1911), 46 settlement, 106 ferry boat system, 122 railroad; 124 bridge over Mississippi, 384 for growth of Lyons.

[2] Annginette's admonishments over Albert's spelling may stem from a learning disability, possibly dyslexia, that Albert may have experienced. People with dyslexia typically struggle with handwriting and spelling.

[3] Annginette's description of the fecundity of the soil no doubt influenced Albert, who was accustomed to the more rocky New England area. P. B. Wolfe quotes from an 1855 letter comparing farming in New England with that of Iowa. Wolfe argued that New England would not grow anything unless the fields were manured and that everyone in a New England household had to work the fields to be able to earn a living from farming. Wolfe, *Wolfe's History of Clinton, County, Iowa,* Vol. I, ibid, 127.

[4] The reference is to Stephen Williams, Sr.[1782-1859] and his wife Betsey (White) Williams [1781-1860].

[5] Annginette Hall (Williams) Sherman; Annginette was known as "Annginette Hall" using her mother's maiden name as part of her given name. Perhaps the emphasis on Hall and not Williams reflects some animosity toward her father subsequent to her parents' separation. See her obituary in the *Long Beach Press*, February 10, 1916, 2, giving her name as Annginette Hall Sherman, eliminating her maiden name Williams. Annginette's own memories of her settlement in Iowa omit reference to both her father and brother; Old Settlers Association, *Proceedings of the Old Settlers' Association of Grinnell,* "March 19, 1895, The Shermans by Mrs. A. H. Sherman," *Proceedings of the Annual Meeting of the Old Settlers of Grinnell,* (Grinnell, Iowa: Signal Printing, 1895), 14-17.

Letter 7

To Albert G. Williams, Cornish, NH
From Annginette Hall (Williams) Sherman

Grinnell October 11, 1856
Dear Brother,

Again do I seat myself to address a few lines to my dear brother although I have received no answer to my last letter but I trust this will receive more immediate attention. I have written to you of the beauties of this western country and have hoped you would visit it at some future day, but have thought of no particular time until quite lately. Newton[1] and I have been talking it over and knowing the advantage of this country over that for young people we thought it best for you to come soon if you would like to and father would consent to have you. N [2] thinks of building a back part to a house this fall for us to live in this winter and build the main house next summer and he also wishes to make some improvements on the land so he will have much to do and will probably be from home considerable and he thinks if you would come out here as soon as your school is through this winter he would do much better by you than you could do there. He says he could afford to pay you good wages just to see to things and stay with me when he is gone he says you could in a little while earn enough to buy you a piece of land and by the time you are old enough to get married you will have a large farm. Now we want you to talk with father also write to mother and see what they think about it but I am sure they both look for your good and if they do they will give their consent for you to come. It may look to [you] like a great ways but it is not so far but what you can go back again if you do not like [it] and it will not seem so far as it now does after you have traveled the road once. I think there is no danger that you will like the western country and I trust you will consider what is for your good both now and in the future and come we would like to have you come this fall only we are not within three miles of a school as yet so we think it would be better for you to go to school there. We wish you to write as soon as you get this, and let us know what you think of it. We are all well now. Be a good boy and read your Bible.
From your sister
     A.H. Sherman[3]
     Direct as I told you before to
     Grinnell Poweshiek County Iowa[4]

---

[1] Luke Newton Sherman, Annginette's husband.

[2] Newton.

[3] Annginette Hall (Williams) Sherman. She was almost nineteen years old at this time.

[4] This is the last letter in the collection from Albert's sister Annginette; the one prompting his move to Iowa within a few months of its receipt. Although somewhat unremarkable to the modern reader, it was none-the-less persuasive to a teenager forced to live away from his parents. Undoubtedly, part of Iowa's attractions laid in the anticipation of again living in a loving traditional family setting with his sister and brother-in-law.

Letter 8

To Albert G. Williams, Cornish, NH
From Melinda (Hall) Williams, Newport, NH

Envelope: [stamped Dec 8 Newport, N.H.]
Mr. Albert G. Williams
Cornish
N.H.

Write very soon and write a long letter M H Williams[1] [written across top of first page of letter]
Dec 7, 1856
My dear Son,

Do you begin to want to hear from your Mother again? I have been thinking of writing this some time. You have no idea how much I think about you. I was invited to Mr. Corbin's[2] Thanksgiving and I believe I should have been quite happy if you could have been with me. But I am longing for the time to come when you will come over and make a good long visit. We will have the best time. What do you think of going west? I don't know what offer they[3] made you but I presume you would be worth as much when you are 25 if [you] went there as you would be at forty if you stayed here.
How is little Frances?[4] does she ever speak of me?[5] I think much of her, but not as much as I do of you. You are now forming a character that will follow you through life. If you are a bad boy you will be a bad man. If you associate with mean people now you will be likely to have the same in ten years from now. But I hope and wish and pray that you will be all that I wish. I should feel very sad to have you go away if I did not think it for your good. I have faith to believe that my last days will be spent with or near you. That I shall have a good and noble Son to lean upon in the downhill of life. As I have been deprived of one that I thought would shield [the word defend was crossed out for shield] me from the cold world, I naturally turn with more confidence to my children and I will not think that Fate will deprive me of their love[6] but Good Bye from your Mother

---

[1] Melinda (Hall) Williams, Albert's mother.
[2] Mr. Corbin may have been either Austin Corbin or Charles Corbin who appear in the Newport, NH 1850 Federal census only four doors away from each other, and 13 years apart in age at 58 and 45, respectively. Both were married farmers with families. Only Austin remains in the 1860 census where his occupation is Pension Agent. Austin Corbin's son, Austin, was considered a wealthy banker, railroad magnate and partner of N. Kendall in the early Windsor, Vermont gun manufacturing business. He was an early developer of Coney Island in New York; Guy Hubbard, *Industrial History*, (Windsor: Windsor Town School District, 1922), 61.
[3] A reference to Albert's sister Annginette and her husband Luke Newton Sherman.
[4] Francis Williams, Albert's youngest sister, then less than six years old.
[5] The poignancy of this question is an intimate reminder of the pain Melinda felt as a mother removed from the daily contact with her children.
[6] Today we might think she is promulgating guilt, but her heartfelt emotion may simply show how difficult the situation was for her. She was consumed by the question of whether or not she would lose her children's love because she divorced their father. Albert was 16 years old at the time of the writing of this letter and Melinda was 39 years old. We would hardly consider her "old" today, but her mind dwelt on her inability to take control of her own life and raise her children as she would have preferred. On some level, Melinda lacked a sense of self; unconsciously deprecating the idea that she could live for herself. She felt she couldn't live only for herself, so her thoughts moved from selfless devotion to a husband to living for her children. See Susan S. Arpad, ed., *Sam Curd's Diary, The Diary of a True Woman*, (Athens, Ohio: Ohio University Press, 1984), 155, who noted that nineteenth century women who were commanded to make a home for others and live for others frequently found that their life "became a repression of all feelings and expressions of individuality."

Letter 9

To Albert G. Williams, Grinnell, Iowa
From Stephen Williams, Jr., Cornish, NH

Tuesday April 28, 1857[1]
My dear Son

It is with the greatest pleasure that I take my pen in hand to inform you of our healths [*sic*] which is very good and hoping these few lines will find you enjoying the same blessings, although separated as we are now. My prayer to God is that we all may enjoy that peace, joy, comfort and happiness that the world can not give nor take away. I received a letter from you Apr 23 with much joy and put one in the office the same night and I had no time to answer it that night so I got GPW[2] to answer the letter. I don't know what he wrote to you, but in regard to your money I feel afraid that you will loose it but if you can make it sure I will send it to you, but after I hear from you again. Francis'[3] birds laid five eggs and has hatched out two little smart birds and if you will come home some afternoon you may have a pair to carry home with you at night. Nothing new has taken place since I wrote to you except I bought a box of shaving soap as a ticket and drew a silver salt spoon. I don't know of but one other prize in town. C. Pike[4] drew a silver thimble for his ticket. As for farmers it has been so cold and windy they have not done much on their farms yet. It been the coldest and windiest they have known for over 20 years. I have been informed that Highby of Newport[5] has cut his throat, but how true it is I do not know. The report is somewhat blind.
So good by for a few days
S. Williams, Jr.
In opening that little napkin [?] I found a line from Annginette[6] and with pleasure I read the contents therein. I had given up the ide [*sic*] of even receiving a letter from her for I had almost thought she had forgotten there was such a being here but may God forgive her as I do. Tell her I will remember her the next time
I write
S W Jr.

---

[1] This is the first letter in the collection from Albert's father, Stephen Williams, Jr. and the first that was sent to Albert in Chester township, Grinnell. It anchors the time frame for Albert's move to Iowa. He moved before this letter was written making him one of the earliest settlers in the Chester township region of Grinnell.
[2] George Philander Williams, Stephen Williams, Jr.'s brother and Albert's uncle.
[3] Francis Williams was Albert's youngest sister, about six years old at the writing of this letter and then living with her father.
[4] There are a number of people surnamed Pike in the immediate area of Cornish. The C. Pike referenced in the letter is probably Chester Pike, a second-generation, prominent citizen of Cornish who served as selectman for the town in 1857, 8 and 9. He would subsequently be elected to the New Hampshire state senate where he served several terms and attained the status of Senate president. Chester Pike would have been 27 years old at this time. William H. Child, *History of the Town of Cornish New Hampshire with genealogical record, 1763-1910,* 2 vols, (Concord, NH.: The Rumford Press, 1910), 159, 285-6. Stephen's reference is to some type of fund-raising or lottery in which only he and Chester Pike drew winning tickets.
[5] Stephen possibly misspelled the name of John Hitchcock Higbee who died at 42 years of age in Newport, New Hampshire on April 25, 1857, three days before this letter was written. He is listed as a trader in the 1850 census, living in Newport with a wife Adeline and family. He was the married father of five children at the time of his death.
[6] Annginette Hall (Williams) Sherman, Albert's oldest sister who had moved to Chester township, Grinnell, Iowa by September of 1856.

Letter 10

To Albert G. Williams, Grinnell, Iowa
From George P. Williams

Cornish May 9, 1857[1]
Absent Friend

I seat myself down to pen you a few lines to you to let you know how we all do out here in the Eastern country. We are all very well at this time and hope that these few lines will find you in the same. Your Father and Fransis [*sic*] was well the last I heard from them. I suppose you have got your sowing and planting all done out there, haven't you, while we have just begun to plough and sow a little. The weather has been very Cold for the last month. The month of April was not so warm and pleasant as the month of March. Albert how is the hard times[2] out there with you? I understand that you feel it very hard there this spring. Has Newton[3] got his house done yet and how does he and Annginette[4] do, pretty well I hope. Well Albert, how many deers [*sic*] have you killed there this winter? Does you like [it] out there now as well as you did? I understand that you have bought some land. Does it lay near Newton? Do you Cultivate it? What are you going to do this summer? Are you going to work for Newton? What wages can you get a month out there this summer? I suppose the hard times will effect the wages some.

Well Albert I am in the shop[5] at work yet but they talk of stopping it in a few weeks if they don't get a new Contract but if they don't get another I don't think they will stop but a short time. They don't pay so large wages as they used to. Albert I have not got much news to write you at this time. George A. Kenyon[6] is dead. I suppose you use[d] to know him and Maria Lewis[7] is married. She has married a carpenter fellow that works in the shop. Marshal Harlow[8] is married too. You knew him. I don't think of any more to write at this time so I will draw this to a close by bidding you good by. Please write as soon as you get this and let us know how you are getting along.

This from your uncle
George P. Williams

---

[1] This may be the letter mentioned by Stephen Williams in the previous letter, Letter 9. He had received a letter from Albert and had asked his brother George Philander Williams to respond to it immediately. This is the first letter in the collection from Albert's uncle.

[2] A reference to the economic malaise that became the Panic of 1857. See Introduction.

[3] Luke Newton Sherman, Albert's brother-in-law.

[4] Annginette Hall (Williams) Sherman, Albert's oldest sister.

[5] This is probably a reference to the Windsor armory factory shop then under the Robbins and Lawrence company, based on Philander's next letter which specifically mentions the armory. If the reference is correct in placing Philander at the Windsor Armory, then his two 1857 letters would have been in reference to employment by Robbins and Lawrence according to the timeline in Joseph Wickham Roe, *English and American Tool Builders*, (New Haven: Yale University Press, 1916), 187. Roe published Lawrence's memories as Appendix A which support production of the Sharps rifle on contract at the Windsor armory, and the failure of Robbins and Lawrence at Windsor after 1856, 281-291. Roe maintained that a failed contract for 300,000 Minie rifles led to the demise of Lawrence and Robbins after the completion of 25,000 of the rifles as per a signed contract for that amount, 192. Thus, Philander probably worked previously on Sharps rifles and then on the Minie rifles prior to the breakup of the company.

[6] William H. Child, *History of the Town of Cornish New Hampshire with genealogical record, 1763-1910,* (Concord, NH.: The Rumford Press, 1910), Vol. 2, 244, recorded a George A. Kenyon, dying in Cornish on April 27, 1858 at 30 years old. Perhaps Child erred in the date which should have been recorded as 1857. There is a baby George Kenyon in the Cornish 1850 census, who would have been about seven years old at this time, but death records are inconsistent with the information in the letter.

[7] Maria Lewis is probably the daughter of Thomas and Mary Lewis noted in the 1850 census of Cornish. Alfred P. Carpenter married Maria Lewis and his occupation was listed as carpenter on his son Martin's death record. In the 1860 census Alfred Carpenter is listed as a machinist residing in Cornish, thus a co-worker of Philander's, as consistent with the letter.

[8] In the 1860 census Marshal Harlow, a 25-year-old machinist was living only two households away from Abijah Williams, Jr. who was a first cousin to Albert's father Stephen and George Philander Williams. Marshal Harlow may have also been a co-worker of Philander's.

Letter 11

To Albert G. Williams, Grinnell, Iowa
From Stephen Williams, Jr.

Cornish [NH] May 31, 1857
My only son,

I take this opportunity to write you a few lines to let you know that my health is very good for me. It has been very good the most part of the time since I last wrote you. I have had one hard touch of the pleurisy[1] but not so hard as the one I had when you lived at J. Taskers,[2] but it was as hard as I wanted to bare. I could not lie on my left side for a number of days. Mr. Cumings[3] has got a picture[4] and I believe he is a going to call it Albert. J. Tasker[5] has got the same, the name I don't know the rest is to be known here after. I have just returned from a fishing voyage to Cananon[6] [sic] to what is called the goose pond.[7] We had good luck and a good time. We had some of your western level muddy roads for a few miles. I thought much of you while there and here too. I had the pleasure of showing that rattle[8] to a great many people while there and I am greatly obliged to you for it. Your letter I received the night before I started our fishing voyage and it gave me a little more pleasure for it was like rolling a sweet morsel under the tongue. Little Fanny[9] is well and appears happy she has not received that letter yet but knows there is one to come for her. Miss Bugbee[10] forgot to take it.
Francis' young birds are dead she felt sad when they died, but the old bird has got 4 more and I hope they will live for her sake if nothing more.
I send you 35 now and I will send the rest next time. 35 20 yours due.[11]
When the above was wrote [sic] I was at the old place.[12]
I am down now
In a hurry
I will write soon
S. Williams Jr[13]

---

[1] Pleurisy is a condition of the lungs that causes sharp chest pain with deep breathing.

[2] There are two James Taskers in the 1860 Cornish census, a father and son. The elder James Tasker (1785-1876) was born in 1785, making him 72 at this time, while his son was 31. The younger James (1826-1903) was a carpenter and builder credited with building the Windsor, VT bridge that connected the town to Cornish; William H. Child, *History of the Town of Cornish New Hampshire with genealogical record, 1763-1910,* Vol. 2, (Concord, NH.: The Rumford Press, 1910), 363-4. Albert could have been bound out to either of these families prior to his leaving New Hampshire. This letter clarifies the family's oral history that Albert had been bound out to more than one person during his youth in New Hampshire. The previous Letter Three, addressed to Albert in care of Bryant, indicates his residence with that family, and now this letter clarifies he had also lived with the Tasker's.

[3] Darwin Comings was born May 13, 1857 to William and Mercy Comings of Cornish, NH. Perhaps Stephen was joking about the name Albert, or was misinformed.

[4] It is possible that Stephen was saying pitcher for picture, and thus using an old slang for child. "Little pitchers have big ears," was a joking way to identify a child.

[5] Arthur Kelly Tasker was born May 21, 1857 to James and Mary Tasker of Cornish, NH.

[6] Canaan, New Hampshire.

[7] Goose Lake was roughly 30 miles, north, northeast of Cornish near the town of Canaan.

[8] Rattle cut from the tail of a rattlesnake that Albert found in Iowa. He sent the rattle to his father. Rattlesnakes are mentioned in another letter, the September 6, 1857 letter from George Philander Williams, Albert's uncle. It was a novelty and worth showing off to many people, as Stephen has revealed. Albert's daughter Lavinia noted that the rattlesnakes had been eliminated in Iowa prior to her childhood on the family farm, Appendix I.

[9] A nickname for Albert's youngest sister Francis. We assume from this letter that Francis is living with Stephen.

[10] The post mistress.

[11] Sending Albert 35 dollars, presumably was quite a chunk of money at the time, on top of the 20 sent previously, if the 35 20 notation is to be believed as money referenced in dollars. The value of 55 dollars in todays' money would be over 2,000 if spent on a purchase.

[12] Implies Stephen is moving between residences.

[13] Stephen Williams Jr., Albert's father.

Cornish July 8 1857

My dear and only son

I take this openturnity
to write you a few lines to let you know
that my health is verry good, except
the rheumatism which I have had for
two days, it is all the sick ones I have
had since I left the shop, I dont know
as I wrote you in the other letter that
I had left of gun work, but I was
a bliged to do so on the acount of health,
and I keepe an old batchelden hall in
Hiram H York house and work out
by days work and I find verry good pickings
at that, I live like pigs in the stover
what I cant eat I can role over, perhaps
I may have a house keeper some time on
other but it twont bee toot toot
as Miss Comings sed, H Freman has a
gall George Weld a gal S Williams
nothing yet I gess I have wrote you nonsence as mutch
as is nesisary at this time

Letter 12 - Stephen Williams to Albert Gordon Williams; July 8, 1857. (First page only)

Letter 12

To Albert G. Williams, Grinnell, Iowa
From Stephen Williams, Jr.

Envelope: Mr. Albert G. Williams
Poweshiek County
Grinnell Iowa
Postmark: Windsor, Vermont

Cornish [NH] July 8, 1857
My dear and only son,

I take this opportunity to write you a few lines to let you know my health is very good except the rheumatism which I have had for two days. It is all the sick [h]ours I have had since I left the shop.[1] I don't know as I wrote you in the other letter that I had left of[f] gun work, but I was obliged to do so on account of health. And I keep an old batch elder[2] hall in Hiram H. York['s][3] house and work out by day's work and I find very good picking at that. I live like pigs in the clover. What I can't eat I can role [sic] over, pack ups [sic]. I may have a house keeper some time or other, but it twon't [sic] be toot toot as Miss Comings[4] said. H. Freeman[5] has a gal. George Weld[6] a gal. S. Williams Jr. nothing yet. I guess I have wrote you nonsense as much as is necessary at this time.

Now I will write you a little about our old maid Francis,[7] for she says so, so I must call her. She has raised three little birds this summer and she feels very proud of them. She came over here last Saturday night and staid with me and helped me to get the breakfast and helped me to do my washing and she is coming over next Saturday night and is a going down to the river with me. She says she wants to come and live with me and she will help me all she can, if I can get Aunt Caroline[8] to make the bread and the pies. Now I would say to you that I have had a good recommend of a lady to come and keep house for me, and I will send you in this letter a part of the recommend, and if you and Annginette will give me a little advice about the same I will abide with your judgement.

I was intending two [sic] write more, but I have not got time, so good by for the present.
Stephen Williams Jr.

Albert I am well now and hope that these lines will find you the same. I came up to Aunt Caroline's last night and am going back tonight. When you write again you will please to write me. So good by from your sister
Francis H. Williams[9]
I am going to school now and there is a girl who cannot read so well as I can.

---

[1] Possibly referring to the David Hilliard gun shop in Cornish, or to the Windsor, VT manufacturing and armory company.
[2] Bachelor.
[3] Hiram York was the son of Uriah and Betsey (Williams) York and Stephen's nephew. Hiram was married, at 39 years old, on January 8th, 1863 to Eliza Walker, having three children in the 1870 census. Hiram became a successful farmer living his entire life in Cornish; William H. Child, *History of the Town of Cornish New Hampshire with genealogical record, 1763-1910*, Vol. 2, (Concord, NH.: The Rumford Press, 1910), 436. In the 1860 census of Cornish he is listed on the same page as Stephen Williams, Jr., so a close neighbor geographically, as well as a relative.
[4] A Miss Comings cannot be identified, but a large Comings family lived in and around Cornish during the 19th century. His previous letter from May mentions the William and Mercy Comings family. Perhaps this is a reference to Mrs. Mercy Comings.
[5] H. Freemen was probably Henry Freeman who was married at the time this letter was written.
[6] An extensive Weld family contained two George Weld's. Both were married at the time of the writing of this letter, and one of the George Weld's had a wife who had just given birth to a baby in June 1857; Child, *History of Cornish*, ibid., 397, 400. It seems that Stephen is just remarking on the ability of these married men to have a housekeeper or a wife, something that he lacks.
[7] Albert's youngest sister Francis who was six years old at the time of this letter.

---

[8] Caroline (White) Williams was the wife of Stephen's brother George Philander Williams, a gunsmith in the 1870 census in Windsor, VT. From the context it appears that Francis is living with George and Caroline, also a first cousin to Stephen, as well as his sister-in-law through marriage. Other letters support the fact that Francis has lived with them at some time. Stephen's acknowledgement, that she would be able to keep up a household for him if only his sister-in-law Caroline made their bread and pies, indicates those tasks were considered too advanced for Francis at six years old. She did make breakfast and help with clothes washing at as his letter attests, seemingly advanced tasks for a child of six.

[9] Albert's sister included a little note at the end of her father's letter. Francis spelled her name with an "i", although her gravestone, marriage and other records, spell her name as Frances with an E. The 1860, 1870, and 1880 censuses spell her name with an I. For consistency Francis with an "i" is used herein.

Letter 13

To Albert G. Williams, Grinnell, Iowa
From Melinda Hall Williams

Clarendon Springs [Vermont][1]
July 12 [1857][2]

My Dear Son,

I received your kind letter last week and seat myself to answer it. I received one from Annginette[3] the week before, but I do not know as that needs an answer. Albert who and what do you live with? Is it Annginette? If I did not occasionally see a letter that she writes to Mrs. Hall[4] I should not believe that those I receive are written by the same person that used to seem to love her Mother so much. What a change matrimony makes! It had been six weeks since I last heard from her. I had written three times. I had written many things that I thought would interest her. I had said "I wonder what Annginette would think of this or that? What will she say to my coming up here?" I had not forgotten how she felt about my going to Concord. But when the letter came there was not one word of inquiry, not one word of sympathy for Mrs. Higbee,[5] not a care too [?] in regard to my health. Finally no more interests manifested for my welfare than she would express for a cat. I cried until I felt sick for two days, but that would not do, for you know that I cannot afford to be sick and there is no pleasure in it when there is no one to pity. Finally, I made up my mind to feel very thankful that my children do not trouble themselves about me any way. I have worried about her arm. I fear it is something bad. Have you had any more sores in your head? Did it make you deaf any? Last night I groaned and cried so in my sleep about Annginette that I waked Mrs. Glidden.[6] I dreamed something dreadful had carried her away and I could hear her cries at a distance and I could not rescue her.[7] Aand [sic] some also worry about you. But I try not to.
Now about that money I expected to hear from Henry[8] when he got out there, but have not, heard <u>one word</u>. I Don't know but there has a letter got lost. I expected to let him have it if he wanted it. I don't know if it will be best for you to have it or not. You know that I should want you to have it if it would benefit you, but I suppose you could not hold the land by law being so young and if I should let you have what little I have got and you should be taken away I could not recover one cent. However, if you feel anxious I shall help you some. Yet I think it would be as well for you to delay buying until another Spring and Winter and Summer there first.[9] Sometimes now Albert I want you to write just as soon as you get this and write just how you feel about every thing. You know me well enough to know that I value the happiness of my children far more than my own. I have almost outlived my usefulness now[10] I don't know as any one that I care for would hardly miss me and if I can do anything that will really help you I want to, but you know that I must eat while I live and it will not do to give away what I have and then come upon the publick [sic] for support.
Now good bye and may you keep in the path of truth and honor is the constant prayer of your mother. I shall not write to A[11] this time as I have been more than a week in writing this, but give my love to her and husband. I hope that she has written before this. Write if you think that your Father will come there. I am feeling rather low spirited and have written rather gloomy, but shall feel better bye and bye.
From your Mother M H Williams[12]

---

[1] Clarendon Springs is roughly 50 miles directly west of Cornish, NH. The Springs are west of Clarendon proper and south of West Rutland. The Springs were established by 1770, as one of the first mineral spring spas in Vermont. The town attained almost 1500 residents by 1790. The healthful properties of the spring water were marketed for visitors and the water bottled. A spa hotel was built in 1835, which still stands, becoming the focal point of the mineral springs which attracted many southerners prior to the Civil War. The hotel could host 200 guests. In the early 1850s the Rutland and Washington Railroad line went through Vermont approximately 3 miles north of Clarendon Springs making easier access to the Springs. The town hit its peak during the 1890s as a resort destination. By 1940 there were only a few families left; Lester Warren Fish, *The Fish Family in England and America*, (Rutland, Vt: Tuttle Publishing Company, 1948), 182; Clarendon House National Register Nomination, May 17, 1976; https://npgallery.nps.gov/NRHP/GetAsset/NRHP/76000146_text, accessed October 25, 2023. From the context of the letter she seems to have been there for roughly six weeks. Presumably she worked as a domestic for the Clarendon Springs spa hotel.

2 Presumably this letter was written before Clara Sherman, Melinda's granddaughter, was born as she does not mention her. It references a death in the Higbee family, so it is placed in 1857.

3 Her oldest child, Annginette Hall (Williams) Sherman, then living in Chester Township, Grinnell, Iowa.

4 Mrs. Hall was whaling captain Worthin Hall wife's, Polly (Lovewell) Hall. See discussion in Introduction.

5 Adeline Higbee was recently widowed when her husband, John Hitchcock Higbee passed away on April 25, 1857 in Newport, New Hampshire. John was a merchant, justice, and a coroner; Edmund Wheeler, *History of Newport, NH, from 1766 to 1878, with a genealogical register,* (Concord, NH.: Republican Press Association, 1879), 12, 210, 211, 418. See also Letter 9 which mentions his death.

6 Mrs. Glidden can't be specifically identified although there are numerous families surnamed Glidden in both New Hampshire and Vermont in the 1850 and 1860 censuses. A Mrs. Joseph "Polly" Glidden resided in Poultney, Vermont about 25 miles west of Clarendon, per the 1850 Federal census. Presumably they are rooming together and working at the Clarendon Springs spa hotel.

7 Melinda was having nightmares about her separation from her children. She had saved herself from a poor marriage, but could not justify in her own mind the separation from her children due to that divorce.

8 Unidentified. This is probably a reference to Henry Sherman [1832-1920], the brother of Luke Newton Sherman, Melinda's son-in-law. Henry Sherman married Almira Dudley in Newport, NH on March 24, 1857. Almira was an adopted daughter of Melinda's cousin Abner Hall [1804-1877]. (See Letter 26) The marriage certificate notes Henry Sherman was a resident of Clinton, Iowa (see Letter 6 from Annginette Hall Williams Sherman from Lyons. Lyons, Iowa became a part of Clinton. The Shermans had settled there in 1854 prior to the move to the Grinnell area.) Similar to his two older brothers, Henry married a New Hampshire woman and then the couple relocated to Iowa. By 1860, they were residing in Chester township, Grinnell, Iowa.

Another possibility is that this is reference to Henry Dudley, an older brother of George Dudley (see Letter 22 from George Dudley) who grew up on a neighboring farm in Newport, NH. He is listed in his parents' household in Newport, NH in the 1860 census at 22 years old. It is possible he went out to Iowa in 1857 and returned prior to the 1860 census. Henry Dudley's father T. Fisher Dudley gave a deposition in the Williams divorce case indicating that the Williams and Dudley farms adjoined. The proximity of the farms and the divorce testimony argue for close ties between the two families. Either Henry Sherman or Henry Dudley could have been entrusted with the money mentioned in the next sentences.

9 This letter was written during the first summer season that Albert spent in Chester township, Grinnell working for his brother-in-law Luke Newton Sherman. She is advising caution in his desire to purchase land, in part due to his age. Albert's first deed for land was created in 1859, but the details of the sale are unknown. It is possible that Albert began making payments on the land prior to the deed.

10 Melinda was about 40 years old at this time.

11 Annginette Hall (Williams) Sherman.

12 Melinda was working in a very tony health spa. In Nathan Hall's log of the voyage of the whaling ship *Elizabeth* there is a page from a newspaper pasted into the log. The newspaper article quotes a letter written by President Franklin Pierce, the only president from NH. The letter was dated January 6, 1860 at Clarendon Springs, making it a well-known spa for the elite of the time. The letter was addressed to Jeff Davis. The newspaper, *Independent Democrat* of Concord, NH published the letter with the comment that Pierce's loyalties to the union should be questioned.

Letter 14

To Albert G. Williams, Grinnell, Iowa
From George Philander Williams

Cornish, [NH] Sept 6" [*sic*] 1857
Absent Friend

I now seat myself down to write a few lines to you to let you know how we are getting along. We are all well at this time and hope that these few lines will find you the same. I received a letter from you which I was very glad to have from you and was very glad to hear that you were so contented out there. I suppose you have some good times a hunting them chickens out there don't you?[1] I wish I was there to ketch [*sic*] some of them with you. Have you ever shot any of them down yet? If not, you have a seen a good many, haint [*sic*] you? Is that a great place for fishing out there ? If so, what kind of fish do you ketch [*sic*] ?
How is it Albert? Do you see many rattle snakes and don't you feel afraid of them? I suppose you kill of them as you can.
Albert how is the wheat crop this summer? I suppose you have thrashed a great deal of it before this time. Do you have much fruit out there? I hope you have more than we do have. We have a few more apples here this year than last year. As for the corn crop, that is very good. If we should have a warm month the potato crop is quite good, but they are rotting very bad. How are they out there, Albert?
I saw your father today. He was well as usual. Francis[2] was home and stayed with us last week. She enjoyed herself first rate. Issac Kinion [*sic*][3] is dead. He died two weeks ago last Saturday.
I suppose you would like to know whether the armory[4] is a running or not. Well that has not got in operation yet, but they have sold it.[5] So they think that it will start now soon. They intended to cut some hands to work last week, but did not get round [*sic*] to it. I don't think of any more news to write at this time. You will give our love to your Brother[6] and Sister[7] and tell them we should be glad to hear from them. Albert, please write us again. Write soon and tell me all about your hunting and fishing and how your crops come in this fall. I will now draw my letter to a close by bidding you good by from your uncle.
G. P. Williams
To A G Williams

---

[1] This reference to wild chickens may imply Albert has been hunting pheasants which are still found in Poweshiek County, Iowa.

[2] Albert's youngest sister, Francis Williams.

[3] Issac Kenyon, a married, 35-year-old farmer in the 1850 census in Cornish, NH, died August 15, 1857 and is buried in Cornish, NH.

[4] He is referring to the gun manufacturing concern in Windsor, Vermont.

[5] Guy Hubbard, "Leadership of Early Windsor Industries in the Mechanic Arts, A Paper Read Before the Vermont Historical Society at Windsor, September 4, 1922," *Essays in the Social and Economic History of Vermont*, (Montpelier: Vermont Historical Society, 1943), 259, found the Lamson & Goodnow Manufacturing Company of Shelburne Falls, Massachusetts purchased the Windsor Armory in 1858 and began manufacturing Windsor Sewing Machines in that year, 260; the White sewing machine is a lineal descendant of these machines. It is possible that Philander is referencing this sale which historians have placed in 1858, thus his letter refines the date when the business was sold, i.e., before September 1857. Machine tools, produced for the Government and private armories, were also made here during this time. When the Civil War broke out, Lamson sold the prosperous sewing machine business to Thomas White, and the Windsor Armory continued under Lamson, Goodnow, and Yale and then under E. G. Lamson in the production of rifles, 260. See also *Vermont Journal*, December 4, 1880, 8, for a short history of the Armory. See Introduction.

[6] Luke Newton Sherman, Albert's brother-in-law.

[7] Annginette Hall (Williams) Sherman.

Letter 15

To Albert G. Williams, Grinnell, Iowa
From Stephen Williams, Jr.

Cornish [NH] November 8th 1857
My dear and only Son

Yours of the 25th was received last evening with much pleasure. I broke the seal to peruse the contents that was within the folds. I have been a looking for a letter for some three months past, but have you have not received my last letter the fault is not yours. I wrote you and Annginette[1] a letter asking your advice on one subject[2] and I did not know but that you took offense at it and would not answer it. I have rewrote one to you asking you to return the last letter, but have not sent it as you have not received my last letter. I will omit that question that as I wrote in my last.

Francis[3] lives with me yet she won't live and go anywhere unless I will go with her.[4] She has learnt to braid straw and has braided a number of yards. She has got a number of meals of vittles, and washes the dishes. She has lost one of her birds. It was a good singer. We miss it much. She has sold one and we have 3 left.

Issac Kennan[5] is dead. One of Jacob Chase's girls[6] is dead. There was a girl that lived at Judge Jackson[7] that hung herself the other day on the account of Horace Bugbe [sic].[8] There are so many stories a float about it we can't get the write [sic] one yet. Henry Bugbee[9] is married, and Louise B[10] is a goin [sic] to be married Thanksgiving day. Rechel Kindric[11] is married. The rest remain as before. I am making shingle[s] this fall and winter. I have ingaged [sic] 20 thousand of shingles to be done in the spring. I have bought 6 thousand feet of timber in the log to be delivered here at 6 dollars a thousand. I have made 15 thousand of[f] shingle[s] this summer and fall.

I have got two small jobs of thrashings to do which will take about 10 days and then I shall go at the shingle. B. F. Tasker has got back from the west and boy.[12] The boy got back before haying. They don't like the west. They don't feed him and let him set and smoke for nothing as they do here. As for your sheep, I have got to sell them for Mr. York[13] can't take them no more. He is a going to buy them if we can fix on a price but he can't pay for them till spring. Money is hard here as well as elsewhere. Corn 80 cts per bushells [sic] wheat 15, potatoes 90, rye 75, beans 150, butter 19, cheese 9 cts per lb, pork fresh 8 cts lb, beef 4 or 5 cts, salt pork remains at 14 cts as usual. Labor is a coming down fast here. Flour has fell from 12.50 to 8 dollars per bushel. It is the hardest time for money now that I have known. The factories all stopped in Claremont [NH] and elsewhere mostly. Hundreds of hands are turned out of work on account of money.[14]

As for myself and Fannie[15] we get a good living yet and I hope we shall. I don't think of much more to write that is worth a mentioning. There is one more I would say. Fanny made some apple sauce the other day. Done the whole herself and it was gooy. If you was here you could have some of it. We do the whole of our work washing, baking, and the whole except sewing,[16] give my best respects to Annginette[17] and her better half. Good by for the present.
Stephen Williams Jr.

---

[1] Annginette Hall (Williams) Sherman, Albert's oldest sister.

[2] Stephen's comment on his previous letter may have been a change of heart over the issue of hiring a housekeeper or finding a "gal", from his previous Letter 12 of July 8, 1857. It reflects some level of stress on his part at the thought of alienating his adult children with the thought of having a woman other their mother in his household. Asking Albert to return the letter exemplifies Stephen's anxiety over words he cannot take back.

[3] Albert's youngest sister, Francis Williams.

[4] This fear of leaving her father is the presumable result of the time spent away from her parents when bound out with Albert. Francis had been traumatized by having to live with other families.

[5] Probably Issac Kenyon, a married, 35 year-old farmer in the 1850 census in Cornish, NH, who died August 15, 1857 and is buried in Cornish, NH.

[6] Jacob Chase's daughter, Sarah, died at 23 years old on September 7, 1857; William H. Child, *History of the Town of Cornish New Hampshire with genealogical record, 1763-1910,* Vol. 2, (Concord, NH.: The Rumford Press, 1910), 73. The Chase family was large and prominent in the area.

[7] Judge Jackson was probably Eleazer Jackson, a member of a large and prominent family; Child, *History of Cornish,* Vol. 2, 224-5. The girl is probably Harriet Newton who was listed as a 10-year-old member of Eleazer Jackson's household in the 1850 census. Harriet died September 27, 1857 and is buried in the Edminster Cemetery in South Cornish, NH. She would have been about 17 at the time of death, roughly the same age as Albert.

[8] Horace Bugbee was Albert's first cousin. Stephen's sister Almira Williams married Benjamin Franklin Bugbee and had 9 children. Horace Bugbee, will appear in later letters as a "ne'er do well" and troubled teen.

[9] Henry Bugbee, Albert's first cousin, was a son of Almira Williams and Benjamin Franklin Bugbee, born October 12, 1832. Henry Bugbee, a carpenter, married Lucy Bryant in October of 1856 according to Child, *History of Cornish*, Vol. 2, 42. Henry married Lucy Barker according to records on Ancestry.com.

[10] The Louise B. is probably Lois Liscomb Bugbee, born November 26, 1836 to Benjamin and Almira (Williams) Bugbee, another first cousin of Albert's. On November 26, 1857, she married Samuel Judd, according to the New Hampshire marriage index on Ancestry.com.

[11] Rachel Kendrick, a first cousin to Albert, was the daughter of Daniel and Mary (Williams) Stearns. Her first husband, Horace Kendrick had died in 1855, thus she remarries in 1857, to John Burbee.

[12] Benjamin Franklin Tasker, born in Cornish about 1804 was a mechanic. He had five sons, any one of whom could have traveled to the West with Tasker; Child, *History of Cornish*, Vol. 2, 364.

[13] This is possibly a reference to Uriah York who was married to Stephen's older sister Betsy Williams.

[14] Stephen's comment about the lack of money, dropping wages, and high unemployment all point to the effects of the Panic of 1857 on his region. New Hampshire was especially hit hard. See Introduction for a discussion of the Panic of 1857.

[15] Albert's youngest sister, Francis Williams.

[16] Francis would have been 3 months shy of seven years old at the time of this letter. She demonstrated a tremendous capacity for work for one so young. What seems exceptional is the hot and dangerous task of making apple sauce on a wood stove. Stephen paints a picture of Francis as an exceptional child devoted to the domestic tasks expected of women at this time.

[17] Albert's oldest sister, Annginette Hall (Williams) Sherman.

Letter 16

To Albert G. Williams
From Stephen Williams, Jr.

Envelope postmarked Windsor [VT] Jan 18
Mr. Albert G. Williams
Grinnell
Poweshiek County
Iowa

Cornish [NH] Jan 10 1858

I have a few moments to spare this evening and I thought I would comenst [*sic*] a letter and finish some other time. I received your letter last evening with pleasure to find you all well. We are all well except Fran.[1] She has got a slight cold. She has been to school every day as yet she improves fast. She is a goin [*sic*] to study arithmetic. Her first book has gone by the board.[2] I have bought two new books since school comenst [*sic*]. She goes bye [*sic*] the whole school so I am told. If you could see her table you would suppose her to be a lawyer. She has a book in her hand all the time almost.

I shave shingle[s] evenings and she stands by the side of the house and reads til 8 o'clock and leaves for bed.[3] Just look over here some evening and see us enjoy ourselves, enough to eat and a good appetite to eat it with. We have a pleasant winter so far a very little snow not much sledding til Jan[uary] has come in. They have turned. Had Bugbee[4] out of school and the sherriff is after him for fighting the master. They are in a peck of trouble stealing chickens, biting master, and sense in turn failing up.[5]

Sunday 17

Since writing the other page they have taken H. Bugbee[6] and fined him 10 dollars and cost, making about 20 dollars, I am told. Stephen D. Ford[7] is dead. He died with the numb palsy.[8] He was sick three days. I took care of him two days and two nights and I hant [*sic*] got over it yet. Fran is quite sick with a cold today, but I hope it will be better tomorrow. If not, she will not go to school. Father[9] has had a light shock of the numb palsy so he can't speak quite so plain as he did before. That disorder is quite common here. [I] know there was one at Windsor [VT] that was taken with it one night and died the next noon. Uncle Abijah[10] is no better. He lays senselessly the most part of the time. I don't think of much more news to write or nonsense. Things remain as usual except that great George Hilliard[11] has got a fox by having someone shoot him for for [*sic*] him.

As for money, I have had the promise of some. I don't know how much I can git. The Bank don't want to pay out much but they say they will let me have a little in two or three weeks and I will be prepared to send it as soon as I can git it, so you may look out for it in three or four weeks.[12] I shall send a draft I think, so you can look out for it. I am in hopes to git it in two weeks, but maybe not under three weeks. So you can calculate on the time the letter will be on the road. Have you sold your rifle?

Fran is asleep now and she appears quite sick. She groans a good deal. If she is no better in the morning I will give my pen another scratch so you will know. So good night.

Stephen Williams Jr.

No better. I think I shall [get] a doctor in the afternoon if no better.

---

[1] Francis, Albert's younger sister.
[2] Francis finished her first reader and progressed into an advanced book.
[3] Francis stood by the side of the house reading while her father cut shingles. Was she afraid to leave his side, or just lonely? This behavior presents a poignant intimate picture of a child possibly traumatized by the life she had been forced to lead away from her parents. See letter 15 which states Francis is afraid to go anywhere without her father.
[4] Horace Bugbee, Albert's first cousin.
[5] Stephen is commenting on Bugbee's lack of common sense, in general.
[6] Horace Bugbee, Albert's first cousin.

[7] Stephen Dana Ford [1805-1858] was a Cornish farmer who died January 13, 1858, only five days before the continued letter on the 17th. Providing care for Ford may explain the gap in the letter writing. Ford was married, but his wife had a small child at the time, perhaps necessitating Stephen William's help.

[8] The term "numb palsy" was in common usage from the mid-1600s to about 1877. The exact cause of death is unknown based on the use of this term. Numb palsy could refer to Bell's palsy, (facial palsy and spasm) a numbness on the side of the face, or it could have referenced a stroke or other convulsive or paralytic disorders.

[9] "Father" was a reference to Stephen Williams, Sr., who died September 13, 1859 at 77 years old. From this letter we can assume his last years were spent with infirmity.

[10] Uncle Abijah refers to Stephen's uncle Abijah Williams who died January 25, 1858, at 82 years old, only a few days after this letter was penned.

[11] The "great" George Hilliard possibly refers to David Hall Hilliard's son George E. who succeeded him in the gun manufacturing industry according to Robert E. Gardner, *Small Arms Makers, A Directory of fabricators of firearms, edged weapons, crossbows and polearms,* (New York: Bonanza Books, 1963), 92, Gardner mistakenly identifies George as a brother of David, but David had no brother George according to William H. Child, *History of the Town of Cornish New Hampshire with genealogical record, 1763-1910,* Vol I, (Concord, NH.: The Rumford Press, 1910), 200. David Hilliard's son was George E. Hilliard who operated the gunshop from 1873 to 78 and put his initials on the underside of each gun barrel, per Gardner, Ibid., 92. David Hilliard's older son Charles Nelson partnered with another Hilliard to operate, in Cornish, a gunsmithing enterprise from 1876-79, later working with the Remington gun makers; Gardner, ibid., 92, Child, ibid., 204. Stephen had previously worked for David Hall Hilliard. The Hilliards became a prominent family through the gun industry, and Stephen's seemingly sarcastic comment on George's hiring of someone to shoot a fox for him may have been fueled by class consciousness and division, or simply Stephen's unflattering opinion of this member of the Hilliard family. George E. was nineteen years old at the time of this letter. See Introduction.

[12] These comments reflect the banking issues related to the Panic of 1857.

Letter 17

To Albert G. Williams, Grinnell, Iowa
From Manson Stevens

Cornish [NH] Feb 12th [1858]
Dear Friend

I will now answer your kind letter which I had ought to have done long before. We are all, I believe, about as when you left. Susan[1] and her Fellow is done I guess. She is to work to Claremont now I believe to Mr. Fletcher's.[2] The school is rather a curious one. The teacher is one John West[3] from Bradford, N. H. He is very quick tempered. Will have a firstrate [sic] to play but don't learn much for it takes him more than half the time punishing them, as all about the same scholars there was last winter. We have [had] three months school this winter next week. The scholars all send their Love to you. The girls in particular. I think we should all like to look out there and see how you last going three miles to school.[4] Bell[e][5] says she should think you mite write their folks as you promised to. Our City is a growing fast and filling up with baby. We have seven here in the City.

It's valentine time now and they are Flying in haste. We have had some changes here. Issac Kenyon[6] died very sudden with the Colic last summer. I suppose you have heard of it without doubt. Stephen Ford[7] died very sudden too a few weeks ago what ailed him don't know for I was gone when he died, to Hanover a visiting. Milton Wyman had a boy[8] killed last week a sledding. The sled broke and ran one of the staves threw his body and he died very quick. He was fifteen years old. You will lose Isabell[9] for she [undecipherable] never was much smarter a fellow in the world I guess. By action she is as happy as a clam in high water. I would like to have you call on our school some day when your school don't keep. George Ayers is married to Jonas Lamson's daughter, of Windsor.[10] Most everyone that are not married is courting someone. They say Norman Bugby[11] is courting Emeline Lewis[12] but how true it is wont know, but he goes very often that is true. I must close now good by.
Yours Truly Manson Stevens[13] Cornish to home

---

[1] Unidentified.
[2] This is possibly David W. Fletcher who was a druggist in Claremont, NH in the 1860 census.
[3] This is possibly a reference to John West [1836-1880], born in Bradford, NH who became a doctor.
[4] Unfortunately, the school Albert attended three miles from his sister and brother-in-law's farm is not known. Presumably it was in the town of Grinnell. His attendance at 17-years old is consistent with other sources. Iowa defined school age children as those between the ages of five and twenty-one, Keach Johnson, "Elementary and Secondary Education in Iowa, 1890-1900," *Annals of Iowa,* Part I, Vol. 45, Issue 2, (Fall 1979), 89. Leonard Fletcher Parker, *History of Poweshiek County, Iowa; A History of Settlement, Organization, Progress, and Achievement,* (Chicago: S. J. Clarke Publishing company, 1911), 327, credits Jennie Howard as the first school mistress in the first school in Chester township in Spring, 1861, held in a private home. He credited the beginning of free schools in Poweshiek County in 1858, 108. In 1857, there were seven teachers in Poweshiek County, six men and one woman, 113. Unfortunately, Parker's history on the specifics of Albert's life in the Grinnell area was mis-informed.
[5] Unidentified.
[6] Issac Kenyon died August 15, 1857. His death was also mentioned in letter 16 from Stephen Williams, Jr. The 1860 census shows a Kenyon family was two doors away from the Manson Stevens family.
[7] Stephen Dana Ford [1805-1858] was a Cornish farmer whose death is mentioned by Stephen Williams, Jr. in letter 16.
[8] Arthur Milton Wyman [1845-1858] died February 5, 1858, William H. Child, *History of the Town of Cornish New Hampshire with genealogical record, 1763-1910,* Vol. 2, (Concord, NH.: The Rumford Press, 1910), 431. "Arthur M. Wyman, aged thirteen, son of Milton Wyman, was sliding in the field near his schoolhouse, when his sled hit a pile of frozen manure, breaking it, and a portion of it was driven into his body several inches. From the effects of this he died after a few hours of extreme suffering," Ibid., Vol. I, 198.
[9] Unidentified.
[10] Jonas Lamson's daughter Almira married George W. Ayers on December 31, 1857 in Windsor, Vermont.
[11] Albert's first cousin, Norman Bugbee married Louisa Gates in 1859.
[12] Emeline Lewis was a 20-year-old in the 1860 census living in a large family headed by her father, Benjamin Lewis, a carpenter. She was born May 2, 1840 and died May 3, 1867, per Child, *History of Cornish*, Vol 2., 260, presumably unmarried.
[13] Manson Stevens [1838-1906], born September 20, 1838 in White River, Vermont, was the son of Joseph and Harriet (Drew) Stevens, and presumably a school classmate. Manson Stevens, a married farmer, was drafted into Civil War service in 1863 according to Child, *History of Cornish*, NH, Vol. I, 105. It is probable that Stevens obtained a substitute or paid three hundred dollars to be relieved of service. He died in New Hampshire in 1906 at 67 years old.

Letter 18

To Albert G. Williams, Grinnell, Iowa
From Stephen Williams, Jr.

Cornish [NH] Feb 3 1858

When I last wrote to you I had a sick girl here.[1] She has been very sick, too, with the lung fever, but she has got well now. So she is a goin [*sic*] to school tomorrow, if she remains as well as today. Things remain about the same as when I last wrote you except Uncle Abijah[2] is dead. I did not attend the funeral for I had a sick child at home. We have about three inches of snow here now. It may last three days and it may not. I expect to send you some money tomorrow if I get it. Your sheep[3] money I will keep for that will not come til spring. I aint in a mood to write tonight so I must bid you good by.
S Williams, Jr.
Has your mother sent out some money and how much?[4]

---

[1] A reference to Francis Williams, Albert's youngest sister. See letter 16.

[2] Abijah Williams [1776-1858], Stephen's uncle, died on January 25, 1858, in Cornish.

[3] Stephen's mention of sheep is consistent with the early histories of the area which discuss the sheep industry. In 1810-11 Merino sheep were imported from Spain because of their wool, considered superior to the older types of sheep then in New England. During the War of 1812 a blockade increased American ingenuity and the development of specialized machinery to handle the longer fibers of the merino sheep. Windsor, VT experienced its first industrial boom with the development of this machinery. After that time, the sheep husbandry was sustained in Windsor, Cornish and the surrounding small towns. See Guy Hubbard, "Leadership of Early Windsor Industries in the Mechanic Arts," A Paper Read Before the Vermont Historical Society at Windsor, September 4, 1922, Proceedings of the Vermont Historical Society, 1921, 22, 23, (Montpelier: Capital City Press, 1924), 164.

[4] Stephen is stressed about Albert's repeated requests for money and his own situation, currently shingle making, rather than gunsmithing work.

Letter 19

To Albert G. Williams, Grinnell, Iowa
From Stephen Williams, Jr.

Cornish [NH] March 20 1858

I take this opportunity to write you a few lines to let you know that we are well and happy under these circumstances, except a cold times is a growing better here at the present. I hope it will continue to better, I have sold 14 lb of shingles for 35 dollars. I have got quite a lot of shingles on hand yet but it ain't quite time to sell yet. I have had a chance to sell 18 lb but the pay did not suit. He wanted to pay half money and the other half in boots & shoes. Your uncle Daniel Stearns[1] is dead. He died town meeting day night. He died at the alms house.[2] He had been on the town about 3 weeks before he died. Daniel Jackson,[3] Evrit [sic] Robinson[4], Cotton Chase[5] is on the town.

Fan[6] is a selling you a copy. It is the first that she has wrote with a pen. She has wrote on a slate to school this winter. She has got a head so fast that she has got your 3 reader the one you read in the last you used here.[7] The school closed Tuesday. She feels quite cross about it. There is no particular change in the Bugbee family yet. Horace[8] Is a bad boy. He was at Jhn Fords[9] auction he cut the table and cut the dried beef and stuck his knife in the cheese and whether his father has settled it or not I don't know. As for old doctor Frank[10] he is at Mr. Hilliards[11] a doing about the same he used to do. As for Mr. Hilliard I have not been into the shop but once since I left. He did not look as though he was a doing great business. The gun shop goes now, but how long it will go I don't know. The sheriff went in one day and see [sic] 6 hundred dollars a laying on the counter and he froze to that. They don't think it will stand it long.

They have got that court house ready for the brick and there it stands. Probably they will make it come up this summer. Our snow has pertemuch[12] all left us now. They have tapped some of their sugar orchard[13] but as it does not act much like sap weather, they won't make much sugar to sell when they can git good molasses for 22 cts per gallon. Cheese 7 cts, corn 8 cts, butter 15, potatoes 34, beans $1.25, pork salt 9 cts. We have got some good apples now if you was here we would have a good feast.[14] So good night.
S. Williams
[On the left side of the letter is written lengthwise]: They are quite feeble at your grandfather's.[15]

---

[1] Daniel Stearns, the son of Daniel Stearns, a Revolutionary soldier, was married to Stephen Williams' older sister Mary. Daniel Stearns was on his own for the three weeks before his death, implying a failed relationship with his wife, and/or an impoverished lifestyle. Mary is listed as the head of the household in the 1850 census, so it is possible that they had been separated for some time previous to his death and that he had resorted to living in the alms house only three weeks before death. Daniel's death was not recorded by historian William Child. Daniel and Mary had eight children per William H. Child, *History of the Town of Cornish New Hampshire with genealogical record, 1763-1910,* Vol 2, (Concord, NH.: The Rumford Press, 1910), 349.

[2] The Cornish Alms house was built in 1838, per Child, ibid., Vol I., 206. Similar stories accompany the other three men that Stephen believed were "on the town," that is, indigent.

[3] Daniel Jackson was a soldier in the War of 1812, aged 73 years at the time of the writing of this letter. Historian William Child related a short history of Jackson's life but ended by observing that Jackson "was a man of good natural endowments but ruined by habitual intoxication." Child, Ibid., Vol 2, 225.

[4] Everett Robinson, a lifetime resident of Cornish, served in the War of 1812, and was 77 years old at the time of the writing of this letter. His wife, Julia Williams, was the daughter of William and Susanna Pond Williams, with whom he had eight children. He died March 2, 1879; Child, Ibid., Vol II, 316.

[5] Cotton Chase, a farmer and mechanic, died in 1872, but Child's *History of Cornish* gives no information on his relative prosperity or accomplishment only noting that the family lived most of their lives in Cornish; Child, Ibid., Vol 2, 81.

[6] Albert's younger sister, Francis.

[7] Francis, just turned seven years old, was doing well with schoolwork. The fact that she was using the same reader that Albert had used the last time he was there, a level three reader, may underscore the family's belief that Albert suffered with dyslexia and/or problems with learning/reading. Albert was roughly 10 years older than Francis and would have presumably used a level three reader at her age, not at the later 16 years old, the last possible age he would have lived with his father.

[8] Horace Bugbee, Albert's first cousin, was 18 years old and living with his parents, Almira Williams Bugbee, Stephen Williams' sister, and her husband Benjamin, at this time. He was somewhat old for the acting out described in the letter, and inconsistent with the cultural norms for children in the Victorian era who were expected to exhibit mature behavior at a young age.

[9] John Ford may have been a reference to John Deming Ford the son of Daniel and Esther Ford, Child, ibid., Vol 2, 165.

[10] Unidentified.

[11] "Mr. Hilliard" was a reference to David H. Hilliard, Stephen's previous employer. Hilliard's gun manufactory in Cornish was well-known for quality pistols and rifles. Hilliard reportedly tested each gun before selling it. Hilliard operated the gun shop until his death in 1877; Child, Ibid., Vol. I, 183, Vol. 2, 202. His rifles had a characteristic under-hammer firing which was cheap, simple, and reliable. Through high quality and low price, Hilliard's guns received a wide reputation comparable to large armory production; Guy Hubbard, "Development of Machine Tools in New England," *American Machinist*, October 18, 1923, Vol 59, Issue 16, 581.; Stephen worked for Hilliard for an unknown amount of time. Hilliard never employed more than 15 men, but they were considered skilled craftsmen; Child, Ibid., Vol. I, 183; Hubbard, *American Machinist*, ibid. The letter collection substantiates Stephen's work for Hilliard and move to the Windsor armory. At the outbreak of the Civil War, Hilliard worked day and night to produce a quantity of rifles which he took to the governor in Concord, NH as his donation to the Northern cause, Hubbard, *American Machinist*, ibid. How many of these guns were used by the North is unknown. Hilliard's two sons continued in the arms manufacturing business. Stephen mentions son George Hilliard in Letter 16 from January of 1858. Stephen appears to have been periodically employed in gunsmithing throughout his life in Cornish.

[12] Pretty much.

[13] "Sugar orchard" refers to maples.

[14] Apples in March were probably secured the previous fall by storage in cellars.

[15] Albert's grandparents, Stephen and Betsy (White) Williams died on September 13, 1859 and March 5, 1860, respectively.

Letter 20

To Albert G. Williams, Grinnell, Iowa
From Stephen Williams, Jr.

Cornish [NH] May 19 1858

We are all well at this time and hoping these few lines will find you enjoying the same. You must excuse me for not writing any more. I am a goin to Claremont[1] today and I thought I would drop you a line. We have been very dry here this spring but it rains and snows now.[2] This is the 2[3] snow we have had since the snow left last winter. Vegetation is very backward this spring. Times is very dull so far this spring. There is no sales of corn or any produce. I fear that we have not seen the hard times yet but I hope I can find enough to eat til the crops come off. I have got 3 large acres planted this spring, 1 of corn, 1 of beans, 1 of potatoes.[4] So if they do well it will keep me and my kind.
You wrote to me for some money. It will be most impossible for me to git it. I can't git it under 3 months if I could in that time I was lucky in gitting [*sic*] what I did for you.[5]
So good by
Stephen Williams, Jr.

---

[1] Claremont, New Hampshire.

[2] Snow in May should seem unusual, but the area is known for cold winters where the average snowfall ranges from sixty to one hundred inches. January temperatures can dip below ten degrees F now during a period of general warming. Historic weather patterns were colder, and one paper noted that in May 1799, hail, snow, piercing winds and ice had slowed the growth of vegetation and disrupted the migration of birds and the movement of animals. Scarcely a week passed during New Hampshire's winter months when the newspapers did not mention snow; Ben Lafferty, *American Intelligence: small-town news and political culture in Federalist New Hampshire,* (Amherst: University of Massachusetts Press, 2019), 116-117.

[3] Second.

[4] As a farmer, Stephen's concerns over what and when to plant to have enough to eat are palpable. Having fields planted before the last snow fall of the season also added to the stress and uncertainty of the season's crops, and lack of disposable income. The poor economic conditions may also reflect the Panic of 1857 with problems lingering into the following year.

[5] This letter is almost curt in its tone. There is no heading of endearment, and it is spaced two months after the previous letter. Stephen references another request for money from Albert, but, frustratingly, he cannot send any. Perhaps the requests for money are overwhelming, as Stephen asked in Letter 18 if Albert had received money from his mother. As he does not mention his daughter Francis it is possible she is not living with him at this time; a situation adding to his stress.

Letter 21

To Albert G. Williams, Grinnell, Iowa
From Stephen Williams, Jr.

Cornish [NH] July [1858]
Dear son,

I take this opportunity to write you a few lines to let you know that we are all well at this time and hoping these few lines will find you enjoying the same blessing. I understood that you had not received a letter from me for a long time. I have sent three letters and the town's report since last March, but whether you have received the book or letters I do not know.[1] We have had very dry weather here, so much so that some fields are past all care. Some pieces of wheat is about spoilt. Corn has stood it better than people could expect. I have three acres that looks very well, potatoes in particular. I have one acre of corn, 1 beans, 1 of potatoes. It has rained some today and we hope that it will continue some two or three days more. Fran[2] has been to school every day yet this summer. She won't stay at home neither hot, dry, sick, or cold, she must go. I wanted her to stay to home one day and go and get her a bonnet, but no go. School was more profit than a bonnet. She boards out this hay season at the widow Demings when I work this season.[3] I do all her work this summer.[4] I don't think of much news to write at this time except the widow Fitch[5] has hung herself. It is the Fitch that worked at father's and knit some stockings for you. She hung herself on a board nail sitting on the bed. She tore a strip of[f] from a sheet to do the deed with. Abbie Fife[6] has got a boy at last. She said she found it up north. I have not got married yet but I come very near it the other day. I made a bow to a lady. That is coming very near to the subject. So good by at the present.
S. Williams, Jr.

---

[1] Sending Albert a book with the latest town report would have kept him tied to the community of his birth, and perhaps substantiate Stephen's opinion of the bleak financial picture for Cornish in 1858.

[2] Albert's younger sister Francis.

[3] The widow Demings was probably Caroline (Jackson) Deming, aged 53 with three children in the 1860 census. Caroline Deming was only two entries away from Stephen in the 1860 federal census, with Lucy and Norman Deming, her brother-in-law and sister-in-law, in between the two. Stephen certainly would have been familiar with the numerous Deming family members who lived in Cornish at the time. See William H. Child, *History of the Town of Cornish New Hampshire with genealogical record, 1763-1910,* 2 vols, (Concord, NH.:. The Rumford Press, 1910), Vol 2, 135 for the Judah [1801-1847] and Caroline Deming [1806-1866] family. The fact that Francis was boarding during hay season may mean that she was using her skills in hay braiding while boarding, and thus working for her board. Hay was burned in some types of stoves instead of wood. Stephen's mention of his work this season may mean he worked intermittently in the gun manufacturing industry or that he worked for local farmer Newton Jackson mentioned in Letter 30.

[4] The implication is that Francis has assigned chores and that the work of a 7-year-old child sustains the upkeep of the home, much the same way that women's domestic work has been addressed by historians. See Glenda Riley, *Inventing the American Woman, A Perspective on Women's History,* (Arlington Heights: Harlan Davidson, 1987), Chap. 3, 63-87, on the proper sphere of women in establishing the home; Nancy Woloch, *Women and the American Experience,* (New York: McGraw Hill: 2011); Nancy F. Cott, *The Bonds of Womanhood, "Women's Sphere" in New England, 1780-1835,* (New Haven and London: Yale University Press, 1977); Jeanne Boydston, *Home and Work, Housework, Wages, and the Ideology of Labor in the Early Republic,* (New York: Oxford University Press, 1990), 144,159, argued for the pastoralization of housework which eventually became culturally invisible. A similar argument might be made for children's work based on what is known of Francis' life. Her work became invisible within the larger history of women and children in nineteenth century America.

[5] The widow Fitch is probably Olive Kimball Fitch [1798-1858] who died July 6th, 1858 in Cornish, at 60 years old. She married Daniel Fitch, had four children, and then Daniel disappeared from the records of Cornish, presumably deceased. Child noted: "There is no known record of his death. It appears he left town for some reason and his name disappears from the records;" Child, Ibid., Vol. 2, 156.

[6] Abbie Fife was 17 years old in the 1850 census living with the Stephen Deming family, a brother of the widow Caroline Deming's late husband. Stephen is commenting on her finding a suitable husband, "a boy" from "up north," at this time when she would have been 25. The name was written in very large script in the original letter, but why Stephen did this is unclear. Abigail E. Fife was married on the 20th of April 1859 to a 65-year-old Judson Packard from Bridgewater, Plymouth, Massachusetts according to the New Hampshire Marriage Records Index on Ancestry.com. They had a daughter Eunice in 1861 per Child, Ibid., Vol. I, 348.

Letter 22

To Albert G. Williams, Grinnell, Iowa
From George Dudley, Newport, New Hampshire

Newport, [NH][1] Oct 22, 1858
Friend Alburt [*sic*],
I received your letter and was very glad to hear from you and I thought it belongs to me to write to you. I have not so many news as you had to write but I thought I would write and let you know that I was alive and kicking. I should like to see you very much but I don't expect to very soon. We used to be great friends once and I hope we always shall. I want you to write as often as you can. I will write as many letters as you will. I suppose you would be glad to hear from Mr. Hall's folks[2]. I believe they are all pretty well. The old lady[3] is pretty slim. I believe they call the crops here pretty good this year but I don't expect they begin with yours where you are. We have just got our fall's work done now but we have enough work to do, you know. I expect to go to Lowell [Massachusetts] next spring to work in a store[4]. If I do you must write to me. I don't know as I have any more to write. Give my love to all the folks that I know. Give my love to your mother and all the rest. Good by now.
Yours truly
Rite soon to George Dudley[5]
[page torn] Newport N H

---

[1] Newport, NH was the location of the home that Albert and his parents shared at the time of their separation in 1852. It is located roughly 20 miles from Cornish, NH. George Dudley [1840-1895] grew up on a farm adjoining the Williams farm in Newport and is presumed to have been a childhood friend of Albert's.

[2] "Mr. Hall's folks" is a reference to the whaling Captain Worthin Hall. Worthin Hall and family resided in Newport after retiring from whaling in 1855 and Worthin represented the area to the New Hampshire legislature in 1866 and 67. See Introduction.

[3] Captain Hall's wife, Polly (Lovewell) Hall.

[4] George's mother, Lucy (Kibbey) Dudley died in 1854, perhaps prompting his departure.

[5] George D. Dudley was the son of Timothy Fisher [1806-1872] and Lucy (Kibbey) Dudley [1809-1854] of Newport, born in 1840 and the same age as Albert Gordon Williams. The 1865 Massachusetts state census places Dudley in the Lowell home of Dennison and Sophia Dudley, his uncle and aunt, with his occupation as wire worker. The 1870 census for Lowell, Ward 2, Middlesex County, Massachusetts shows George as a member of a boarding house, at 30 years old. He is boarding in the house of Edwin Heath who was a store clerk, George a laborer. At 33 years old, he married in Lowell, Massachusetts. It was his first marriage and the second for his wife Mary Norton Stewart. His occupation was listed as wire worker. He died June 20, 1895, at 55 years old in Lowell, Massachusetts, occupation machinist. Other Dudley family members worked in the factories of Lowell, as perhaps did George. Letter 26 mentions Almira (Dudley) Sherman, a cousin of George's. Almira (Dudley) Sherman married Henry Sherman who was the brother of Albert's brother-in-law Luke Newton Sherman, thus the close ties between the Halls, Williams, and Dudley families. George Dudley's father, T. Fisher Dudley, a farmer, gave a deposition in the divorce case of Albert's parents. He had known them for 10 to 12 years in 1852 and lived on an adjoining farm. He testified that in the summer and fall of 1852 he had conversed with Stephen in the field and by the roadside of their farms. Stephen told him he refused to allow Melinda to come back home and refused to live with her again, subsequent to their separation in July of that year. See Introduction.

Letter 23

Deed
To A.G. Williams
From L. N. Sherman

Bond for Deed L. N. Sherman to A.G. Williams[1]

Know all men by these presents. That I, L. N. Sherman[2] of Poweshiek County, in the State of Iowa, in consideration of the sum of one dollar in hand paid by A. G. Williams of said Poweshiek County, do hereby agree to sell and convey, (by good and sufficient deed free from encumbrance) unto the said Williams the following described real estate, to wit- - The West half of the Northeast quarter of section number fourteen (14) in Township number eighty one (81) North of Range number Sixteen (16) West – containing eighty acres, more, or less –
On condition that the said Williams shall pay me, the said Sherman, the first day of December A. D. 1860, the sum of one hundred ten dollars and eleven cents ($110.11)
Witness my hand this sixth day of December A. D. 1859.[3]
L. N. Sherman

---

[1] Written on the exterior of the folded deed.

[2] Luke Newton Sherman, Albert's brother-in-law, the husband of Anginette Hall (Willliams) Sherman.

[3] The deed substantiates what is believed to be Albert's first purchase of farmland in Chester township, Poweshiek County.

Letter 24

To Friend
From A. W. Hobbs and Albert G. Williams[1]

1 1860
Albion, Marshall County[2]
Dear Friend[3]

I received your letter dated Dec 17ᵗʰ. I was glad to hear from you. Although I feel heartily ashamed of myself for not writing to you before but I hope you will forgive me when I tell you the reason I have not written. Last summer I labored so hard I almost forgot Grinnell,[4] last September was severely kicked by a horse so that I could not write, however I am all right now. I am attending the Iowa Lutheran College at Albion.[5] We [have] 75 students & three teachers. I think we have a better building than Grinnell.[6] My studies are Algebra, Higher Arithmetic, Philosophy, Grammar, and Bobking [*sic*][7].

Now A. G. wants to ask a few questions.[8] Is Lyman[9] and Emma Bross[10] in Grinnell this winter? Is Cordell and Lucy married?[11] What has Rollin and Sarah done since I left last spring?[12] Is Sarah Ellis[13] single yet? Is Charlie Cooper [14] and Lucy[15] there yet? With these few questions I hope you will have with patience. Now in regard to business you may sell that book if you want and if not do whatever you like with it, and I will be satisfied. But it is time to close. The bell is ringin [*sic*] for Dr. Kimball[16] is delivering a full course of lectures here. Give my love to all inquiring. Yours with repentance.
Write Soon
    A. W. Hobbs
    A. G. W.[17]

---

[1] This letter is the only one in the collection from Albert Gordon Williams, although it appears that it was written by Albert's friend and fellow student A. W. Hobbs. Albert W. Hobbs, a son of John and Emily Hobbs of Albion, Iowa, was 18 years old in the 1860 census taken on June 13 of that year. The census indicates he is a farmer who had attended school during the year. He was the second oldest of seven children all born in Iowa. His older sister Sarah was recorded as a school teacher. Albert Hobbs enlisted in the Union ranks as a Private in Iowa's Eleventh Infantry on September 16, 1861 and died of disease while serving on April 25, 1863.

[2] This letter was written in Albion, Marshall County Iowa which is roughly forty miles north of Grinnell. Albion was founded in 1852, adopting the name Albion in 1858. The letter was written during the first semester of the operation of the Iowa Lutheran College of Albion, Marshall County, Iowa.

[3] Unidentified.

[4] The University of Grinnell started in the winter of 1859-60 in a few unfinished buildings. The name Grinnell University was dropped when the University merged with Iowa College from Davenport in 1860 and took the name Iowa College. If Albert attended Grinnell University or Iowa College before Iowa Lutheran College in Albion, he would have been one of the first students there in the winter of 1859-60. The Old Settlers Association mentions Albert attending Iowa College in Grinnell, substantiating this interpretation of the letter; Old Settlers' Association President, *Annual Meeting of Old Settlers' Association of Grinnell, Iowa,* 1900, President's Opening Address, 31.

[5] The Iowa Lutheran College was established in 1860 in Albion as a coeducational college. Albert was almost 20-years old at the time of this letter and it appears that he and Albert Hobbs had attended Grinnell University together. Then, at the time of the writing of the letter, they both were in attendance at Iowa Lutheran in Albion. The Iowa Lutheran College at Albion was founded in 1860 with a mixed student body of both men and women; David M. Camp, editor, *American Yearbook and National Register for 1869,* (Hartford: O.D. Case and Company, 1869), 198. Unfortunately, records do not exist listing the names of students. The first term was December of 1860 making this letter consistent with the notion that Hobbs and Albert were among the first students; *Marshalltown Times Republican,* June 30, 1953, 3-C for opening date of Dec 5ᵗʰ, 1860. The *Tipton Advertiser,* August 15, 1861, 3, reported the Iowa Lutheran College is "flourishing." In 1866 the president of the school was charged with a failure to conduct the school in the appropriate Lutheran fashion; *Tipton Advertiser,* December 6, 1866, 2. The Iowa Lutheran College, originally designed to be a seminary, closed in 1870, apparently also suffering from financial problems; Mary Qually, "United Lutheran Synod in Iowa," *The Palimsest,* Vol. 35, no 6, (June 1954), 257. It reopened in 1872 as a Methodist seminary and operated at the site for many years. The original college building was torn down in 1915; *Marshalltown Times Republican,* June 30, 1953, 3-C. Most of the Iowa academies sponsored by protestant churches were coeducational; Forest C. Ensign, "The Era of Private Academies," *The Palimsest,* Vol. 27, no 3., (1946), 82.

[6] Grinnell University, subsequently Iowa College in Grinnell, now Grinnell College. From this comment we can presume that Grinnell University had only one building then.

[7] Possibly bookkeeping.

[8] The handwriting does not change. Presumably Albert Williams dictated his portion of the letter to Hobbs who continued writing.

[9] Unidentified.

[10] The people mentioned in the letter appear to have been of the proper age and residents of Iowa to have made them also students at Grinnell University/Iowa College. An Emma Jane Bross was a resident of Bear Creek township, Poweshiek County Iowa in the 1860 census, at 15 years old.

[11] Cordell and Lucy are unidentified.

[12] Rollin and Sarah are unidentified.

[13] A 22-year-old Sarah Ellis lived in Grinnell according to the 1860 census. She married Arthur G. Clifford in Poweshiek County on 29 November 1860.

[14] At least four Charles Coopers lived in Iowa in 1860 according to the census.

[15] Unidentified.

[16] Unidentified.

[17] Albert Gordon Williams. The letter substantiates Albert's desire for an education as well as the support he must have received from his sister and brother-in-law in pursuing it.

Letter 25

To Albert G. Williams, Grinnell, Iowa
From George Philander Williams

[Envelope]: Postmarked Windsor, Vermont June 25, 1861
Mr. Albert G. Williams Grinnell Iowa

Windsor [VT] June 25th 1861
Absent but not forgotten friend

It is with pleasure that I sit myself down to write a few lines to you in answer to yours of the 19th of May which has just reached me. I was very glad to hear from you. I have been looking for a letter from you for a long time. As for our health, they are all very good at this time and has been since I last wrote you. I was glad to hear that your health is so good and I hope that these few lines will find you still in the same enjoyment. As for your father[1] he was here at my house yesterday and his health was quite good and he said that he was looking for a letter from you as he had written to you some time ago. I suppose that before this reach you you [sic] have heard what he has done with Francis. He has given her to Miss [sic] Worthin Hall.[2] Your mother has written the particulars to you I suppose so I will not write them. I feel very sorry to have her go away as we shall not be very likely to see her much more. I think a great deal of Francis. She seems like one of our own children but I don't know that it is for the best.

Albert we are having a very backward spring here but things look very well indeed considering the cold and wet weather that we have had. The grass never looked better in the world than it does now. We shall have [a] great crop of hay this year. Fruit, we are not a going to have much.

Business is very dull here in the eastern states. There is no business but gun work that is of any account, and that they are driving it very hard as they are in wants of all the guns they can get to carry on the war[3] with. There is great Excitement here. There is 2 regiments gone from Vermont and 2 from New Hampshire. There is a goodly number gone from both towns of Windsor [VT] and Cornish [NH] and they are calling out the militia in all of these eastern states to do military duty and preparing them for war. The papers are talking about peace. I hope they Compromise and settle the trouble without any more loss of lives but I am afraid they will not. Albert you will see by this that I am at work at Hartford, Conn.[4] I am now at home on a visit and when this reach[es] you I shall be back at my work again. I am to work on guns as they[5] are not doing much here. I should be glad to hear from you often. You write and I will do the same. I will now Close this by bidding you good by.

From your uncle
G. P. Williams[6]
You will please direct your letter
Broad St (S) Hartford
Conn

George Philander Williams, Windsor VT; about 1890s

[1] Stephen Williams, Jr., the letter author's brother.

[2] Mrs. Worthin Hall was Polly (Lovewell) Hall the wife of the whaling Captain Worthin Hall, Albert's uncle. See Introduction.

[3] The Civil War started on April 12, slightly more than a month prior to this letter.

[4] Hartford, Connecticut was at this time the sight of two gun manufacturers, Colt and Sharps. Although he doesn't mention the name of his employer, it can be assumed Philander either worked for one of these companies on guns destined for the Civil War. Both companies had ties to the Windsor gun and machine tool manufacturing companies. Philander would have been a well-paid, skilled machinist by 1861. The Colt armory in Hartford doubled in size in 1861, making it the largest private armory in the world at the time; Joseph Roe, "Early American Machinists; The Men of the Hartford Shops," *American Machinist* Vol. 41, No. 8, (August 20, 1914), 332. Revolver production increased from roughly 38,000 in 1859 to over 111,000 in 1862; City of Hartford, *Hartford Connecticut as a Manufacturing, Business, and Commercial Center,* (Hartford: Published by the Hartford Board of Trade: 1889), 91). Every Civil War soldier carried a revolver; most of those produced by Colt. Invented by Christian Sharps in 1848, the Sharps rifle was the first successful breech loading rifle. Sharps brought his rifle invention to Robbins and Lawrence of Windsor, VT who perfected the use of interchangeable parts and were responsible for the ultimate precision of the Sharps' gun. Christian Sharps split from the company in Windsor, Vermont in 1855 and moved his operation to Hartford where it continued until 1876. From the beginning of the Civil War through June 1862, the Northern Army purchased 3,213 Sharps rifles and 13,000 Sharps carbines. It proved the obsolescence of the older muzzle-loader types of guns, as estimates place over 100,000 Sharps' guns in use during the War; Winston O. Smith, *The Sharps Rifle, its history, development and operation,* (New York: W. Morrow and Company, 1943), 6, 7, 25. It seems most likely that Philander was employed by Sharps in Hartford, based on all information known about his life.

[5] A reference to the Windsor, VT armory. Lamson, Goodnow, and Yale Company operated the armory at the outbreak of the Civil War. The sewing machine resources of the armory under previous operators, Robbins and Lawrence, were sold off and manager Henry Stone began to recruit men for a switch to the production of arms, primarily Springfield rifles, Carrie Brown, "Guns for Billy Yank, The Armory in Windsor Meets the Challenge of Civil War," *Vermont History*, Vol. 79, no. 2 (Summer/Fall 2011) Vermont Historical Society publication, 145-147. By August 1861, co-worker William Hale Foster wrote that the company would not begin work on guns for two to three months in the future. Ibid., 148. By September 1861, the newspaper reported that the armory would employ 300 men to produce arms, *Vermont Journal*, September 28, 1861, 8. Presumably Philander was employed by the armory after this time, as he appears in an 1863 draft document as employed by the armory.

[6] Albert's uncle, George Philander Williams was a farmer in the census record of 1880. George married his first cousin Caroline White, and they had one child, Ella. He was born in Cornish, NH on March 31, 1823. He died February 16, 1902 of pneumonia at almost 79 years; *Vermont Journal*, February 22, 1902, 8. This is the last letter in the collection from him.

Letter 26

To Albert G. Williams, Grinnell, Iowa
From Melinda Hall Williams

Newport, [NH] [April] 14th [1861]

My Dear Son

I received your kind letter on Tuesday last. I had looked a long time, but in vain the last before letter before this [*sic*] you said you intended to write very <u>often </u>then delayed five weeks!! I don't know what to think of your plan of improving. Cousin Daniel[1] has said a number of times that you ought to improve, that you was losing the interest on your land that <u>I</u> ought to discourage you to do so – With I think I should be as happy with you in improving as I ever expect to be or ask but I foresee there would be a continual fear that when we had got a cozy little home[2] you would bring some one there that would think that it was a great deal of trouble to have <u>Old people about</u>. I did not comprehend your time of building next spring or one year from then? If you should think best to improve & want money before Newton[3] would wish to pay I think you can have three or four hundred at ten per cent to buy as long as you wish from a friend of mine. Perhaps it would be the best way then I could have mine to buy the furniture & stock, etc., etc. <u>Think</u> & report. I am not sorry on the whole that you do not work for Newton, but I pitied A[4] for I thought she would miss you. But perhaps not. <u>I should</u> if I was there. Do you feel as though you would like a farm in Chester as well as Grinnell? I sometimes think it will be as well for you but perhaps not quite as pleasant. I think you might make any change if you thought best, but enough of this. You will see by the last letter to A[5] that I have been quite unwell five weeks that I was not able to do hardly a thing sometime could not make my bed. If I used my arms any, I would be so troubled for breath. But am nearly well. I am doing Aunt Fanny's[6] sewing now. Have been here a week, shall stay one week.
Mrs. Hall[7] has been quite unwell and is so now, but improving. I don't think they will start until the middle of May.[8] They have a pleasant Couple here Mr. Crowell[9] and wife. Tell Almira[10] if you see her for Mrs. Hall says that she don't know as she shall ever write. Have you bought you any clothes since I left? Did you have to take any of that note? I wish I could think of something pretty to send you, but I can't only a lump of sugar. Mrs. Gilmore[11] came and spent the day here last week. Not a word about money. She is almost homesick it don't seem like home & she can't have money to dress like others and that troubles her. Where it don't me one atom. I buy all I want and that is not much. I have earned nothing since I came East.[12] I <u>shall</u> this summer. Do you read your papers that I send? Do you like them? Does Annginette miss me any? She has never said one word as though Newton ever mentions me & I presume he don't. I never lived a month[13] with any one that I thought took so little interest in me as he does. I have sent a number [of] little messages to him but never received one. Does Clara[14] grow beautiful or pretty? I do want to see the little thing & all the rest of you a great deal & finally I would like to make a visit to Grinnell if it were not more than [illegible] miles. People are not making as much sugar this spring as usual.
Henry Dudley[15] is married to Chauncey Wellington's daughter.[16] I guess there is not much sprawl [?] to him. He has been there all Winter. I have not heard from Frances[17] since I wrote before. I fear her Father has found out that she writes & has put a stop to it. I want you should see what I have written to A[18] about her for I can't write twice the same thing. Now I have got nearly to the bottom of the sheet. I will wind of[f] by a little advice you have not heard for a number of years Will those that do not love you before <u>now</u>. Well I presume you will not be censured more than you have been, but your faults will not be as easily forgiven you must be cautious about expressing your views of matters & men. You are young and liable to err but don't be servile—everyone must have some independence of <u>thought</u> at least do not do anything that would cause your Mother shame for I have a keen eye to the faults of my Children <u>you</u> know. Good bye & may God bless you & keep you until we meet. MHW[19]

---

[1] Cousin Daniel was probably Daniel Hall [1802-1885], the son of Abijah and Mary (Read) Hall and Melinda's first cousin. He was a farmer who lived his entire life in the Croydon, NH area.

[2] Melinda and Albert have obviously talked about a time when she and Albert will live together in a home on his farm land in Chester Township, Grinnell.

[3] Luke Newton Sherman, Albert's brother-in-law, the husband of Annginette Hall (Williams) Sherman.

[4] Annginette Hall (Williams) Sherman, Albert's oldest sister.

[5] Annginette Hall (Williams) Sherman.

[6] This appears to be a reference to Melinda's cousin, Abner Hall's, wife Fanny. Abner was the son of Abijah Hall [1754-1812] who was Melinda's father's older brother. Melinda wrote Aunt in the margin above the name Fanny, perhaps to identify the older lady from Albert's youngest sister Francis, frequently nicknamed Fanny. Abner Hall [1804-1877] and wife Fanny (Hurd) Hall [1800-1879] lived in Newport, NH. Fanny was roughly 61 years old at the time of writing of this letter. The attachment of the sobriquet Aunt may be understandable due to the generational distance between Melinda, then almost 20 years younger than Fanny.

[7] Mrs. Worthin (Polly) Hall, wife of the whaling captain and Melinda's sister-in-law.

[8] Presumably this refers to a journey that Worthin Hall and Mrs. Polly Hall would take with Albert's sister Francis to bring Francis out to Grinnell to live with her older siblings. Francis Williams Hays' obituary said she moved to Grinnell in 1861. Perhaps this was a means by which the Hall family could ensure that Melinda would be able to live with her children in Iowa, without Stephen Williams' consent, and subverting the law and custom then in effect which gave the divorced husband control over his children.

[9] Crowell and wife have not been identified, presumably visitors.

[10] Almira (Dudley) Sherman [1836-1904] was married to Henry Sherman [1832-1877] who was the brother of Anginette Hall (Williams) Sherman's husband, Luke Newton Sherman. Almira had been raised in the Abner Hall family household (see footnote 6 above) after her mother's death when Almira was two years old. Almira was left one thousand dollars in Abner Hall's will, treating her as an adopted daughter and a valued member of the family. Letter 23, from George Dudley, who was a first cousin to Almira, substantiates the close ties between the Dudleys and the Halls.

[11] Unidentified, possibly a previous employer of Melinda's.

[12] Melinda means that since she returned to New Hampshire after visiting her children in Grinnell in 1860 where she was recorded in the Federal census.

[13] Melinda must have stayed a month with Luke Newton and Anginette Williams Sherman in Grinnell when she was recorded in the 1860 Federal census taken in August.

[14] Clara Sherman [1858-1872] was the daughter of Luke Newton and Anginette Hall (Williams) Sherman.

[15] Henry Dudley was a son of Timothy Fisher Dudley, a resident of Newport, NH who lived on the farm adjoining the Stephen and Melinda Williams farm. T. Fisher Dudley gave a deposition in their divorce proceedings. Henry was a cousin to Almira (Dudley) Sherman, mentioned in this letter and a brother to George Dudley whose letter to Albert is preserved in this collection as letter 23.

[16] Henry F. Dudley married Martha Jane Wellington on March 30, 1861 in Claremont, NH. The groom was 22 and the bride was 16. They were divorced in July 1867 for alleged abandonment and willing absence of Henry, by Martha's petition as libelant.

[17] Melinda spelled Frances' name in the traditional fashion for girls with an E, while Francis signed her name with an "i" in the only letter preserved by her. See Letter 13 from Stephen Williams, Jr. which bears a short note from Francis at the end.

[18] Annginette Hall (Williams) Sherman.

[19] Melinda (Hall) Williams. This is the last letter in the collection from Albert's mother. The letter seems scattered, and the author troubled by numerous issues including her health, Albert's activities with his farm, a lack of communication from Francis, and the lack of recognition from Annginette and Newton Sherman. Perhaps the lack of control over her life and the numerous uncertainties are taking a toll. Perhaps she was ill from this early time, four years before her death. She moved to Iowa sometime after this letter in 1861 and before her death in 1865 at 47 years old.

Letter 27

To Albert G. Williams
From Stephen Williams, Jr.

Envelope stamped Windsor, [VT] January 30
Albert G. Williams
Grinnell
Poweshiek County Iowa

Windsor [VT][1] Jan 30 1862[2]

I send you the money. Write as soon as you receive it. You may have the use of it free.[3] You may send me the note if you please dated April 10 1862. There is no change since I wrote to you only we have a great body of snow about 3 and a ½ feet.
S Williams[4]

---

[1] Stephen wrote this letter in Windsor, Vermont, the location of the Windsor Armory, and the home of his younger brother George Philander Williams. Perhaps his location in Windsor indicates that he is at work at the Windsor Armory, then in high production mode due to the Civil War.

[2] There appear to be missing letters between Stephen's last one dated 1858 and this one.

[3] Without interest.

[4] Stephen Williams, Jr. Albert's father.

Letter 28

To Albert Gordon Williams; Grinnell, Iowa
From Stephen Williams, Jr.; Cornish, New Hampshire and Windsor, Vermont

Cornish [NH] Nov 2 186[2]

I sent you a draft of one hundred dollars[1] over three weeks ago and I have not heard from it. I begin to think it is lost so I thought I would drop you a line and see if you had received it. You will answer it as soon as convenient. I have no news worth note except Silas Spalding[2] has gone to war. Henry Freeman[3] enlisted and they sent him home.[4] The town pays a bounty of one hundred dollars to each soldier that is mustered into the service. Direct to Cornish Flat
I am tough and hearty
Write soon
Stephen Williams
Windsor[5] [VT] Nov 6 1862
Tell Francis[6] that Lyman Fitch[7] little girl is dead and Norman Deming's wife and Mattie is dead.[8] They lay in one grave. It is dark. I write soon.

---

[1] The value of one hundred dollars in 2023 purchasing power would be over three thousand dollars according to measuringworth.com. Stephen had sent money in January and again in October according to Letters 27 and 28. Stephen's ability to send these large sums of money argue for his well-paid employment with the Windsor Armory during the Civil War years.
[2] Silas Spaulding [1824-1863] volunteered for service and was mustered in on September 21, 1862 in the 16th regiment of New Hampshire volunteers. "Rough in manners and language, yet kindly in nature," Spaulding died September 20, 1863 according to William H. Child, *History of the Town of Cornish New Hampshire with genealogical record, 1763-1910*, Vol. 2, (Concord, NH.: The Rumford Press, 1910), 343. According to New Hampshire military records, Spaulding became ill in April 1863 and was hospitalized. He was then mustered out of the service approximately one month before his death in Cornish, NH, Ancestry.com.
[3] Henry Freeman [1829-1899], a Cornish, NH farmer, and "respected citizen and obliging neighbor," apparently did not serve in the Civil War, Child, *History of Cornish,* 170.
[4] Draft registration records for New Hampshire substantiate his attempt to enlist. He was rejected with no further information as to cause.
[5] The fact that Stephen continued the letter in Windsor means he was working for the Windsor Armory at this time, as can be clarified in the next letter. The 1860 census provides Stephen's occupation as laborer.
[6] This note to Francis substantiates Francis Williams Hays' obituary which states that she moved to Grinnell, Iowa in 1861, or at least prior to this letter. She was a class member of the 1862 Chester township school.
[7] In this letter, Stephen Williams is commenting to his daughter Francis on the deaths of his neighbors' children whom his daughter Francis knew. Lyman Fitch [1825-1914] and family are listed immediately after Stephen Williams' listing in the 1860 census, thus close neighbors. Lyman Fitch's daughter, Lena Leverna Fitch, was born July 19, 1858 and died November 1, 1862. Two of her brothers also died in November 1862, within a week of her death. William Child records "malignant diphtheria" as the cause of death for the Deming children, which also occurred in November of 1862. Presumably the disease spread to the Fitch family, also. Child, *History of Cornish,* Vol. 2, 156, 137. Malignant diphtheria, not well understood at this time, was characterized by sudden and severe onset with subsequent cardiac failure.
[8] Norman Deming [1824-1899] and family are listed in the 1860 census in Cornish Flat in the house immediately preceding Stephen Williams' home. Lucy Ann (Bartlett) Deming died in Cornish on November 3, 1862, and her five-year old daughter Martha (Mattie) died the following day. Both succumbed to "malignant diphtheria". Norman Deming was considered a thrifty farmer and held several political positions in Cornish including selectman. His son Harvey followed his mother and sister's death on November 10, four days after this letter was penned; Child, *History of Cornish,* Vol. 2, 137.

Letter 29

To Albert G. Williams
From Stephen Williams, Jr.

Envelope:
Postmark: Cornish Flat
Albert G Williams
B box
A. G. Williams Poweshiek County, Iowa

Cornish [NH] January 23rd 1863

I have a few leisure moments to spare so I thought I would write a few lines to let you know how we are. We are all well except George P. Williams.[1] He has been very sick with the croup. He had three doctors at one time. They thought of cutting a hole in his throat and put in a silver tube, but they tried one remedy more and saved him as yet, but he is very sick yet. I am at the gun shop[2] yet but I don't know how long I shall stay. The job is not [a] very long one, but I get pretty good pay, 1.50 a day.[3] I pay 2.00 per week for board, at most places they charge 3.00 a week for board.[4] Your Aunt Lois[5] sends her best respects to all inquiring friends. Board is so high I think I shall keep house by myself in the spring. I shall have time to do my work[6] for we go in to the shop[7] at 7 in the morning and come out at 6 at night.[8] So you see that in warm weather I shall have plenty of time to tarry(?) about. You wrote for some more money. I am a going to Cor flat[9] to day and if I do get some will send it. I don't get no pay at the shop till I have been there two months then I draw once a month.[10] I have indorsed the interest on the note as you [torn paper]. As to your notes you can do as you please it will make more cost because there will be the stamp but I will give the dates.[11]

April 6 1863 of 15.00
Nov 1th of 1863 of 20.00
Stephen Williams
Tell them all to write and I will answer if I can. Fran[12] must excuse me for not writing to her this time so good morning[13]

---

[1] George P. Williams was Albert's uncle and Stephen's youngest brother.

[2] Windsor Armory in Windsor, VT.

[3] A rough estimate of Stephen's monthly salary would be 30 dollars. Measuringworth.com translates this salary into a *labor value* at $6,630.00 (using the unskilled wage) or $11,200.00 (using production worker compensation). This is within the range that one historian estimated for the monthly average salary for small arms workers in 1860 in Connecticut at $37.50; Felicia Johnson Deyrup, *Arms Making in the Connecticut Valley; A Regional Study of the Economic Development of the Small Arms Industry, 1798-1870*, (York, Pennsylvania: George Shumway, pub., 1970), 249, 8, 9, The average annual wage of small arms workers was well above that of other industrial workers from 1850 through 1940.

[4] A notice in the December 4, 1858 *Vermont Journal*, 4, verifies that a boarding house was part of the Amory property at Windsor, a complex totaling ten acres at that time. Cornish Flat was over eight miles away from Windsor and would have created a long commute in winter.

[5] Lois White Williams [1815-1867] the wife of Charles Williams [1820-1894], one of Stephen's younger brothers.

[6] He may be referring to work on Newton Jackson's farm, mentioned in Letter 30. His work on Jackson's farm seems to overlap with his work in the gun shop.

[7] The *Vermont Journal*, December 4, 1858, 4 contains an ad for the sale of the Windsor Armory under Robbins and Lawrence in 1856 contained the "Armory and Machine Shops." Stephen's consistent use of the descriptive "shop" presumably means he is located at the machine shop portion of the Armory.

[8] Co-worker William Foster noted that he worked from 6 am to 6 pm in 1861; William Foster to Maria Foster, Foster Private Letter Collection, August 21, 1861. In September 1861 he noted that the shop would be fitted with gas works to enable the men to work overtime, William Foster letters, September 8, 1861. The extreme hours are in response to the need for weapons for the Northen Civil War forces.

[9] Cornish Flat, NH.

[10] This practice of holding back a month's pay at the Windsor Armory is substantiated in a letter from Stephen's co-worker, William Hale Foster to Maria Foster, August 21, 1861, Foster Private Letter Collection. Foster mentioned that pay for days worked in July would not be paid until October. Mention of this practice leads to the conclusion that Stephen has been employed at the Windsor Armory since his previous letter, Letter 29, dated November 6, 1862 from Windsor.

[11] Presumably these are dates when interest is due on the money sent to Albert as a loan.

[12] Stephen's daughter Francis Williams.

[13] Printed on right side of letter facing sideways of main text.

Letter 30

To Albert G. Williams
From Stephen Williams

Envelope stamped Cornish Flat N. H. March 30
Albert G. Williams
Grinnell
Poweshiek County Iowa

Cornish [NH] March 29 1863

Yours of the 22 of Feb was received at a late hour and I [had] begun to think that you had no want of money so that I have disposed of it on a pant outfit, but I think I shall have some more come in in [*sic*] the course of two or three weeks but it will be in small lots so perhaps I can send you some. I am expecting some tomorrow and if so I will send 15 or 20 dollars in this letter. If I don't receive it it [*sic*] will go [to]day. I am at work at Newton Jackson where I have been for the last 4 years.[1] I work for 16 dollars a month by the year. My work is light in the winter and not very hard in the summer. Tell Francis[2] she must write to me as oft as she can if I don't write. And you must do the the the [*sic*] same. I thot I would have a little sport this winter so we got up a sleigh ride to Newport [NH] and we got out 48 couples. The day was pleasant so we had a fine time.
Stephen Williams
A letter will do some good.[3]

---

[1] Newton Jackson (1908-1871) was a third-generation Cornish resident and a farmer, according to William H. Child, *History of the Town of Cornish New Hampshire with genealogical record, 1763-1910,* Vol. 2, (Concord, NH. The Rumford Press, 1910), 226. Jackson had three daughters and no sons to help with the farm. This letter stated he worked for farmer Newton Jackson for the past four years; 1859-1863, although other letters place him in the gun manufacturing factories. Stephen Williams is listed as a laborer in the 1860 census for Cornish Flat. No personal wealth was listed for him.

[2] Albert's youngest sister who was then living with her mother on either Albert's farm or Anginette Hall (Williams) Sherman's farm in the Chester township of Grinnell.

[3] Written in pencil at the bottom of the second page.

Letter 31

To Albert G. Williams, Grinnell, Iowa
From Stephen Williams

Cornish [NH] Oct 21 1863

Yours of Sept 27th was received in due time and I was happy to hear you was doing well. In reply to those that was drafted in this town they all but two got a substitute.[1] One skedaddled and the other can't raise the money. The town pays each draft on his substitute three hundred dollars each. They have to pay each substitute 400.25 to 400.79.[2] Those substitutes are mostly French men.[3] I remain at Jackson's[4] yet but I don't know how long I shall stay. My year is up the 1 of last Sept. It seems a little too hard for an old man 51 years old[5] to work out by the year the old legs draw round hard some nights. I enclose 20 dollars. It is all that I feel like sparing this time. Money is rather hard as yet.[6] Perhaps I may do a little better by and by.

I intended to write to you all but I feel too lazy to write. So you may give my respects to them all and tell them to write and I will try to answer the same. They have got pertemuch[7] through harvesting here. Corn is quite good in this section of the country, oats rather light, potatoes are light. Some fields they don't dig them. Almost all rotten. Mr. Jackson[8] has not got even 40 bushels from over one acre. I now close by bidding you all good by, one and all.[9]

S Williams

---

[1] Albert has obviously asked his father about the effect of the draft on the townsfolk. The fact that only two men were unable to come up with the money suggests that the town was in good shape financially at this time, and moreover, there was a reluctance to serve.

[2] Stephen's notation on the dollar amounts of substitutes are probably $400.25 to $400.79 dollars. The point to be made was that to avoid the draft, one had to have more than one hundred dollars above what the draftee received to pay the substitute.

[3] Although Stephen credits the substitutes as French men, a number of men from Ireland and Scotland, as well as France and those from Canada were used as substitutes. Historian William Child downplayed the use of substitutes from Cornish, many of whom subsequently deserted. He lists a total of over 1200 New Hampshire men serving in the Civil War, of those, he credits 161 to Cornish; William H. Child, *History of the Town of Cornish New Hampshire with genealogical record, 1763-1910,* Vol. 1, (Concord, NH.: The Rumford Press, 1910), Chapter VII, Cornish in the Civil War, 85-106.

[4] Farmer Newton Jackson mentioned in previous letters as employing Stephen.

[5] Stephen had just turned 51 only three days before writing this letter. Perhaps his birthday reminded him of his insufficiencies.

[6] His comment that times were still hard in Cornish underscores the stability that the Civil War brought in contrast to the Panic of 1857 and its aftermath.

[7] Pretty much.

[8] Newton Jackson.

[9] Albert's mother and Stephen's ex-wife, Melinda Hall Williams, was living at this time in Iowa with her son. Stephen's closure to all may be a sign of acknowledgement of her.

Letter 32

To Frances H. Williams [*sic*], Grinnell, Iowa
From Stephen Williams, Jr.[1]

Cornish [NH] May 28, 1864[2]
Dear Daughter,

I was pleased to hear from you again and glad that you remember me so far away. I am glad you got along so well in your studies. But if you do not begin to keep school[3] quite yet it may be just as well. You are young and there is a great deal to be learned yet and as you go to school more you will find a great deal to do to prepare for a successful teacher. I should like to come and see you when you do keep school and hope I may. I conclude by what Albert wrote that you are going to herd the sheep again this summer. I think you will be entitled to the name of shepardess. I hope to see you again some time and wish you to continue to write to me.
Your father
Stephen Williams[4]

---

[1] This letter is noteworthy because it was written on fine lined paper. The spelling, punctuation, and legibility are far above that used by Stephen in other letters, suggesting this letter was written by Stephen's new wife Rhoda Lamberton. From the extant letters, there is no mention of Rhoda whom he married on February 13, 1864.

[2] Stephen married Rhoda only three months before this letter was written.

[3] Francis was living with her mother and brother, Albert Gordon Williams, at this time. She was 13 years old, and seemingly too young to be a school teacher.

[4] This is the only letter in the collection from Stephen to Francis, which begs the question of why the letter is in the collection. Did Francis reject the letter?

Francis Williams (Hays); about mid 1850s

Letter 33

To Albert Gordon Williams, Grinnell, Iowa
From Stephen Williams and Rhoda M. Williams

Cornish [NH] Dec 28, 1866
Dear Son:

We were very glad to hear from you again. You seem to have a great deal of work on your hands. It is a good thing enough to have enough to do, but not so agreeable to be drove with work. We are all very well and so are all the friends here. Cousin Abijah Williams[1] died Thanksgiving day of fever.[2] I have constant employment in the shop[3] at painting. They are making all sorts of machines and have more hands than they had last year, but not near so many as when they were making guns. They have been making a wonderful drilling machine to work in stone quarries. It is said to do nearly as much labor in a day as a hundred men could do. It was sold, with the engine to work it, for eight thousand dollars[4] and they have begun another. Winter has held off pretty well but has begun in earnest now. It was unusually warm till the middle of this month. We had a light fall of snow the 17th and the 21st and 22nd were very cold. Thermometers went down as low as 15o[5] below zero. For Christmas we had a rain which left the ground bare but yesterday and last night we had a foot of snow and it seems likely to be good sleighing. Hay was a light crop last summer and the weather we have had has saved a great deal and it is not so high now as it was in hay time. Pork is down to 10cts. Beef and butter are some lower than last winter. Butter is about 40cts. Flour is from 14 to 18 dollars according to quality. Northern corn has been $1.50 and western $1.35. We kept a pig this year. Killed it at eight months old weighed 307 lbs. Sheep seem to be as high with you as there are here. Hope you will be prospered [sic] with yours. Wool is doing better than it was one spell. Mr. Tasker & Fletcher have got the bridge all done.[6] It is four feet higher than the old one and will be likely to stand. You little sister[7] is getting along nicely and has to be quite a great girl and is a very busy body. Hope you will see her some time.
Philander[8] had a letter from Frances[9] last week saying that Anginette[10] [sic] had another daughter.[11] Give our love to Frances and tell her We shall write to her before long. I suppose you find enough to do winters to keep you busy, but when you have leisure write to us. Give our best respects to your wife.[12]
Yours with regard
Stephen Williams
By Rhoda M Williams[13]

---

[1] Cousin Abijah Williams (1808-1866) is a reference to Stephen's cousin, the son of Abijah Williams, his father's older brother.
[2] Abijah died November 28, 1866.
[3] Windsor, VT armory. The shop Stephen worked in refers to the Windsor Manufacturing Company under E. G. Lamson in Windsor, Vt., across the river from Cornish. After the Civil War the company switched to the manufacturing of Cases's Patent Diamond Rock Boring Machine to be used in stone quarrying, as well as tools, tool machines, sawmills, and guns, specifically Springfield rifles. A catalog from 1866 pictures the Lamsom Stone Channeling machine for use in quarrying. As Stephen noted, the shift from guns to machine tooling and related specialty equipment helped Windsor become a hub of technological innovation. Guy Hubbard, "Leadership of Early Windsor Industries in the Mechanic Arts," A Paper Read Before the Vermont Historical Society at Windsor, September 4, 1922, Proceedings of the Vermont Historical Society, 1921, 22, 23, (Montpelier: Capital City Press, 1924), 181. See also Letter 34 from 1872 in which Stephen comments on the business partnerships. From these two letters it is assumed Stephen worked for the Lamson company in various iterations and reorganizations from at least 1866 to 1872. See Letters 28 and 29 for his employment in the Windsor shop in 1863.
[4] Eight thousand dollars in 1866 is roughly 150,000 dollars in 2023 if made on a purchase. Measuringworth.com
[5] o indicates degrees.
[6] The Cornish-Windsor bridge would have been of utmost importance to Stephen in providing the main thoroughfare from home to work. Cornish was flooded on several occasions to the extent that bridges were wiped out and needed to be rebuilt. In March of 1866, the third bridge at the Windsor-Cornish location was lost to flooding. James Tasker and Bela Fletcher finished a new bridge across the Connecticut river between Windsor, Vt. and Cornish in late 1866 with a span of 470 feet. William H. Child, *History of the Town of Cornish New Hampshire with genealogical record, 1763-1910,* vol. 1, (Concord, NH. The Rumford Press, 1910), 215-6. Tasker and Fletcher's wooden, covered bridge still stands.

---

[7] Stephen and Rhoda had one child, daughter Martha E. Williams (1865-1917), nicknamed Mattie, and born October 24, 1865 in Cornish. The 1880 census shows Rhoda, divorced, and Mattie, 13 years old, living in Cornish in a dwelling by themselves. Mattie grew up to become a school teacher, and she and her mother eventually relocated to Kansas. Mattie married a doctor, John Chambers, in 1894 in Brown, Kansas, and soon the couple moved to a small farming community in the northern part of the state where John was credited as the city physician. Rhoda joined her daughter in Hanover, Washington, Kansas in 1897 where she developed a close-knit group of friends. By 1900 the three lived in one household. The marriage produced no children, and Mattie devoted her life to lodge and society endeavors. Rhoda died suddenly in 1914 and Mattie lingered with an unstated illness for several years until finally succumbing in 1917; *Hanover Herald*, February 13, 1914, 1; *Hanover Herald* January 26, 1917, 1. John Chambers remarried in 1919 to Emma Artemesia "Artie" Hobbs of Cheyenne Wyoming, a childhood sweetheart. They remained in Hanover, until retiring to Sulphur Springs, Arkansas where John Chambers died in 1934; *Hanover Herald* August 22, 1919, 1.

[8] George Philander Williams (1823-1902), Stephen's brother.

[9] Francis (Williams) Hays, Albert's youngest sister.

[10] Annginette Hall (Williams) Sherman, (1837-1916), Albert's oldest sister.

[11] Annginette's second child, Anna May Sherman (1866-1868).

[12] This letter was written after Albert and Eliza's marriage on March 13, 1866.

[13] Rhoda (Lamberton) Williams (1827-1914), Stephen's second wife.

Letter 34

To Albert Williams, Grinnell, Iowa
From Stephen Williams, Jr and Rhoda Lamberton Williams

Cornish [NH] Feb 6th 1872
Dear Son,

We were very glad to get a letter from you had been thinking for some time about it but knew you must be very busy this winter. We have received your papers[1] and ought to have sent you some and will endeavor to before long. We are in usual health. Your father was not very well yesterday and staid at home. There is plenty of work in the machine shop[2] now, and most of the hands are back again. Mr. Jones[3] thought he could not attend to the business of the shop and was going to shut down, but Mr. Stone[4] has gone in with Lamson[5] and as he has a share of the profit instead of a salary it is probable they will have work.

Mattie[6] goes to school only when the weather permits and learns quite fast. Our teacher is a young gentleman from Croydon named Powers.[7] We have had a very pleasant winter so far and excellent sleighing. We have not had much more than a foot of snow in all, till last Saturday, but it has been cold enough not to thaw any, without much severe cold weather. Saturday we had from 15 to 18 inches of snow. The wood and lumber men in the back part of the towns have been very busy.

James Tasker[8] is filling his mill yard to its utmost capacity and Welcome[9] of Newport has got a steam mill somewhere in the mountain and its furnishing lumber to the railroad. The people at Cornish Flatt and Meriden are just now quite excited about getting a railroad through their respective places. It is a route that has been contemplated for some time and was to go from Windsor to Nashua. Now it is proposed to carry it to White river Junction instead of Windsor and it will come from Claremont up through these places. It is quite certain that the road will be built as far up as Claremont. They have got committees appointed and will try to get a charter this summer.[10] I heard today that John Weld[11] was very sick with a complaint of the lungs and his friends were quite alarmed about him. I hear that Mrs. Stone[12] of Newport has left her husband and has been over here at Martin Williams[13] all winter. Did not learn the cause of the trouble. We are much obliged to Newton & Anginette[14] for their pictures and think they are very good ones. We never shall feel really satisfied with ours but I hope sometime to have some better ones. We are going to stay here another year. Our relatives are all well as far as I know. There has not been much change in prices of things. Pork is now 7cts it was but 6cts the first of the winter. We shall be glad to hear from you as often as you can get time to write and shall always remember your visit[15] with pleasure. Give our love to your family and the others.
Yours with respects
Stephen Williams
& R M Williams
Mattie H. Williams Mattie H Williams
Mattie wants to write her name and so she has.[16]

---

[1] Presumably this is a reference to local newspapers. It was a practice in the mid-1800s for people to share newspapers.

[2] Windsor Vermont Manufacturing Company previously the Windsor, VT armory.

[3] Russell Jones. In 1869, E. G. Lamson had formed a partnership with Russell Jones, turning the Windsor armory building into a cotton mill, with associated machine tool manufacturing under Henry Stone operating in buildings across the brook from the main factory building; Carrie Brown, "Guns for Billy Yank: The Armory in Windsor Meets the Challenge of Civil War," *Vermont History*, Vol 79, no 2 (Summer/Fall 2011), 147-8, 156. Historian Guy Hubbard noted that in 1870 prior to his partnership with Russell Jones, Lamson sold his gun manufacturing company to the Winchester gun company. Jones and Lamson, & Co. of Windsor, VT, were credited with fine engine-lathes, screw milling machines, drill presses and turret lathes exhibited at the 1876 centennial celebration. The main factory of this large complex is now the American Precision Museum. See Guy Hubbard, "Leadership of Early Windsor Industries in the Mechanic Arts," A Paper Read Before the Vermont Historical Society at Windsor, September 4, 1922, Proceedings of the Vermont Historical Society, 1921, 22, 23, (Montpelier: Capital City Press, 1924), 180.

---

[4] Henry Stone. He had been with the Lawrence, Kendall, and Robbins partnership since the mid-1840s; David R. Meyer, *Networked Machinists, High-Technology Industries in Antebellum America,* (Baltimore: John Hopkins University Press, 2006), 250-2. Stone, along with Frederick Howe supervised the Windsor gun manufacturing center from the 1853 departure of Richard Lawrence to Hartford, CT where he took manufacture of the Sharps rifle. He supervised the construction of most of the equipment at the Windsor plant. In 1854, the Windsor company produced a machine that created rifles with the long, precise spiral groves on the interior of rifle barrels. The invention, riffling, gave rifles their name as well as their accuracy. By September of 1861, the factory employed 300 men with manufacturing operations running day and night; Brown, "Guns for Billy Yank" ibid., 146-7. By 1861, Henry Stone was running the gunsmith shop in Windsor, Vt. which turned out 50,000 Springfield rifles, as well as the machine tools necessary for interchangeable parts, and would have been Stephen's and Philander's supervisor at the shop. Henry D. Stone with partner Frederick W. Howe and were co-creators of the modern turret lathe considered one of the most important modern machine tools, Hubbard, ibid, 177.

[5] E. G. Lamson. Under this partnership, the center processed cotton, manufactured guns and made machine tools for manufacturing interchangeable gun parts and sewing machines. Beside these accomplishments they also made sawmills, drill presses and wood turning lathes. Exactly which of these many production units was the site of Stephen's work is not known, but his experience in gunsmithing under Hilliard, and the comment about the "machine shop" would point to Stephen as an employee of the machine tool aspect of the concession, or the manufacture of guns. This letter specifically demonstrates the post-Civil War ties between the three owners, Jones, Stone, and Lamson, that produced uncertainty for Stephen's employment.

[6] Younger half-sister of Albert. Martha (Mattie) [1865 -1917] was the daughter of Stephen Williams, Jr. and Rhoda Lamberton Williams.

[7] Powers has not been identified. The Powers family included early settlers of Croydon and contained numerous members; see Edmund Wheeler, *Croydon, NH 1866, Proceedings at the Centennial Celebration on Wednesday June 13, 1866,* (Claremont, NH: Printed by Claremont Manufacturing Company, 1867), 130.

[8] James Tasker [1785-1876] ran a sawmill in Cornish, per William H. Child, *History of the Town of Cornish New Hampshire with genealogical record, 1763-1910,* 2 vols, (Concord, N.H.: The Rumford Press, 1910), 182, 363.

[9] Probably Abner P. Wellcome [1817-1893] of Newport who was involved in several businesses including a dairy, livery stable, stagecoach driver, justice of the peace, per Edmund Wheeler, *History of Newport, New Hampshire, from 1766 to 1878, with a genealogical register,* (Concord, NH: Republican Press Association, 1879), 83, 88, 212, 563.

[10] For a history of antebellum railroads in the Connecticut Valley see: Thelma M. Kistler, "The Rise of Railroads in the Connecticut River Valley," *Smith College Studies in History,* Vol XXIII, Nos 1-4, (October 1937-July 1938), 5-289. The decade 1840-1850 was the most feverish railroad construction in New England, 38, producing three major railroad lines in competition after 1850, 196. The line referred to was probably a branch line of the earlier main lines through New England.

[11] John Weld [1811-1899] Stephen's cousin by marriage. John Weld married Anna Bartlett [1819-1898], a first cousin of Stephen Williams, Jr. Anna Bartlett's mother was Polly Williams, a sister of Stephen's father. John Weld was credited with retentive memory, sound judgment and respected by all. See William H. Child, *History of the Town of Cornish New Hampshire with genealogical record, 1763-1910,* 2 vols, (Concord, NH. The Rumford Press, 1910), Vol I., 396; Vol. II, 19. See also letter 35 which again mentions Weld.

[12] Mrs. Stone, unidentified. Only one family surnamed Stone is listed in Wheeler, *History of Newport,* ibid., James and Harriet Dinsmore Stone, 540.

[13] Martin Williams [1839-1910], was Stephen Williams, Jr.'s first cousin once removed, the son of Abijah Williams, Jr.[1808-1866].

[14] Newton Sherman and Albert's sister Annginette Hall (Williams) Sherman.

[15] The visit may have allowed Albert to bring small trees back to his Iowa farm. Family lore establishes New Hampshire as the origin of evergreen trees still growing on farm Albert Williams established. At the time of the writing of this letter, Albert's Chester Nursery would have been in full operation.

[16] Mattie appears to have written her name twice at the bottom of the letter with a one sentence acknowledgement from her mother. The letter was written in Rhoda's handwriting.

Letter 35

To Albert Williams, Grinnell, Iowa
From Stephen Williams, Jr.[1]

Cornish [NH] April 18th 1872[2]
Dear Son;

We received your letter some time ago and felt very sad to hear of Clara Sherman's death.[3] Her father & mother[4] must be greatly afflicted at her loss and must miss her so much. I hope they have got better. We are all in usual health now. Mattie[5] was quite sick a month ago with the influenza, but has got well and is enjoying running outdoors again. The spring seems backward and there is a good deal of snow in the woods yet. The ice did not break up in the river until till last Saturday the 13 inst.[6] The season has been bad for sugar making and there will not be a great quantity made in these parts. Sleighing was good here until the second week of this month. I suppose you are beginning your springs [*sic*] work by this time. You must write us how your plants and trees that you carried home get along.[7] We remain where we are another year and I have plenty of work at the shop.[8] They are running the cotton mill to its utmost capacity. Have run nights most of the winter. We receive your papers[9] quite often and we are much obliged. They contain a good deal of useful reading.

I have not heard from John Weld[10] for some time. It is thought he is going into consumption. Your Uncle Charles' wife[11] has been very sick with a lung complaint but has got better. Ed Bryant and wife[12] are rejoicing in an addition to their family of a little daughter.[13] There does not seem to be much news for me to write. All the new thing we hear of now is the milk association a company forming to send milk to Boston. They have held a good many meetings at Windsor and think they will get in operation by the first of May. A great many farmers here will send their milk if it works. They have cars with ice in hot weather and think they can carry it to Boston and have it sweet. They will pay farmers 3 ½ cts in summer and 4 ½ cts in winter for [a] quart and the farmers think that will pay better than making butter.[14]

Give our love to Newton & Anginette[15] and your family. Write again soon as you can make it convenient.
Yours with regard
Stephen Williams

---

[1] The handwriting is that of Rhoda Williams.

[2] This is the last letter in the collection from Stephen Williams, Jr., Albert's father. In 1879 Rhoda and Stephen divorced. In the 1880 census, Stephen was recorded as a 67-year-old, divorced laborer in the household of George W. Sargent of Cornish, NH. Rhoda sued Stephen in Poweshiek County Iowa in 1882 and 1883 indicating his move to live with Albert occurred between 1880 and 1882. Stephen Williams, Jr. was living with Albert and family on the farm in Grinnell according to the 1885 Iowa state census.

[3] Clara Sherman [1858-1872] was Stephen's granddaughter. Luke Newton and Annginette Hall (Williams) Sherman's daughter Clara died on March 10, 1872 in Grinnell.

[4] Luke Newton and Annginette Hall (Williams) Sherman.

[5] Albert's half-sister, the daughter of Stephen and Rhoda. Mattie was a nickname for Martha [1865-1917].

[6] Inst was an abbreviation used to mean during the current month. The writer is saying last Saturday, the 13th of April.

[7] A reference to a trip Albert made to New Hampshire. He brought back tree saplings for his Iowa orchard, the Chester Nursery, and the evergreens that still grow on the farm there. See Letter 34.

[8] Stephen was working at the Windsor Manufacturing Company, previously the Windsor, Vermont Armory. Part of the complex was devoted to cotton mills. See Introduction and Letter 34, notes.

[9] Presumably local newspapers.

[10] John Weld [1811-1899] was married to Anna Bartlett [1819-1898]. Anna was a first cousin of Stephen Williams, Jr. Anna Bartlett's mother was Polly Williams, a sister of Stephen's father. John Weld was credited with retentive memory, sound judgment and was respected by all; William H. Child, *History of the Town of Cornish New Hampshire with genealogical record, 1763-1910,* 2 vols, (Concord, NH.: The Rumford Press, 1910), Vol I, 396; Vol. 2, 19. See also Letter 34.

[11] This is a reference to the second wife of Charles Williams [1820-1894], Sarah (Leet) Draper Williams [1829-1873], who died January 25, 1873 of consumption at 44 years old, giving the impression that consumption was not always diagnosed, nor effectively treated. Charles Williams was a younger brother of Stephen Williams, Jr.

---

[12] Edward [1837-1909] and Julia (Gilkey) Bryant [1842-1889], residents of Cornish, NH were parents of several children. Edward was the son of Daniel Bryant [1803-1864] to whom Albert was bound out as a child. See Letter 3.

[13] Daughter Julia Bryant was born March 1, 1872, per Child, *History of Cornish*, Vol 2, 39-40.

[14] See Child, *History of Cornish*, Vol I, 183-185 for a discussion of local creameries' importance to farmers.

[15] Luke Newton and Annginette Hall (Williams) Sherman, Stephen's son-in-law and daughter.

Letter 36

Document
Teaching Certificate for Eliza Blair

There are five one cent stamps in the upper left hand corner of the document.

This is to certify that I this day examined Eliza Blair in Orthography, Reading, Writing, Arithmetic, Geography and Grammar and believe her competent to teach the same, and being satisfied of her good moral character and capacity to teach, she is hereby licensed to teach in the common schools of the County for a term of Six Months from this date, unless the same be sooner revoked.
J. Root Jr[1]
Supt Com Schools
Iowa Co., Iowa
Dated Marengo[2]
Apr 30th, 1864.[3]
2nd Class.[4]

---

[1] The 1870 census for Marengo, Iowa contains James Root, Jr. a vineyardist, aged 39 years old, born in New York living with wife and family. Born and educated in New York state before moving to Iowa in 1854, Root's obituary indicated he had served two terms as Superintendent of Iowa County, while spending 40 years in the classroom; *Emmetsburg Democrat*, December 14, 1905, 5, Obituary.
[2] Marengo is the county seat of Iowa County, directly east of Poweshiek County.
[3] The date is on the bottom left side of the page and the signature are at equal levels on the document. Eliza may have taught for six months in Iowa County then moved to the Chester school system in Poweshiek County, where she was teaching when she met Albert Gordon Williams. As she was married in 1866, the possibility exists that she taught school for two years before marrying. Albert's youngest sister Francis was a pupil of Eliza's. See Introduction.
[4] Second-grade certificates were good for one year and generally required only three months of successful teaching before certification, Suzanne L. Bunkers, *"All Will Yet Be Well", The Diary of Sarah Gillespie Huftalen, 1873-1952*, (Iowa City: University of Iowa Press, 1993), 286n2.

Letter 37

To Eliza (Blair) Williams, Grinnell, Iowa
From Nettie Rusco

Patterson
Feb 3th [*sic*] 1866[1]

Dear Cousin;[2]

It is a long time since we heard from you and Mother[3] would like to hear from you very much. She sent Cousin Ted's[4] letter to you last Summer but we have back no reply. We have another letter from him which we will inclose [*sic*] in this.
Now I will tell you a little news. We have got a dear little Baby, a sister. She was born the 20th of October.[5] She is as fat as a little pig [?] and very fair complexion. And Mother says you can guess who she looks like. She has small blue eyes and red hair but we all think she is pretty and we love her very much. Mother has been very sick since the baby has been born. She has got pretty smart now. Father is well and all the rest of the family. We are a going to remain here another year.[6]
We had a Christmas tree for the Sabbath school. Chloe[7] got the present camp[8] which was a beautiful Bible with gilt-edged and silver clasp. She learnt the best lessons in the school. Emma[9] got a very pretty doll and a pair of mittens and a pocket handkerchief. I got a workbox filled with tools to work with. Hart[10] goes to school in the forenoon and works in the afternoon on the cars.[11] Love to cousin Albert and to yourself.
Affectionate Cousin
Nettie Rusco
Patterson Station Putnam County New York[12]

On the side of the letter written are two words: write soon (?).

----

[1] Written about one month before Albert and Eliza's wedding, possibly in response to an invitation or notification of the upcoming wedding.
[2] This February 1866 letter from Annette, nicknamed Nettie, (Rusco) [1853-1870] is the only one in the collection that appears to have been directed to Eliza (Blair) Williams. Nettie Rusco was the daughter of Henry (Harry) Ruscoe (Rusco) [1831-1889], and Helen (Lewis) Ruscoe [1828-1879]. In 1860 they lived in Southeast, Putnam County, near Patterson with the following children: Hart Ruscoe, aged 8, Ann E. (Nettie) aged 6, Sarah, aged 4, Chloe, aged 3, Melissa, aged 8 months, 1860 Federal Census South East, Putnam County page 18, family 156). Ann E. (Annette) was the only child born in Connecticut; all others were born in New York. Nettie was 12 years old when she penned this letter to her cousin. Nettie's exuberant letter reflects the first Christmas that her father would have enjoyed with the family after his return from the Civil War. The seemingly meager gifts to the children appear huge and sumptuous when viewed through the eyes of the 12-year-old Nettie. This is probably her only writing to have survived. Nettie died at 16 years old on March 22, 1870, but the newspaper report did not state the cause. Annette (Nettie) is buried in the Old Methodist Cemetery in Brewster, Putnam County, New York in a plot near her mother Helen and two girls named Sarah F.; presumably both had died in infancy or early childhood. No birthdates are available on the cemetery website at www.putnamgraveyards.com. *Find a Grave* gives the first death date for Sarah F. as January 12, 1861. If this is correct, then the baby girl mentioned in the letter was probably the second Sarah F. who died June 12, 1872.
[3] Helen Lewis Rusco[e] [1828-1879] born in St. Albans, Hertfordshire, England was presumably a younger sister of Ann (Lewis) Blair, Eliza's mother.
[4] Cousin Ted has not been identified. He may have been Edward Blair, an older brother of Eliza's with the nickname Ted. Edward appears in the English 1851 census as an older brother of Eliza's.
[5] October 20, 1865.
[6] Possibly a reference to a return to Connecticut.
[7] Nettie's sister, Chloe [1857-1938].
[8] Possibly related to the church organization or group for the children.
[9] Nettie's sister, Emma [1861-1945].
[10] Nettie's brother, Hart [1851-1920].
[11] Train cars, as Patterson Station was a train stop.

[12] The 1850 census for Southeast, Putnam County, New York, provides information for the Ruscoes, who at that time were borders with the Crosby family of shoemakers; US Federal Census, 1850, 21, family 318. Henry Crosby, shoemaker, and his wife Rebeka, both aged 49 in 1850 headed a household with 13 other people, some children, but some obviously borders, or employees of a shoemaking facility. Six children, Hart, Henry, George (16), Francis, Ann E., Annette, Sarah, and Charles were the Crosbys noted in the census. Others in the household included: Henry Ruscoe, age 20, Oliver Smith, 15, Thomas Meade, 30, Ellen Lewis, 23. Henry's personal estate totaled 100 dollars and his occupation was shoemaker. From this information it is presumed that Ellen Lewis was Helen, later wife of Henry Ruscoe. Henry and Helen married in June 1851 at the South East Presbyterian church. The census for Southeast shows a number of Ruscoes, Crosbys, and other shoemakers. See Introduction.

Nettie's father, Henry Rusco[e], served in the Civil War as a volunteer in the New York Fourth, Regiment 4, company A, H heavy artillery. Thirty-two years old in 1862, a mechanic by occupation, he began service on September 1, 1862, as an enlisted private from Southeast, New York in Putnam County. Henry was 5 ft 5 inches, dark complexion with dark hair and hazel eyes; New York Civil War muster roll abstract, 4627. (Spelled Rusco on service record). He began service only 16 days before the battle of Antietam. He served until June 1865 when mustered out by General Order number 26. He is briefly mentioned in a book length history of the heavy artillery; Hyland C. Kirk, *Heavy Guns and Light, A History of the Fourth New York Artillery*, (New York: Dillingham pub, 1890), 489. The Heavy Artillery was formed as a separate branch of the army tasked with placing, manning, and working places of heavy ordnance in permanent fortifications and in Siege Trains where they accompanied an Army in the field in engineering work; Captain Augustus C. Brown, *Diary of a Line Officer*, (New York, 1906), 2.

Henry's group was mustered in as the 135th regiment of infantry, later to be designated 6th regiment of heavy artillery. Company A became Battery A of heavy artillery. His regiment made up part of the Army of the Potomac, under Major General George Meade, assigned to the eastern theater of war. They protected the upper Potomac River and defended Washington, D.C. from the time of Henry's entry into service until March, 1864. Then the regiment saw fighting in Northern Virginia for the remainder of Henry's service. He may have been involved in a number of the most famous and decisive battles including the Battle of the Wilderness, the battle at Spotsylvania Courthouse, Cold Harbor, and the siege of Petersburg. A total of 454 men were lost from the 4th regiment during the three years Henry served, mostly from disease. By late 1864, U.S. Grant supervised General Meade's Army of the Potomac which saw warfare at the Battle of Cold Harbor and the Appomattox campaign; www.nps.gov. Henry was mustered out June 3, 1865, near Alexandria, Virginia, relieving him of his Civil War service. The Fourth Regiment, New York heavy Artillery was considered one of the most distinguished regiments in the service; Kirk, *Heavy Guns and Light*, ibid, 454. The number of men serving in this regiment totaled over 3,000. Rusco was discharged to South Norwalk, Connecticut, only 40 miles from Patterson, New York. It may be that the family was staying in South Norwalk and as Nettie's letter mentions staying another year, they would be returning to Connecticut. South Norwalk is only 8 miles from Wilton, Fairfield, CT where a number of Ruscoes, presumably relatives, were engaged in shoemaking.

APPENDIX I

From a Hand-Written Account by Lavinia (Williams) Grattan

"My father, Albert Gordon Williams, was born in Cornish, New Hampshire, Nov. 18, 1840, and went to Grinnell in the Spring of 1856, at 16 years of age.[1] His father put a $20 dollar gold piece in the heel of each boot he wore. He stayed overnight in Chicago, and father sort of picked up a Pal on the train, or the man had attached himself to father. When they got a room for the night, the man undressed himself and went to bed. Father was suspicious of the man, and did not want to take his boots off and so he lay on the bed fully dressed and got to sleep. They rode the train to Iowa City as far as the railroad was completed. They were supposed to ride the stage for 75 miles, but as the roads were deep mud, and there were small horses and a full coach, the men walked most of the way, taking several days to make the trip.

His sister Annginette had married Newton Sherman, and they lived 3 1/2 miles northeast of Grinnell. He walked out there, and his feet were so sore and tired he did not get his boots back on for several days, but had his feet tied up in old rags. He worked summers for them for three years, then worked for Dr. Holyoke[2] for one more year, and by this time had earned enough to buy a quarter section of land. The year at Dr. Holyoke's, he broke two stears [sic], so had an ox team in the Spring of 1860 to go to Chester and break sod. The first land broken was west of the house, and he planted crops (and grass) there. All Summer was spent in breaking sod. That was slow work, as the grass had deep roots. He worked for some of the neighbors some of the time.

At that time they thought a road would go by them north and south, and that was the reason they faced the house to the south. Father tried to buy of Mr. Sheff [sic] a few acres just northwest of the home across the road, to plant quick growing trees as a break against the wind, the northwest winds blew days at a time.[3]

There were only three other houses in Chester at that time: Jason Sherman on what is now Lidkas, Henry Sherman on what is now Schnells, and Wilson Sherman, one mile west. They had been on their places one or two years, and had small houses.[4]

The Winter of 1860-61 father with Sylvester H who settled a half mile east of father's, put up a log hut just big enough to have a bed, stove and table, and cut down black walnut trees and got lumber for a house.[5] They had two horses at this time, but one day one horse fell down into the river and got very wet, and it was cold they thought it best to bring the horse into the hut, and there was just enough room between the bed and the stove and table for the horse to stand until he dried off, which did not take very long.

The Summer of '61 by degrees the house was built. Father had to hire the plastering done only. Meantime he put up a shed for his horses, corn, and a pig or two and chickens. He got poles from trees growing in the grove, and made sheds that were open on the south side but kept the stock from the north winds and snow. He sort of wove the poles together and covered them with hay or straw, and then dirt on top, and then more poles on top of that. This kind of shed had to be repaired each year and made bigger for some years, before father could build a barn. I remember a turkey made a nest up on the shed, one year, and when she got ready to set, the turkey gobbler wanted to set on the eggs. He would pick at the hen turkey until she left the nest. Then he would sit down on the eggs, but he did not quite know how, and the result was he broke the eggs, a loss. We had quite a time over it. That turkey gobbler would chase me, but if I had a stick and run after him, he beat it in a hurry.

I was early taught not to be afraid of anything. I was never afraid of the dark, and am not today. So many folks are. When father finally got the house up, his mother and ten years' younger sister came to live with him.[6] His mother could make men's clothes, and so got work in Grinnell. Most men's clothes were home-made then. The younger sister kept house for father.

Meantime my mother had come down from Fort Dodge to go to school.[7] She wanted to teach in the country, and taught in our district the Fall of 1865, and the Winter of '65 and '66 boarded with father and Francis [sic]. She did a lot of

Albert Williams, Grinnell IA; at age 53 in 1893

Jane Eliza (Blair) Williams; about 1890s

the house work to live in a decently clean home. Francis [*sic*] went to school under her. Then father and mother were married in March, 1866.

My mother was very high strung, nervous, high-tempered, sensitive, and seemed under tension and tears all the time, always worrying about disaster coming to them. Mother was born in London, England, January 8, 1841. She was 51 days younger than father. When Mother lived in England an Aunt in New Jersey[8] said, "Send one of the children," so Mother was chosen to be the one.[9] In those days passengers had to be provided with food for the trip over on the sailing ship, and it consisted mostly of dry bread. This ship was becalmed three weeks, and the food ran low, and there was terror among the passengers. I think that experience accounted for much of my mother's high tension. It was very hard for her to live the economical life of the pioneers. That first Summer she had the mistaken idea she was not getting food enough to nourish the baby coming – ME. She and father were so different, they never did understand each other, and never came to a common ground. It took a sort of work-hardened kind of woman to live through those pioneer days and get any joy out of it.

Now it has taken all this preliminary to get to my early memories. In my mind I can see shadowy pictures of this and that I cannot put into words. So the clearest first memory is going into the bedroom to see my new little brother born May 30th, 1870.[10] I stood by the bed and looked at him and mother in bed. Then I climbed onto a chair and wanted to hold him, and he was placed in my arms, and I thought of him so little and at the time so big, for he did weigh 12 pounds.

It was a wild prairie north of the house, and father's milk cows ran them [*sic*], so one had to go after them at night. A Robert Rutherford worked for father that Summer, and he walked for them if they were anywhere near, but if they were some distance away he would ride a horse.[11] Either way I went with him. If he walked he would carry me in his arms, or if he rode the horse, the same, I remember. That prairie was covered with flowers from Spring until Fall. The air was filled with flocks of birds. What a noise their chattering made! When father would plough a flat of land, the birds would settle down on the fresh-turned earth to try to find worms and grubs, and I, following behind father, would try to catch a bird. Of course I never did. But there was such swarms of them, I felt I almost did catch one. I always wanted to be out doors wandering around. I knew where the bird nests were, and I climbed many a young orchard tree to look into the nests and see the young birds of various ages, and degrees of length of feathers, from the time birds were naked until they were full-feathered and ready to fly. Also the frogs and toads, turtles and snakes. When father said they would not hurt me or harm me in any way, I would catch them and play with them. I tied a string to their feet and played with them. This my mother thought horrible, and that it was strange that those creatures were of interest to me.

There was little work done on the roads. Folks drove anywhere between the side fences. The small culverts usually had a mud puddle on each side. We drove through the mud puddles, and bumped up over the culverts, and thus the mud puddles on either side developed deep ruts, and if a snake got in one of those ruts, he had to go some distance sometimes to get out, and as I went to school (a half mile east of the house)I could pick up the snake by the tail and snap him, breaking his neck. These were the garter snakes. There were rattle snakes in the early days of the development of the country, but none were left in my childhood. However, there were a few blue racers, a dark-colored snake that moved faster than the rattle snake, and would wiggle along with head and three or four inches of neck raised upright. They were really hard to catch up with. As I went to school, I watched for all the reptiles, and that day was counted lost that I did not encounter one of some kind.

There was no barbed wire in those days, and men planted cotton wood, willow or maple along the roadside. They would click branches close together, and they usually grew and made a hedge-tight fence. So as we rode along, it was between the rows of trees. When the barbed wire fence came the trees were mostly taken out, or the wire was nailed to the trees. I used to walk along that kind of fence when the road was muddy, on my way to school. In the Winter we would walk on the snow-drifts. They would be hard-packed by the wind, with spots of soft snow that would let us down, almost burying us deep in snow. The uncertainty of where and when we would step into the soft spots made the going adventurous.

From left: Worthin Grattan about 2 years old; Worthin's mother Lavinia (Williams) Grattan; Stephen Williams (seated) aged 84; Worthin Williams; Eliza Williams with baby Henry Grattan; Albert Williams standing. Photo taken November or December 1896.

The outstanding memory of the country school is the big, hot stove in the center of the room, and the cold seats near the window and in the back of the room far from the stove. They did not know that if they had put a sheeting around the door it would have distributed the heat better to all parts of the room. But the little red school houses, two miles apart throughout the countryside, was a wonderful idea, and served to make our citizens a literate people. In the Winter terms of 3 ½ months, when we had a man teacher, nearly all the big boys under 21 years of age went to school. At the end of the school year we had an "extriction" [sic]. We sang all the patriotic songs from Civil War days, spoke pieces, had dialogue and some charades. Parents came with lanterns to hang on the walls, and a big time was had. My father used to take a lot of apples as a treat for everyone. We girls used to have big pockets in our dresses. I would take two or three apples in my pocket to trade with Will Hafkey[12] for doughnuts he had in his pockets. My mother did not make doughnuts often, but did make fritters that we ate with hot maple syrup.

Once in a while I would find a nest of young rabbits, and once I saw quite a big garter snake shedding his skin as he wriggled in the rubbish. I was able to get it out carefully and take it to the house. My mother tried so hard to get me interested in being a nice little lady in the house, to learn to cook and sew and do housework. All that was so distasteful to me. I did everything I could to avoid it. They got the Singer sewing machine when I was quite small, and I could put in the round shuttle that Mother could not seem to do. I learned to run the machine, and stayed in the house just to run the machine. In those days mother made father and brother's shirts, pants, and underwear. The underwear was of heavy fleece-lined cotton flannel, and took so long to do when washed. Mother hung them on lines over the stair and hall, and let them dry at their leisure. She bought a bolt of grey flannel from the Amana Colony's plant, made the men's shirts, my bloomers, petticoats and dresses. It seems now that we were loaded down with clothes, but remember the house was cold. Only the living room and kitchen were heated part of the day, and to go from one room to another was often like going outdoors. We slept in such cold rooms!

Mother knit stockings for all of us. We could buy Summer stockings – they were all black. I did not have a boughten ready-made dress until I was grown. I don't remember if mother ever had a ready-made dress.

I did not go to school until the Spring I was 7 in January. Mother taught me at home. When she taught country school she had such children sent to school, and had them take a nap afternoons. In the school the day opened by Bible reading and a Sunday School song or hymn, and we were asked to memorize some verse. The teachers were rather strong on that. I am not clear in my mind about the lights we had. I remember mother making candles out of beef tallow. There was a frame for 12 candles. She had to thread the cotton cord in each, and heat the tallow, and pour it real hot into the frame, and when they had cooled they were easily taken out. I carried a candle to bed after I was grown up. We did not have kerosene at first, but a something called naptha, that took three matches to make it hot enough to light. We had to make a little light go a long way. It was not light enough to read by, or sew by, but women would knit with half a light. As long as we could see each other, and where a table or chair was, it was enough. Folks eat in the dark many times. You don't need a light to see to talk.

We did not go to town oftener than once in two or three weeks, and had no way to keep food or meat. So beef, as well as pork was put down in brine; or any other fresh meat. We had dry, salted codfish – it came in big slabs. It had to be soaked overnight, and then made into codfish gravy.

Folks wore their Sunday clothes for years. My mother had a bunch of big pansies she would put on a black Winter bonnet, and then on a Summer light straw bonnet, for several years. When she finally discarded them father felt so disappointed! Children's coats and dresses were handed from one to another. I wore an alpaca dress – a big plaid with much color in it – blue, red and black. It was very heavy cloth and came to me from a girl who had outgrown it. I wore it until it was too small, then gave it to Edna Sherman[13] and she wore it. Our head coverings were knit hoods or scarfs, and we little folks took them off in church. I had a fur cap I wore for several years, with pads that came down over my ears. Before I went into church I took the cap off, tucked the tabs into the flap of my cap and put the cap back on again. And today I cannot get used to the idea of having so many clothes, dresses and hats. I still think one good outfit for Sunday (take it off the minute you get home!) is enough. Why have any more?

Mother was always careful about her clothes, and tried to make me think about clothes. But to me it was all bosh. I remember on Sunday morning she said "Get dressed for church". I put on a clean, everyday dress and was quite determined to wear it to church over her objections. She never said, "What will folks think, or what will they say?" It was always "This is the right way to do." And I never did get the idea of how folks do think of what you have on, or how you look, or what they will say. The idea was, "Are you clean", and "will you be careful to keep clean and not tear your clothes."

Folks tried to raise gardens, as there were no canned vegetables. And in the fall vegetables were stored in the cellars. We raised all kinds of beans, and thrashed them out in the fall. Most raised some cane, and put it through Mr. Shiff's[14] cane crusher and boiled it down into thick molasses. That seasoned the baked beans and corn bread; also was on most tables in the kitchen. There was very little fruit of any kind. I suppose plums were about the first. So when father had fruit in his nursery, he had plenty of customers who wanted to pick on shares. There was little cash in any of our pockets, but men exchanged work, or would work for a day or two for something.

They had lumber wagons and it was a day's trip from our house to town and back – nine miles in one day. It wore mother out. When folks could afford it, they got spring wagons. We had a big three-seated one, and filled it when we went to church. With hired man, hired girl, the school teacher (that mother always boarded) our going to church on those days was as sure as eating on Sunday. Everybody went but two or three families. The folks were young married folks, and there were babies aplenty. That church used to be filled, and when we had Sunday School we all formed around into classes, but we sat next to another class. We had suppers and socials in the church. The annual church meeting and dinner was well attended. Folks did not have phones or daily papers, and Sunday was a day of much visiting, before and after service. The women talked together, and the men talked also, and the young folks. Many a date was made on Sunday, or gay man given the mitten! [*sic*] Mother's method for us children was to keep such watchful care over us, and clasp a lid down on us. If she did not know where we were it would frighten her into conniptions. One day I was upstairs in the P.M. and went to sleep on the floor. She had begun to hunt for me outdoors. Then father began to look in the house and found me, and woke me, and took me downstairs. Mother made a bid to-do over me. So in a day or two I was playing the corn crib, and she called me. I kept still, and she began to hunt for me, calling and calling. I still kept still, and soon she saw me looking through between the boards, and came in and got me, and then broke off a branch of a tree, and whaled me to a fare-you-well. I never tried that again! Just one other time did she whip me. That time with her slipper. I was just about nine, and had been to the next door neighbor, and was giving her a report on how we girls had played. As I think of it now, we are not doing anything very bad, but she thought so, and as I was telling it she jerked me across her lap, took off her slipper, and again beat the band! I screamed! When she was through I went outdoors and thought: "I will never tell her anything again. She really effectually shut my mouth. I wandered around outdoors, crying and mad. I they went into supper, then right to bed, still weeping.

The next morning she was going to comb my hair to get ready to go to school. I would not go near her, but tried to comb my own hair. It was to be in two braids down my back, but the way it worked out, each braid stuck straight out by my ears. When I went to school the girls laughed at me, and I asked them to braid it again. And that was the way my hair was cared for from then on. And I never felt cordial toward my mother again. And I did not tell about anything now at home. I felt I was whaled for telling – so don't ever punish a child for telling you what he has done.

When I was quite young, father made me a sled, and Worthin one. It was really too big for us to handle, but I had some good times on it, even when I was grown up. It would hold three children. Father had a straw stack on the southeast quarter, and he would put the rack on runners. The hay rack extended out and I could tie the sled rope on to the corner of the hay rack and ride on the snow. There had been a thaw, then a freeze, and there was a crust on the snow, so the sled stayed on top without breaking through. So I rode my sled when he went for straw. We boarded the school teacher, when I was grown, and in bad weather we would hitch a horse to my sled, and I would take the teacher to school. Also go after her. When the horse trotted, he would throw the snow in our faces.

We had no bed mattresses in those days, but straw ticks filled with straw. There were the bed slats, then the straw ticks, not too bad before the straw got broken up. They were high when first filled, but settled down finally – no springs in those beds! I can see mother making the beds, putting her hand into the tick, and moving the straw around to make the most comfortable kind of bed.

I went to Cedar Falls to school[15] in 1888 and 1889, and we had straw ticks. They got pretty hard after a while, and usually, come a nice day in mid-Winter, father would take the ticks down to the straw stack and refill them. I can see the hay rack with five big straw ticks so full it looked like a big load. Most folks kept ducks so as to have pillows and feather-beds on top of the straw, which made them warmer and nice. In the summer the feather beds were put under the straw ticks, as they were too warm. None were sorry for themselves because of these primitive ways. It was the way the best of folk had to do – everybody was doing it.

One time mother bought calico to make me a dress. It was a medium blue with polka white dots so big! When the dress had been washed a time or two the dots became halos. And she did not know what to do. I didn't care – it didn't bother me. She was always afraid I would feel hurt or sensitive, but I wasn't a lot, before she thought it was so bad. We used to go to town in the later afternoon, so as not to take time during the day, and trade in the evening. Mother bought herself goods for a Sunday dress. It was a light grey in the night light of the store. The next day it proved to be green, light green. She was heart-sick and kept it quite a while before deciding what to do with it. She was not as skilled at dyeing cloth as some were. So finally she gave it to Ruth R. Wells[16] grandmother, and pretty soon Ella (Ruth's mother) came out with a very nice black dress.

I have a peculiar ear. My left one – the lower lobe part of the ear sticks out straight. And folks would ask what happened to your ear? I would answer, "Nothing. It has always been that way." Mother would squirm and try to change the talk to something else. She thought she had marked me with a birth mark or defect. We know now there is no way a mother can mark a baby. I have always looked my babies over to see if their ears were the right kind – and they were.

I had got to be quite a big girl, 11 or 12, and in my walking over the farm east of the hay barn I found and killed a real big snake. After supper I was telling about it, and spread my arms to show how long it was. Mother poohed me, rather said it just looked that way, so I said I would get it. The night was quite dark, save a little moonlight, but I found it and picked it up by the tip of the tail and dragged it home. When I walked into the dining room, mother let out one of her screams, and father exclaimed. My story had not been exaggerated at all.

Father planted apple seeds in his nursery in the spring – a pail full he sent off for. In the fall he dug them up. They would be little trees six inches high. He would put 100 in one pack, and pack them in a box of mulch dirt in the cellar, for the winter.

He would go through the orchard and cut off scions from the apple trees. A scion is a branch 1 ½ to 2 feet long. This was cut in short sticks and grafted onto the little apple trees. He had a grafting box on legs that were in front of him as he sat on a chair, and this he did all winter, and he had one man who stayed with us through the winter to do chores. He would graft sometimes, too. One man, Will H __ was very high strung. I would run and play around him. I did not know I was bothering him, but once he hit me across the face with a scion. I screamed, and so did mother. I had a deep red mark across my face for several days, and it was sore indeed. Neither father nor mother made any remarks. I surely stayed away from that man and his work!

I always wanted my brother to play with me, to run and jump and scuffled with him. He never could, and not until I had little boys of my own did I realize that my brother had what I now believe was a weak heart. He never could run more than a few steps, and I always outwalked [sic] him when we went to school. He never could lay much with the boys at school. He would try for a minute or two and then quit. Nowadays we would take a child to a doctor, if he was so inactive. He was a large child and looked well.

Everyone was interested in politics in those days. And Chester was solid Republican for years. Noted men would speak in Grinnell, and there would be torch-light parades. A torch would be made of rags wired to the end of a long pole or stick, soaked with kerosene, then lit, and a dozen men would join the parade, singing, and parading until the blaze went out. Father would go into town to hear the speaker, and see the celebration, but it was too far and too hard a trip for mother.

The slough south of the home was wide so a lot of land was not producing any crop. Father had a mole ditch put through to the bridge on the road running north and south on the outside of the farm. Two men came and set up the rig. The oxen would go round and round pulling the rope that pulled the mole through the ground underneath the surface. It was perhaps a foot in diameter and 6 feet long. It was very slow work. What I remember about it was that one of the oxen was very tame, and one of the men would put me on top of him, and I would ride down to their work after dinner, and go and meet them coming home for supper. After supper the oxen would lie down. I would sit down on the tame oxen. He was too tired to care. The next year there were the same heavy rains, and that mole ditch washed out, and it made an open ditch that was all to the good.

I was not a very big girl when on a damp day father and the men went down in the field and dug out the big stones that we used as stepping stones to get into the spring wagon when going to church. They proved to be much bigger than father thought they would be. When they were brought to the house they no longer bothered with the field work.

Superstitions still linger with folks. My grandfather[17] would say: "You know it is said, if planted in the dark or light of the moon, so and so will happen." I don't believe it. I was talking with Mrs. ____ last night about it. She said she did not have any superstition, she was sure. I recalled what they used to think, and finally spoke of how they would witch for water. She at once exclaimed: "Now that, I know, has something in it! The water in the ground draws the branch down!" But in my disbelief and blindness I had my say, anyway, if water had a pulling power, we could not put bridges across rivers.

We did not have screens for some years, and then it was mosquito netting. It was a lot of work to fight flies. The food was put on the table in tureens, and bread was covered with a napkin. No food without a cover, except the home-keeper would stand with a branch of a tree, and move it back and forth over the table. They used to put asparagus branches across the walls and over doors for the flies to roost in. People used to put on new paper and whitewash the ceiling in the fall, after the frost had killed the flies. No one had a carpet for some years. They made mats or rugs from men's old suits or braided or crocheted cotton rugs. It was a big event when mother finally got her first rag carpet. She has saved rags from worn-out dresses for a long time. And finally took them to a woman who had a loom and wove them into strips. Then the sewing of the strips together and getting it put down on the floor and tacked down.

One time mother had a neighbor girl help her. It was winter, I think, because there was deep snow. She had a very bad cold, one day. She was so sick in the morning, mother had her stay in bed. Father went over to Mrs. Skiff's[18] and told her she seemed very sick, but he thought that children made a fuss over a cold. The next morning mother went up to see her, and when she came down she was agitated and whispered to father. He went upstairs to her room. Then he came down and went over to Mrs. Skiff's. The girl had died during the night. Mr. Skiff came with a team and sleigh. Then mother kept me in the bedroom downstairs so I could not see them bring her downstairs, and I wanted to see what was going on.

It was in 1877 when the east part of the house was put on. I think the bay window was put on about 1874.

Father had sheep in the early days, and as usual there were some lambs to raise by hand. They would have the run of the place, and would come to the east door, and if mother did not chase them away, they would scamper through the house and out the west door, and I would chase them further away.

The Chester[19] people were very devoted to their church, and made real sacrifices to build the church, and keep it going without any help from back east.[20] We had one minister fourteen years – Mr. White. I remember very well some of his talks, manners, and strictness. He was walking one day and heard boys talking the other side of a hedge. So he investigated and found they were playing cards. He was horrified and made a to-do over it. We always sat in the one seat right in the front. Father would almost memorize a sermon as it was given. I did not like to sit so near the front, and when we were going home I explained about it. Said I did not believe a word he said, and that it was just talk, talk, talk, and I didn't like it. That was quite a bomb-shell for my parents – and they gave me the silent treatment. No one had anything to say at dinner or in the afternoon. Their disapproval fairly shrieked. They had no idea their little girl was such an unbelieving sinner.

One time a skunk was in the cellar under the old part of the home. We didn't know how to get at it. It wanted to stay. Father said that if he shot it we would have a stink around. But mother was sure we would have a stink anyway. So father shot it, and what a stink we did have! Father got it out, then shoveled a lot of dirt down into the cellar. We moved the cook stove out into the yard, and mother cooked, and we ate out there. But we had to go into the home to go to bed. And the odor was terrible, and lasted so long!

The men wore beards – father shaved his upper lip and a little on his lower lip. Some of the young men began to have a full beard as soon as their faces would grow one.

Father's idea to grow and have all possible food produced on the farm included bees and pigeons. He made a place for the pigeons inside a granary on a shelf, where they could make nests, and where we could get a juicy squab when needed. He used to out 75 swarms of bees in the cellars over winter. We always had honey on the table.

We had good food in those days, if we didn't have salads. They were always sharp cucumber pickles. We dried fruit, if we had any fruit. There was no canning in the early days.

I remember the to-do over a young man's drowning. He lived in Chester a year or two, and was always talking about his folks back home, when he drowned, and they went through his things, there was no name or address of anyone to write to or mail to. Made a lot of talk.

My grandfather had about six box rabbit traps around, and he would go the rounds and get the rabbits out, kill them, and feed them to our many cats in the barn. One time he had a bad cold, and we thought he had better not go out into the snow. I don't know how old I was – but about grown up. So I put on some pants and started out and what a time I had in the deep drifts. I had to go through the sheep yard. He told me to carry a big stick and the buck would not bother me, but I did not. I got across the yard and was climbing over a big tall gate, and was on top of it, when he ran and bumped it, sending me into a six foot deep soft drift. How I floundered around and struggled out of that situation!

Men used to whittle evenings. We children were so impressed. We boarded a man school teacher, one Winter, and he whittled every evening. I was always curious to know what he was making. But at the Christmas tree there was for me a little wooden doll in a wooden cradle he had whittled.

Neither father nor mother had very much schooling, but both had the inquiring mind that educates itself. I was a little girl not yet able to read when father bought a big dictionary. I was allowed to look at pictures in it only when he was nearby, every day. Every day after dinner he would open it at random, look over a word, study it and similar words nearby, and so master the use of the word and its meaning.

I can remember being out in some heavy rain. Mother and I had started home from town in the little one-seated buggy and it began to just pour down. It wet our laps. We drove into a place and up to the door. The man came out and helped us into the home. The lady said I had better take off my dress, as the skirt of it was sopping wet. So they did, and I was embarrassed. We sat down to supper. I felt as though a trick had been played on me.

Father had a way of saying "This or that will be the best way to do." Once I had been into mischief, and he took hold of my arm and said, "Will I have to speak cross to you?" That was enough. Mother never let me get rough house. If I began to, she would say, "Go into the pantry and sing as loud as you want to until you can be quiet when you come out." Both father and mother were quite refined and maintained that kind of a house. There was never any kind of criticism of each other, and anyone could come into the home at any time and there would not have been anything going on they would have been ashamed of, or wanted to cover up. They never seemed to be making an effort to live up to such a standard, but it was just their way of life. They thought it a terrible lack of self respect for folks to speak sharp words to each other.

I have gone over this and it is quite a jumble. When you type it, shape it up into paragraphs. It will take a lot of sorting. I hope you can make three or four copies at one time, one for Ralph's[21] and one for ?? Eva[22] is getting used to using one hand, but it is in a hurry to use the other.

Last known photo of Albert Williams, sitting at the beach at Santa Cruz CA; about 1921

[1] Lavinia is incorrect as to the year. Albert left in the winter of 1856/7, as is verified by the letter collection. He arrived during or before Spring, 1857.

[2] T. E (Thomas) Holyoke was a 41 year-old physician living in Grinnell in the 1860 and 1870 Federal census.

[3] This appears to be a misspelling of Cornelious Skiff's name. Skiff, a native of Connecticut, was the adjacent neighbor in the 1860 census to the Luke Newton Sherman farm where Albert is listed as a farm laborer. In this census, Skiff's wife is Emma, and their oldest daughter, Isabella, is 6 years old, with four other children.

[4] These three men were brothers of Luke Newton Sherman, husband of Albert's oldest sister Annginette.

[5] No Sylvester H has been identified. This is possible a misspelling of Salvador Hayes who appears in the 1860 Federal census as a farm laborer and appears in the 1870 census at three dwellings' distance from Albert Williams and family. Salvador Hayes is credited as settling in Chester Township in 1859 in G. H. White, *Historical Sketch of Chester Township*, (Grinnell: Cravath and Shaw Steam Printers, 1881), 3.

[6] This is a reference to Melinda (Hall) Williams and Francis Williams.

[7] The Catalogue of Iowa College for 1864-5 lists Jane Eliza Blair as a junior from Fort Dodge. The 1865-66 Catalogue of Iowa College lists Jane Eliza Blair as a junior from Fort Dodge, then deficient in Latin. She was in the Ladies Course of studies which would have provided a diploma, but not a degree. In the ladies department junior year courses included English Analysis, Ancient Geography, Histories of Greece and Rome, Physical Geography, Elements of Natural Philosophy, Algebra, Caesar and Cicero. She apparently withdrew from the college by 1867 and later was considered an alumni of Grinnell College with a forwarding address in Campbell, California.

[8] See Introduction. Aunt Helen (Lewis) Ruscoe and family lived in South East Patterson, New York according to the one letter in the collection from her daughter. Presumably Lavinia was confused as to Patterson, New Jersey and Patterson, New York.

[9] See also Letter number 37, Nettie Rusco to cousin.

[10] Worthin Hall Williams.

[11] R. S. Rutherford was listed as a farmer working in the household next door to Albert Williams and family in the 1870 federal census.

[12] William Hafkey, Jr. was three years old in the 1870 census living with his parents in La Claire township, Scott County Iowa. In the 1880 census they were living in Chester township, Poweshiek County, Iowa.

[13] Edna Sherman [1869-1948] was the daughter of Jason Winchester Sherman and Jane (Wheelock) Sherman. The Sherman family intermarried with the Williams' family when Annginette Hall Williams married Luke Newton Sherman in 1856.

[14] Cornelious Skiff, wife Roxy Ann, and family are listed as the next farm adjacent to Albert Williams' farm in the 1870 census.

[15] Lavinia would have been 21 and 22 years old. Presumably she was attending the Iowa State Normal School in Cedar Falls established in 1876, which is now the University of Northern Iowa.

[16] Ruth Wells, 10 years old, appears in the 1880 census with her parents H. N. and Elizabeth Wells in Clay, Grundy, Iowa.

[17] Stephen Williams, Jr.

[18] Cornelious Skiff and his oldest daughter, Belle, were both listed in the 1870 census as born in Connecticut. Isabelle E. Skiff [1853-1872] died April 24, 1872 and is buried in the Chester, township cemetery. Lavinia would have been roughly five years old at the time of her death. Cornelious Skiff had another daughter, Harriet Skiff [1863-1882] who also died in youth, but Lavinia would have been about 15 years old at the time of Harriet's death, so presumably she was recalling an event concerning the older Isabelle. There are other farms listed in the 1880 census that would have been between the Skiff's and Williams' farms.

[19] Settlement nearest the Williams farm; Chester township is a part of Grinnell.

[20] The Chester Congregational church was organized on June 15, 1865 with the first church building constructed in 1868; G. H. White the most recent minister; *Grinnell Herald*, July 5, 1881, 2.

[21] Ralph was Lavinia's youngest son.

[22] Eva (Horn) Grattan was the first wife of Worthin F. Grattan, thus Lavinia's daughter-in-law.

PRICE CIRCULAR
—OF—
CHESTER NURSERY.

FALL OF 1873 AND SPRING OF 1874.

Nursery 6 Miles North and 2 Miles East of Grinnell, Ia.

A. G. WILLIAMS, Proprietor.

I would say to my patrons that I propose to continue my trade on the same terms as before, insuring all my stock to grow ; and I would inform my last Spring's customers that I will furnish Trees and Plants to replace all that failed to grow. I believe my stock to be as good as can be grown, and my prices very low. My Hedge Plants are grown on rich manured ground, my Grape Vines are all layers from bearing vines, and my stock is all grown and handled by myself.

STANDARD APPLE TREES, 6 to 8 ft., 10 cts. each.
" " " 4 to 6 ft., 8 " "
" " " 2 to 4 ft., 5 " "
* " " " 1 to 2 ft., 3 " " $20 per 1000.
NO. 2—Thrifty, but lacking in form; 4 to 8 ft.; 4 cts. each.
SIBERIAN CRAB—Several varieties; same price as Standard.
EARLY MAY CHERRY—3 to 5 ft.; 25 cts. each.
PEAR TREES—1 year; 15 " "
PLUM TREES— 15 to 25 " "
CURRANTS—Red Dutch; 1 year; 30 cts. per doz.
" " " 2 years; 50 " " "
GOOSEBERRIES—Houghton Seedling; 1 year; 20 " " "
BLACKBERRIES—Kittatinny; 40 " " "
PIE PLANT—Best variety; 25 " " "
RASPBERRIES—Several varieties; 20 " " "
GRAPE VINES—Concord, Clinton, Delaware; 1st class, $1.75 per doz.
" " —2nd class; strong vines; $1.25 per doz.—$8.00 per 100.
" " —3d class; 75 cts. per doz.—$5.00 per 100.
OSAGE HEDGE PLANTS—No. 1 assorted, spring delivery, $2 per 1,000.
" " " No. 2, small roots, 75 cts. per 1,000.
" " " *No. 1, fall delivery, $1.75 per 1,000.

I can also furnish, in limited quantities,
GREENHOUSE and BEDDING PLANTS, MOUNTAIN ASH, FLOWERING CURRANT, ROSES, SYRINGA, SNOW-BALL, HONEYSUCKLE, LILIES, and a general assortment of Ornamental Plants and Shrubs, 10 to 15 cents each.
MIXED TULIPS—For fall planting, 30 cents per dozen.

*Fall delivery, without warrant.

I employ no Agents and pay no commissions. I deliver all articles at Grinnell, without extra charge, and pack and deliver at railroad station, with no extra charge, except cost of material for packing.
Address

A. G. WILLIAMS,
Grinnell, Iowa.

PRICE CIRCULAR
—OF—
The Chester Nursery.

NURSERY, 6 MILES NORTH AND 2 MILES EAST OF GRINNELL, IOWA.

A. G. WILLIAMS, Proprietor.

In presenting my ANNUAL PRICE LIST, I would invite all who contemplate planting Nursery Stock to examine and compare my stock, prices and terms, with the same offered by others in the trade. My stock is all grown and handled by myself. My list is not large, but comprises such as are noted for hardihood, early bearing, and quality. I have no "rare kinds" at fancy prices. *I warrant my stock to grow*, by furnishing to replace all that fails to grow through any fault of the plant or the season. I deliver all articles at GRINNELL, and pack and deliver at Railway Station without extra charge, except the larger sized (6 to 8 ft.) trees, which are too large for shipping.

☞ I will be found at my Nursery during the season for handling trees on every week day, except Saturday.

PRICE LIST

STANDARD APPLE TREES...4 to 8 feet, 8 cents each; 3 to 4 feet, 5 cents
CRABS...Leading varieties same price as Standard each
EARLY MAY CHERRY ....3 to 5 feet, 25 cents each
PLUM TREES..Miner and Wild Goose, 3 to 5 feet, 25 cents each
CURRANTS..................................Red Dutch, 1 year, 30 cents per dozen; 2 years, 50 cents
RASPBERRIES.................Doolittle, Mammoth Cluster, Purple Cane. Turner and Philadelphia, 20 cents per dozen; $1 per 100
GRAPE VINES....Concord (layers), 1st class, $1.25 per dozen, $8 per 100; 2d class, $1 per dozen, $5 per 100; 3d class, 50 cents per doz
DWARF JUNEBERRY...1 year, $1.25 per dozen
PIE PLANT..Best variety, 25 cents per dozen
CHESTNUT...4 to 7 feet, 10 cents each
BUTTERNUT (White Walnut)..2 feet, 5 cents each
RUSSIAN MULBERRY...3 feet, 20 cents each
ROCK MAPLE (from New England)...........................4 to 6 feet, 15 cents each; 6 to 8 feet, 20 cents
NORWAY SPRUCE (without warrant)..........................4 and 5 feet, 30 cents each; 2 to 4 feet, 20 cents
BALSAM FIR " " ....4 feet, 30 cents each; 2 feet, 20 cents
SCOTCH PINE " " ....6 to 8 feet, 50 cents each

I also have, in limited quantities—

EUROPEAN LARCH,	SNOWBERRY.	SNOWBALL,	FLOWERING CURRANT,
FLOWERING ALMOND,	HONEYSUCKLES,	SYRINGA,	HARDY HYDRNGEA
LILAC,	PEONIES,	LILIES,	CATALPA.

10 to 25 cents each.

Address

A. G. WILLIAMS, Chester Center, Iowa.

APPENDIX III

HOW MY WIFE EARNED HER GUILD SOCIAL DOLLAR
By A. G. Williams[1]

It was not long ago by some mishap
That my wife and I got into a scrap,
As it was something neither of us intended,
I'll tell how it began and how it ended.

Like most such affairs where there's naught to provoke,
It began out of nothing and ended in smoke.
We were talking over the events of the day,
How I'd been working for wages and gotten my pay.
I told her I thought it a pretty good plan
To earn a few dollars now and then,
For these small amounts
Will help in the living, and giving, and expense accounts.
Then she went on to say" We church ladies were beginning
To think it high time that we had our inning,
And we have determined the matter and got it clinched
That the Guild room is too small and the kitchen too pinched.
So it has finally been settled by the Woman's Guild
That there's no way out of it but to build.
The rooms must be made larger and fixed up just right
With doors from the parlor and more windows for light.
It must all be done neatly and not look like a patch,
With the woodwork and painting and ceiling to match.
Now this must be done with other needed repairs,
So we'll have things down pat for our social affairs.
Now it will be quite an expense to bring this about
So this is the very best time for you to shell out.

Then I said in a joke as anyone might see—
Not knowing that I was touching a key—
"That in this advanced and progressive age
When new ideas were all the rage,
When the women aspired to a larger sphere,
Had momentous schemes to manage and engineer,
They will lecture, and canvass, and caucus and go to the polls
And abolish all wrongs and close up the bad holes.
That with woman's rights and the franchise secured
All the ills of the world will speedily be cured.
The reward you will get for your diligent pains
Will be to sit in high places and hold the reins,
While we men are expected to sort of retire
And look on and behold and admire.
But now remember as I have heard folks say
That big reforms do not come in a day,
But have their beginning in a very small thing,
Which if persistently followed, success will bring,

135

Now in this age of scramble, and greed, and strife,
When to gather in money seems the end of life,
To prestige, power, influence and fame,
Thinks nothing that equals that Dollar that you could name.
And, if you have a part in this glorious work to do,
Of those dollars, hadn't you better earn a few?
If you can't find a job that gives promise of pay,
For milking the cow, I'll give you a cent a day,
And a like amount you may have to keep,
If you'll build the fire and let me sleep."
This was as far as I got for she took her turn
And said, "Do you mean to tell me that I don't earn?
Whose kept the house with so little waste,
And cooked all the vittles to suit your taste?

Haven't I washed and scrubbed and worked in the suds,
And worn myself out to care for your duds?
Whose sewed on your buttons and mended your rips,
And patched your pants and brought in the chips?
Forty years have I done this with all my might,
And now to do your work you offer a stingy mite.
I have served you faithfully, as everyone knows,
And have stayed at home when you went out to the shows.
I have cared for the home without even a thinking,
And trained up the kids and done all the spanking.
You think yourself wise and know everything true,
But folks hunting a model would not pick you."

"Well," I said, "I give my attention to outside cares,
And carefully look after the secular affairs.
In all matters of profit I am always alert,
And manage my business in a manner expert.
And as to my being picked out among model men,
They might think I've already been picked by a hen!"

"Will you get down to business and quit your brag,
And hand over that chink and quit chewing the rag?
Have'nt I a right to a nickel that's mine to give?
It is only half mine when you die but none while you live?
Have'nt I pinched and saved so that nothing be lost,
And pieced out and fixed over to save the cost?
Have'nt I scrimped in my shopping to yield to your freak,
Then set in the buggy while you went in the Unique?

Your foolish notions, they make me sick,
If you keep it up you'll go to the Old Nick.
Now if you don't give in and mark the line with your toe,
And get down in your Jeans and dig up that "Dough,"
And put it right into my hand with a plunk,
And keep down your temper and none of your spunk—
I'll cook your grub as dry as a chip,
As hard as a rock, and as hard as a whip,

That you can not get down without using a swab.
That will feel in your stomach like you'd swallowed a cob.
Then I'll report you to the Parson,
To his wife and the Woman's Guild,
And sound it abroad till with shame you're filled.
And if that will not do, I'll unmuzzle, turn loose and sick 'em on you,
The Woman's Club and the W. C. T. U.,
And I'll [missing word] if there's not power in the Pulpit, the Press and the T'en
To silence and squelch these obstreperous men.

She kept on with her talk till she filled me with dread,
For I was awfully afraid that she'd do as she said.
To keep even with her is sure a lost cause,
Which I could not prevent except I'd stayed as I was
So I gave up the money, good friends must part,
It is just what I got for trying to be smart.
It was a bitter pill for me to swaller,
But that's the way she earned her dollar.

To keep peace and quiet I have done my best,
But I guess I told too much truth to be taken I jest,
So I smoothed it all over as well as I could
So now it's a thing of the past and we both are good.

---

[1] This humorous poem was written by Albert Williams in about 1906 based on his comment that he and his wife were married for forty years. The original was typed on one page, single spaced, in two columns with reproductions of a male figure in suit clothes with arm outstretched in a pleading fashion in between the two columns. It is not known it was published. The poem validates Eliza's membership and work with the local Woman's Guild and Women's Christian Temperance Union organizations. It also hints at the stresses that men of the time felt at a perceived loss of authority due to the work of women in the suffrage movement.

Bibliography

Abbott, Collamer M., "'Gramp' Abbott's Life, Farming in Central Vermont, 1865-1913," *Vermont History* 39, (1971), 31-42.

Alexander, Mary Charlotte, *Dr. Baldwin of Lahaina*, (Berkeley: Stanford University Press, 1953).

Aley, Ginette and J. L. Anderson, editors, *Union Heartland, The Midwestern Home Front During the Civil War*, (Carbondale: Southern Illinois University Press, 2013).

Anderson, Robert Charles, *The Great Migration Begins: Immigrants to New England, 1620-1633, Volumes 1-3, (New England Historical and Genealogic Society, 1995)*.

Anderson, Robert Charles, *The Great Migration, Immigrants to New England, 1634-1635,* Seven volumes, (Boston: Great Migration Study Project, New England Historic Genealogical Society, 2007).

Anderson, Rufus, *History of the Sandwich Island Mission*, (Boston: Congregational Publishing Company, 1870).

Anonymous, *Portrait, and Biographical Record of Johnson, Poweshiek, and Iowa Counties, Iowa* (Chicago: Chapman Bros., 1893).

Anonymous, *The History of Poweshiek County, Iowa,* (Des Moines: Union History Company, 1880).

Arnesen, Eric, "Inventing a Heartland," *Middle West Review* 9, no. 2, (Spring 2023): 91-104.

Arpad, Susan S., ed., *Sam Curd's Diary, The Diary of a True Woman*, (Athens, Ohio: Ohio University Press, 1984).

ASME, *Landmarks in Mechanical Engineering,* (West Lafayette, Indiana: Purdue University Press, 1997, American Society of Mechanical Engineering).

Baker, Paula, "The Domestication of Politics, Women and American Political Society, 1780-1920," *The American Historical Review* 89, no. 3, (June 1984): 620-647.

Baker, Thomas R ., *The Sacred Cause of Union, Iowa in the Civil War*, (Iowa City: University of Iowa Press, 2016).

Barlow, George, *The History of New Hampshire*, (Concord, NH: published by J.S. Boyd, June 4, 1842).

Barron, Hal S., *Those Who Stayed Behind, Rural Society in Nineteenth-century New England*, (Cambridge: Cambridge University Press, 1984).

Bartlett, Emery, "Letter to Grinnell: Emery S. Bartlett to his children and grandchildren," *Annals of Iowa* 44, no. 6, (Fall 1978): 419-440.

Basch, Norma, *Framing American Divorce, From the Revolutionary Generation to the Victorians*, (Berkeley: University of California Press, 1999).

Batchellor, Albert Stillman, *Revolutionary Documents of New Hampshire*, Vol 30, State Papers Series, Manchester, NH Printed for the State, 1910.

Beaglehole, Ernest, *Social Change in the South Pacific, Roatonga and Aitutaki*, (New York: McMillan Company, 1957).

Bishop, Sereno Edwards, *Reminiscences of Old Hawaii, with a brief biography by Lorrin A. Thurston*, (Honolulu: Hawaiian Gazette Company Limited, 1916).

Bly, Antonio, "A Prince Among Pretending Free Men, Runaway Slaves in Colonial New England Revisited," *Massachusetts Historical Review*, Vol 14, 2012, 87-118.

Bogue, Allan G., *From Prairie to Corn Belt*, (Chicago and London: University of Chicago Press, 1963).

Boyd, Mrs. Tom "Lou", et. al., "A Diary of the Cherokee Strip," *Journal of the Cherokee Strip* 16, no. 9, (1974): 1-20.

Boydston, Jeanne, *Home and Work, Housework, Wages, and the Ideology of Labor in the Early Republic*, (New York: Oxford University Press, 1990).

Breen, T. H. and Stephen Foster, "Moving to the New World: The Character of Early Massachusetts Immigration," *The William and Mary Quarterly* 30, no. 2 *(*April 1973): 189-222.

Brown, Captain Augustus C., *Diary of a Line Officer*, New York, 1906.

Brown, Bob, *Echoes from Middle Iowa's Historic Past,* (Fort Dodge, Iowa: Messenger Printing, 2002).

Brown, Carrie, "Guns for Billy Yank: The Armory in Windsor Meets the Challenge of Civil War," *Vermont History* 79, no 2 (Summer/Fall 2011) Vermont Historical Society publication: 141-161.

Brown, Carrie, *Arming the Union, Gunmakers in Windsor, Vermont*, (Vermont Historical Society, 2012; American Precision Museum, Windsor, VT 2012).

Browne, J. Ross, *Etchings of a Whaling Cruise: With Notes of a Sojourn on the Island of Zanzibar* (New York: Harper, 1846).

Bunkers, Suzanne L., *"All Will Yet Be Well", The Diary of Sarah Gillespie Huftalen, 1873-1952*, (Iowa City: University of Iowa Press, 1993).

Busch, Briton Cooper, *"Whaling will Never Do For Me," The American Whaleman in the Nineteenth Century*, (Lexington: University of Kentucky Press, 1994).

Calomiris, Charles W. and Larry Schweikart, "The Panic of 1857: Origins, Transmission and Containment," *The Journal of Economic History* 51, no. 4 (December 1991): 807-834.

Camp, David M., editor, *American Yearbook and National Register for 1869*, (Hartford, CT.: O.D. Case and Company, 1869).

Chambers-Schiller, Lee Virginia, *Liberty, A Better Husband, Single Women in America: The Generations of 1780-1840,* (New Haven and London: Yale University Press, 1984).

Chandler, George, *The Chandler Family; The Descendants of William and Annis Chandler who settled in Roxbury in 1637*, (Worcester, MA.: Charles Hamilton Press, 1883).

Child, William H., *History of the Town of Cornish New Hampshire with genealogical record, 1763-1910,* 2 vols, (Concord, NH.: The Rumford Press, 1910).

Cook, Robert, "A War for Principle? Shifting Memories of the Union Cause, 1865-1916," *Annals of Iowa,* 74, no. 3, (Summer 2015): 221-263.

Cordier, Mary Hurlburt, *Schoolwomen of the Prairies and Plains,* (Albuquerque: University of New Mexico Press, 1992).

Cott, Nancy, *Public Vows: A History of Marriage and the Nation,* (Cambridge and London: Harvard University Press, 2000).

Cott, Nancy F., *The Bonds of Womanhood, "Women's Sphere" in New England, 1780-1835,* (New Haven and London: Yale University Press, 1977).

Creighton, Margaret S., *Rites and Passages, The Experiences of American Whaling, 1830-1870,* (Cambridge: Cambridge University Press, 1995).

Cutting, T. A., *Cutting Kin,* (Campbell, CA.: Private Publishing, 1939).

Cutting, T. A, *Historical Sketch of Campbell,* (Campbell, CA: R. H. Knappen, Press, 1929).

Damon, Ethel M., *Koamalu; a story of pioneers on Kauai, and of what they built in that island garden,* 2 vols., (Honolulu: Private Publishing, 1931).

Danbom, David B., *Sod Busting, How Families Made Farms on the 19th - Century Plains,* (Baltimore: John Hopkins University Press, 2014).

Decker, William Merrill, *Epistolary Practices, Letter Writing in America before Telecommunications,* (Chapel Hill and London: University of North Carolina Press, 1998).

De Pauw, Linda Grant, *Seafaring Women,* (Boston: Houghton Mifflin, 1982).

Derby, Samuel Carroll, *Early Dublin: A List of Revolutionary Soldiers of Dublin, New Hampshire,* (Columbus, Ohio: Press of Spahr and Glann, 1901).

Deyrup, Felicia Johnson, *Arms Making in the Connecticut Valley; A Regional Study of the Economic Development of the Small Arms Industry, 1798-1870,* (York, Pennsylvania: George Shumway, pub., 1970).

Dolin, Eric Jay, *Leviathan, The History of Whaling in America,* (New York and London: WW Norton and Company, 2007).

Druett, Joan, ed., *"She was a Sister Sailor," The Whaling Journals of Mary Brewster, 1845-1851,* (Mystic, CT.: Mystic Seaport Museum, 1992).

Druett, Joan, "Whaling Wives, Sister Sailors," *Sea History Magazine,* 74, (Summer 1995): 20-22.

Druett, Joan, *Petticoat Whalers; Whaling Wives at Sea, 1820-1920,* (Auckland, New Zealand: Collins Pub., 1991).

Dudden, Faye E., *Serving Women: Household Service in Nineteenth-Century America,* (Middletown, CT.: Wesleyan University Press, 1983).

Ensign, Forest C., "The Era of Private Academies," *The Palimsest* 27, no 3, (1946): 75-85.

Epstein, Barbara Leslie, *The Politics of Domesticity: Women, Evangelism, and Temperance in Nineteenth-Century America*, (Middletown, CT: Wesleyan University Press, 1981).

Fink, Deborah, *Open Country Iowa, Rural Women, Tradition and Change,* (Albany: State University of New York Press, 1986).

Fish, Lester Warren, *The Fish Family in England and America*, (Rutland, Vt: Tuttle Publishing Company, 1948).

Fisher, Philip A., *The Fisher Genealogy, Record of the Descendants of Joshua, Anthony and Cornelius Fisher of Dedham, Mass, 1636-1640*, (Everett, Mass: Massachusetts Publishing Company, 1898).

Folmer, John Kent, ed. *"This State of Wonders", The Letters of an Iowa frontier Family, 1858-1861*, (Iowa City: University of Iowa Press, 1986).

Forbes, David W., Ralph Thomas Kam, Thomas A. Woods, *Partners in Change, A Biographical Encyclopedia of American Protestant Missionaries in Hawaii and their Hawaiian and Tahitian Colleagues, 1820-1900*, (Honolulu: Hawaiian Mission Children's Society, 2018).

French, Allen, *Charles I and the Puritan upheaval: a study of the causes of the great migration*, (Boston: Houghton Mifflin Company, 1955).

Fulbright, Jim, *Trails to Old Pond Creek, The Early Days of Trade and Travel in Northwestern Oklahoma*, (Goodlettsville, Tenn.: Mid-South Pub., 2005).

Games, Alison, *Migration and the origins of the English Atlantic world*, (Cambridge, Mass.: Harvard University Press, 2001).

Gard, Wayne, *The Chisolm Trail*, (Norman: University of Oklahoma Press, 1954).

Gardner, Robert E., *Small Arms Makers, A Directory of fabricators of firearms, edged weapons, crossbows and polearms,* (New York: Bonanza Books, 1963).

Garner, Stanton, ed., *The Captain's Best Mate, The Journal of Mary Chipman Lawrence on the Whaler Addison, 1856-1860*, (Hanover and London: University Press of New England, 1966).

Ginzberg, Lori D., *Women and the Work of Benevolence: Morality, Politics, and Class in the Nineteenth-Century United States*, (New Haven and London: Yale University Press, 1990).

Gordon, Linda, *Heroes of Their Own Lives, The Politics and History of Family Violence, Boston 1880-1960*, (New York: Viking, Penguin Books, 1988).

Gray, Susan E., *The Yankee West, Community Life on the Michigan Frontier*, (Chapel Hill: University of North Carolina Press, 1996).

Grimshaw, Patricia, "'Christian Woman, Pious Wife, Faithful Mother, Devoted Missionary,' Conflicts in Roles of American Missionary Women in Nineteenth-Century Hawaii," *Feminist Studies* 9, no. 3, (Fall 1983): 489-521.

Grinnell, Josiah Bushnell, *Men and Events of Forty Years, Autobiographical Reminiscences of an Active Career from 1850 to 1890*, (Boston: D. Lothrop Co., 1891).

Gue, Benjamin, *History of Iowa From its Earliest Times to the Beginning of the Twentieth Century*, Vol I, (New York City: Century History Company, 1903).

Halford, Francis John, *Nine Doctors and God*, (Honolulu: University of Hawaii Press, 1954).

Hall, Charles S. Hall, *Hall Ancestry, A Series of Sketches of the lineal ancestors of the children of Samuel Holden Parsons Hall,* (New York and London: G. Putnam, 1896).

Hall, David B., *The Halls of New England, Genealogical and Biographical*, (Albany, N.Y.: Private Publishing, Printed for the author by J. Munsell's Sons, 1883).

Hammond, Isaac W. ed., *State of New Hampshire, Rolls of the Soldiers of the Revolutionary War, 1775 to May 1777, with a appendix embracing the diaries of Lt. Jonathan Burton*, (Concord. NH: P. G. Cogswell, 1885).

Hampsten, Elizabeth, *Read This Only to Yourself; The Private Writings of Midwestern Women, 1880-1910*, (Bloomington: Indiana University Press, 1982).

Hansen, Marcus L., "Official Encouragement of Emigration to Iowa," *Iowa Journal of History and Politics*, XIX, no. 1, (1921): 159-195.

Hartford, City of, *Hartford Connecticut as a Manufacturing, Business, and Commercial Center,* (Hartford: Published by the Hartford Board of Trade, 1889).

Herndon, Ruth Wallis, and John E. Murray, *Children Bound to Labor, The Pauper Apprentice System in Early America*, (Ithica and London: Cornell University Press, 2009).

Herriott, Frank L., "Seventy Years in Iowa" *Annals of Iowa* 27 (1945), 97-118.

Hightower, Michael J., *Banking in Oklahoma before Statehood,* (Norman: University of Oklahoma Press, 2013).

Hohman, Elmo P., *The American Whaleman*, (New York: Longmans Green, 1928).

Hooper, Jayna Huot, *Celebrating Community Newport, New Hampshire, 1761-2011, 250 Years and Beyond*, (Newport, NH: Newport Historical Society, 2011).

Hooper, Jayna, ed., *Jacob Wheeler's Journal of Matter and Things in General, 1847*, (Newport, NH.: Newport Historical Society, 2016).

Hooper, Jayna and Larry Cote, eds., *The Diary of Charles Emerson*, (Newport, NH: Newport Historical Society, 2021.

Howard, Robert A., "Interchangeable Parts Reexamined: The Private Sector of the American Arms Industry on the Eve of the Civil War," *Technology and Culture* 19, no. 4 (Oct. 1978): 633-649.

Hubbard, Guy, "Development of Machine Tools in New England," *American Machinist*, October 18, 1923, Vol 59-61 (1923-24), series of twenty-three articles; Issue 16: 579-581.

Hubbard, Guy, *Industrial History*, (Windsor, VT: Windsor Town School District, 1922).

Hubbard, Guy, "Leadership of Early Windsor Industries in the Mechanic Arts," A Paper Read Before the Vermont Historical Society at Windsor, September 4, 1922, Proceedings of the Vermont Historical Society, 1921, 22, 23, (Montpelier: Capital City Press, 1924): 159-182.

Hubbard, Guy, "Leadership of Early Windsor Industries in the Mechanic Arts, A Paper Read Before the Vermont Historical Society at Windsor, September 4, 1922," *Essays in the Social and Economic History of Vermont*, (Montpelier: Vermont Historical Society, 1943), 239-264.

Hurd, D. Hamilton, *History of Cheshire and Sullivan Counties, N.H.*, (Philadelphia, PA: J. W. Lewis, 1886).

Huston, James L., "Western Grains and the Panic of 1857," *Agricultural History* 57, no. 1, (January 1983): 14-32. Hutchison, William R., *Errand to the World: American Protestant Thought and Foreign Missions*, (Chicago: University of Chicago Press, 1987).

Iowa College, *Catalogue of Iowa College, 1864-65, Grinnell Iowa,* (Montezuma, Iowa: Printed at the Republican Office, 1864).

Iowa College, *Catalogue of Iowa College, 1865-66, Grinnell Iowa,* (Montezuma, Iowa: Printed at the Republican Office, 1865).

Jacobs, Margaret, "Western History: What's Gender Got to do With it?" *Western Historical Quarterly* 42, no. 3 (Autumn 2011): 297-304.

Joesting, Edward, *Kauai, The Separate Kingdom*, (Kauai: University of Hawaii Press and Kauai Museum Association, 1984).

Johnson, Joan Marie, *The Woman Suffrage Movement in the United States,* (London and New York: Routledge, 2022).

Johnson, Keach, "Elementary and Secondary Education in Iowa, 1890-1900," *Annals of Iowa,* Part I, Vol. 45, Issue 2, (Fall 1979): 87-109.

Kaplan, Amy, "Manifest Domesticity," *American Literature* 70, no. 3 (September 1998): 581-606.

Kaufman, Polly Welts, *Women Teachers on the Frontier*, (New Haven and London: Yale University Press, 1984).

Kessler-Harris, Alice, *Out to Work, A History of Wage-Earning Women in the United States*, (Oxford: Oxford University Press, 2003).

Kirk, Hyland C., *Heavy Guns and Light, A History of the Fourth New York Artillery*, (New York: Dillingham pub., 1890).

Kistler, Thelma M., "The Rise of Railroads in the Connecticut River Valley," *Smith College Studies in History*, XXIII, Nos 1-4, (October 1937-July 1938): 5-289.

Laegreid, Renee M. and Sandra K. Mathews, ed., *Women on The North American Plains*, (Lubbock: Texas Tech University Press, 2011).

Lafferty, Ben, *American Intelligence: small-town news and political culture in Federalist New Hampshire,* (Amherst: University of Massachusetts Press, 2019).

Lauck, Jon K., *The Good Country, A History of the American Midwest, 1800-1900*, (Norman: University of Oklahoma Press, 2022).

Lauck, Jon K., *The Lost Region, Toward a Revival of Midwestern History,* (Iowa City: University of Iowa Press, 2013).

Leonard, Levi W. and Josiah Seward, *The History of Dublin, NH,* (Dublin, NH: Published by the town of Dublin, 1920).

Lepore, Jill, "Historians Who Love Too Much: Reflections on Microhistory and Biography," *Journal of American History* 88, Issue 1, (June 2001): 129-144.

Lund, Judith Navas, *Whaling Masters and Whaling Voyages Sailing From American Ports, A Compilation of Sources,* (New Bedford: New Bedford Whaling Museum, Ten Pound Island Book Co., 2001).

MacKay, Anne ed., *She Went A-Whaling, the Journal of Martha Smith Brewer Brown from Orient, Long Island, New York, Around the World on the Whaling Ship Lucy Ann, 1847-1849,* (New York: Oysterponds Historical Society, 1993).

McDermott, Scott, *The Puritan ideology of mobility: corporatism, the politics of place and the founding of New England towns before 1650,* (London: Anthem Press, 2022).

McGuire, Mary Lou, *Croydon, New Hampshire, Two Villages Under the Mountain: Four Corners and East Village,* (Croydon, NH: Croydon Historical Society, 2022).

Meyer, David R., *Networked Machinists, High-Technology Industries in Antebellum America,* (Baltimore: John Hopkins University Press, 2006).

Mulford, Prentice, *Prentice Mulford's Story,* (Oakland, CA: F. J. Needham, NY, 1889; California Relations #35, reprint, bio books, 1953).

Norling, Lisa, "Ahab's Wife, Women and the American Whaling Industry, 1820-1870," IN *Iron Men, Wooden Women, Gender and Seafaring in the Atlantic World, 1700-1920,* ed. Margaret Creighton and Lisa Norling, (Baltimore and London: John Hopkins University Press, 1996): 70-91.

Noyes, Katharine Macy, *Jesse Macy: An Autobiography,* (Springfield, Ill and Baltimore, Maryland: Charles C. Thomas, 1933).

Old Settlers' Association, Proceedings of the Old Settlers' Association of Grinnell, "March 19, 1895, The Shermans by Mrs. A. H. Sherman," *Proceedings of the Annual Meeting of the Old Settlers of Grinnell,* (Grinnell, Iowa: Signal Printing, 1895).

Old Settlers' Association President, Annual Meeting of Old Settlers' Association of Grinnell, Iowa, 1900, President's Opening Address, *Proceedings of the Annual Meeting of the Old Settlers of Grinnell,* (Grinnell, Iowa: Signal Printing, 1900).

Old Settlers' Association President, Annual Meeting of Old Settlers' Association of Grinnell, Iowa, 1902, *Proceedings of the Annual Meeting of the Old Settlers of Grinnell,* (Grinnell, Iowa: Signal Printing, 1902).

Olmstead, Francis Allyn, *Incidents of a Whaling Voyage,* (New York: Appleton and Company, 1841).

Parker, Leonard Fletcher, *History of Poweshiek County, Iowa; A History of Settlement, Organization, Progress, and Achievement,* (Chicago: S. J. Clarke Publishing company, 1911).

Pillsbury, Hobart, *New Hampshire, Resources, Attractions, and Its People, A History,* Five volumes, (New York: The Lewis Historical Publishing Company, 1927).

Qually, Mary, "United Lutheran Synod in Iowa," *The Palimsest*, 35, no. 6, (June 1954): 243-260.

Radke-Moss, Andrea, "'Willing Challengers'; Women's Experiences in the Northern Plains, 1862-1930," IN *Women on The North American Plains* ed by Renee M. Laegreid and Sandra K. Mathews, (Lubbock: Texas Tech University Press, 2011), 48-67.

Richter, Amy G., *At Home in the Nineteenth-Century America, A Documentary History*, (New York: New York University Press, 2015).

Riley, Glenda, *Building and Breaking Families in the American West*, (Albuquerque: University of New Mexico Press, 1996).

Riley, Glenda, *Divorce, An American Tradition,* (New York and Oxford: Oxford University Press, 1991.

Riley, Glenda, *Female Frontier, A Comparative View of Women on the Prairie and Plains*, (Lawrence: University Press of Kansas, 1988).

Riley, Glenda, *Frontierswomen, The Iowa Experience*, (Ames: Iowa State University Press, 1994).

Riley, Glenda, *Inventing the American Woman, A Perspective on Women's History*, (Arlington Heights: Harlan Davidson, 1987).

Riley, Glenda, "Not Gainfully Employed: Women on the Iowa Frontier, 1833-1870," *Pacific Historical Review*, 49, no. 2, (May 1980): 237-264.

Robotti, Frances Diane, *Whaling and Old Salem*, (New York: Bonanza Books, 1962).

Roe, Joseph, "Early American Machinists; The Men of the Hartford Shops," *American Machinist* 41, no. 8, (August 20, 1914): 331-335.

Rondeau, Mark, "Vermont Gunmakers Armed the Union," *Bennington Banner*, June 13, 2012, https://www.benningtonbanner.com/stories/vermont-gunmakers-armed-the-union,178994).

Rouleau, Brian, "Maritime Destiny as Manifest Destiny, American Commercial Expansion and the Idea of the Indian," *Journal of the Early Republic*, 30, (Fall 2010): 377-411.

Ruggles, W. Oakley, "Early Reflections of Fort Dodge," *Iowa Journal of History*, 49, (April 1951): 168-84.

Sage, Leland L., *A History of Iowa*, (Ames: Iowa State University Press, 1987).

Savage, James, ed., "Times Hard but Grit Good, Lydia Moxley's 1877 Diary," *Annals of Iowa*, 47, (1984): 270-290.

Schultz, Martin, "Divorce in Early America: Origins and Trends in Three North Central States," *Sociological Quarterly*, 25, no. 4, (Autumn 1984): 511-525.

Schwieder, Dorothy, *Iowa, The Middle Land,* (Ames: Iowa State University Press, 1996).

Secomb, Daniel F., *History of the Town of Amherst, Hillsborough, NH Hillsborough County, New Hampshire (first known as Narragansett Township Number Three, and subsequently as Souhegan West)* (Concord, NH: Evans, Sleeper & Woodbury, 1883).

Shiels, Richard, "The Feminization of American Congregationalism, 1730-1835," *American Quarterly* 33, no. 1, (Spring 1981): 46-62.

Smith, Dean Crawford, Melinde Lutz Sanborn, *Vital records of Croydon, New Hampshire, to the end of the year 1900,* (Boston, Mass.: New England Historic Genealogical Society, 1999).

Smith, Merritt Roe, "The American Precision Museum, Windsor, VT," *Technology and Culture* 15, no. 3, (July 1974): 413-437.

Smith, Merritt Roe, "John H. Hall, Simeon North, and the Milling Machine: The Nature of Innovation among Antebellum Arms Makers," *Technology and Culture* 14, no. 4 (Oct. 1973): 573-591.

Smith, Winston O., *The Sharps Rifle, its history, development and operation*, (New York: W. Morrow and Company, 1943).

Soike, Lowell J., *Necessary Courage, Iowa's Underground Railroad in the Struggle Against Slavery*, (Iowa City: University of Iowa Press, 2013).

Speakman, Cummins E. Jr., *Mowee, An Informal History of the Hawaiian Island*, (Salem, Mass.: Peabody Museum of Salem, 1978).

Squires, J. Duane, T*he Granite State of the United States; a history of New Hampshire from 1623 to the present*, (New York: American Historical Company, 1956).

Stabler, Lois K., *Very Poor and of Low Make; the Journal of Abner Sanger*, (Portsmouth, NH: Historical Society of Cheshire County, 1986).

Stackpole, Edouard A., *The Sea-Hunters, The New England Whalemen During Two Centuries, 1635-1835*, (Philadelphia and New York: J.B. Lippincott Company, 1953).

Stansell, Christine, "Women on the Great Plains, 1865-1890," *Women's Studies*, 4, (1976): 87-98.

Starbuck, Alexander, *History of the American Whale Fishery*, reprint (Secaucus, NJ: Castle Books, 1989).

State of Iowa, *Census Returns of the different Counties of the State of Iowa for 1856, Printed by the Authority of the Census Board*, (Iowa City: Crum and Boye Printers, 1856).

Stewart, Geoffrey S., *Arming the World, American Gun-Makers in the Gilded Age*, (Essex, Ct.: Lyons Press, 2024)

Stone, Ronald H., *Eber: Pioneer in Iowa*, (Iowa City, Iowa: Camp Pope Bookshop, 2008).

Strasser, Susan, *Never Done: A History of American Housework*, (New York: Pantheon Books, 1982).

Terry, Constance J., compiler, *In the Wake of Whales, The Whaling Journals of Capt. Edwin Peter Brown, 1841-1847*, (Orient, Long Island, NY: Old Orient Press, 1988).

Tufts, Warren, et. al., "The Rich Pattern of California Crops," IN *California Agriculture*, Claude B. Hutchinson, editor, (Berkeley and Los Angeles: University of California Press, 1946), 113-238.

Vermont Provost Marshall General, Record of the Provost Marshall General, State of Vermont, Consolidated List Class II, Second District Vermont, Records of the Provost Marshall General's Bureau, Civil War, Vol. II, 1863-65.

Vickers, Daniel with Vince Walsh, *Young Men and The Sea, Yankee Seafarers in the Age of Sail*, (New Haven and London: Yale University Press, 2005).

Virkus, Frederick Adams, *Immigrant Ancestors, A List of 2,500 Immigrants to America before 1750*, (Baltimore: Genealogical Publishing Company, 1963).

Wade, Hugh Mason, *A Brief History of Cornish, 1763-1974*, (Hanover, NH.: University Press of New England, 1976).

Warren, Wendy, *New England Bound, Slavery and Colonization in Early America*, (New York: Liveright Publishing Corp., 2016).

Watson, Jeanette, *Campbell, the Orchard City*, (Campbell, CA: Campbell Historical Museum, 1989).

Welter, Barbara, "The Cult of True Womanhood, 1820-1860," *American Quarterly*, 18, no. 2, Part I, (Summer, 1966): 151-174.

West, Elliott, "Child's Play: Tradition and Adaptation on the Frontier," *Montana, The Magazine of Western History* 38, no. 1, (Winter 1988): 2-15.

West, Elliott, *Continental Reckoning, The American West in the Age of Expansion*, (Lincoln: University of Nebraska Press, 2023).

West, Elliott, *Growing Up With the Country, Children on the Far Western Frontier*, (Albuquerque: University of New Mexico Press, 1998).

Wheeler, Edmund, *History of Newport, New Hampshire*: from 1766 to 1878, with a genealogical register, (Concord, NH: Republican Press Association, 1879).

Wheeler, Edmund, *History of Croydon, New Hampshire*, (Claremont, NH: Printed by the Claremont Manufacturing Company, 1867).

Wheeler, Edmund, *Croydon, NH 1866, Proceedings at the Centennial Celebration on Wednesday June 13, 1866*, (Claremont, NH: Printed by Claremont Manufacturing Company, 1867).

White, G. H., *Historical Sketch of Chester Township*, (Grinnell: Cravath and Shaw Steam Printers, 1881).

Whiting, Emma Mayhew, and Henry Beetle Hough, *Whaling Wives*, (Boston: Houghton Mifflin Company, 1953).

Wickham, Joseph, *English and American Tool Builders*, (New Haven: Yale University Press, 1916).

Williams, Harrison, *Life and Ancestors of Robert Williams of Roxbury, 1607-1693*, (Washington, D. C.: W. F. Roberts, Co. Press of Washington Company, 1934).

Williams, Major William, ed Edward Breen, T*he History of Early Fort Dodge and Webster County, Iowa*, (Fort Dodge: KVFD-KFMY, 1950).

Williams, Stephen West, *The genealogy and History of the Family of Williams in America; More Particularly of the Descendants of Robert Williams of Roxbury*, (Greenfield: Printed by Merriam and Mirick, 1847).

Williamstown Historical Society, *Williamstown My Own, The History of Williamstown, Vermont, 1781-2012*, (Williamstown: Williamstown Historical Society, 2012).

Wilson, Harold Fisher, "The Roads of Windsor," *Geographical Review*, 21, (1931): 379-397.

Wohl, R. Richard, edited by Moses Rischin, "The Country Boy Myth and Its Place in American Urban Culture, The Nineteenth-Century Contribution," *Perspectives in American History*, III, (1969): 77-156.

Wolf, P. B., *Wolfe's History of Clinton County Iowa,* Vol I, (Indianapolis, Ind.: B. F. Bowen and Co., 1911).

Woloch, Nancy, *Women and the American Experience*, (New York: McGraw Hill, 2011).

Zeigler, Sara, "Wifely Duties: Marriage, Labor and the Common Law in Nineteenth-Century America," *Social Science History*, 20. no. 1, (Spring 1996): 63-96.

Unpublished

Alexander and Baldwin families, Letters and Papers of Alexander and Baldwin Families in Hawaii, Hawaiian Mission Children's Society Library.

Dublin, New Hampshire town records, 1768-1830, Microfilm, LDS Genealogical, Family History Library Salt Lake City; Microfilm of records in the New Hampshire State Capital, Concord.

Elizabeth log, Whaling Log, 1844-1848, First mate Martin Arey, log keeper, Log # 546, Peabody Essex Museum.

Elizabeth, Majestic, Natchez log, 1844-1855, Nathan Hall, log keeper, Log # 1490, Peabody Essex Museum.

Foster Letters, William Hale Foster to Maria Foster letters, August 9, 1861-January 23, 1863, private collection.

Grattan Divorce, Lavinia Williams Grattan v. John Grattan, State of Colorado, County of Jefferson, District Court, No 2026, Filed June 2, 1917, Separate Maintenance.

"Johnson, Lois S. Hoyt - Journal - 1836-1838," *Hawaiian Mission Houses Digital Archive*, accessed February 8, 2022, http://hmha.missionhouses.org/items/show/81.

Majestic and Natchez log, 1848-1855, Nathan Hall, log keeper, Log # 1741, Peabody Essex Museum.

Natchez Log, Hall, 1851-1855, Worthin Hall, log keeper, Log # 827, New Bedford Whaling Museum.

Poweshiek County, Iowa, U.S. Probate, School and Court Records, 1850-1954.

Reaper log, Whaling Journal, 1835-1837, Unknown log keeper, Log # 378, Peabody Essex Museum.

Sullivan County, Registrar of Deeds, Newport, New Hampshire.

Whitney, Mercy Partridge, Journals 1 and 2, 1848- 1852; 1852-1855, Hawaiian Mission Houses Museum and Library, Honolulu.

Whitney, Mercy Partridge, Letter collections, online, Hawaiian Mission Houses Museum and Library, Honolulu.

AG. Williams, probate records, District Court of Iowa in and for Poweshiek County, Iowa Judicial Branch 2, A.G. Williams estate, Probate number 4454.

Williams Divorce, Melinda H. Williams v. Stephen Williams, Jr. Divorce Decided July, 1856, Sullivan County Superior Court Records, New Hampshire State Archives, Concord.

Williams Divorce, Rhoda M. Williams v. Stephen Williams, September 2, 1879, Sullivan County record of divorce, 37, State of New Hampshire State Archives, Concord.

Newspapers

Avalanche Echo (Glenwood Springs, Colorado)
Bennington (Vermont) Banner
Campbell (CA) Weekly Visitor
Campbell (CA) Interurban Press
Columbia Centinel (Boston, Mass.)
Emmetsburg (Iowa) Democrat
Fort Dodge (Iowa) Republican
Fort Dodge (Iowa) Sentinel
Grinnell (Iowa) Herald
Grinnell (Iowa) Signal
Hanford (CA) Sentinel
Iowa Northwest (Webster, Co., Iowa)
Long Beach (CA) Press-Telegram
Marshalltown (Iowa) Times Republican
National Eagle (Claremont, New Hampshire)
New Hampshire Argus And Spectator (Newport, NH)
New Hampshire Sentinel (Keene, NH)
San Jose (CA) Herald
San Jose (CA) Mercury News
Tipton (Iowa) Advertiser
Vermont Journal (Windsor, Vermont)
Vermont Phoenix (Brattleboro, Vermont)
Whalemen's Shipping List and Merchant's Transcript (New Bedford, Mass)
Whip and Spur (Newport, NH)

Internet

Ancestry.com
Family Search.com
Hawaiian Mission Children's Society Museum and Library, Honolulu, Digital Archive
NPS Civil War website

Index

Lamson Goodnow, Yale Company, 6, 33n56, 33n69, 71, 95
Lamson, Almira, 77
Lamson, Jonas, 77
Lawrence, Richard, 6, 32n42, 114
Lepore, Jill, historian, viii
Lewis, Annie Finch, 20
Lewis, Benjamin, 77
Lewis, Emeline, 77
Lewis, Maria, 63
Lewis, Thomas, 20
Lewis, William, 20, 40n238
Lovell, James, 36n141, 37n159
Lowell, Massachusetts, 87
Lutheran College, 19, 91
Lyon (ship), 2,
Lyons, Iowa, 38n180, 55, 70
Machine tool industry, 3, 5, 7; organizational changes, 33n69
Macy, Jesse, 41n248
Majestic (ship), 10, 11, 12
Malignant Diptheria, 101
Manifest destiny, 10, 34n96
Marengo, Iowa County, Iowa, 117
Maui, Hawaii, population in 1846, 35n112
Medford, Oklahoma, 26
Melzard, John, 11, 35n114
Meriden, NH., 113
Metacom (ship), 36n141
Mexican American War, 6,
Microhistory, viii
Midwest, characterization, 24, 42n306; settlement, 30, 39n187
Nashua, NH., 113
Natchez (ship), 10, 13, 14, 35n102, 51
National Hydraulic Company, 5
New Bedford, MA, 10
New England, 1; literacy, 3; industrial revolution, 3; settlement, 2; see also arms manufacturing
New Hampshire, population, 1
Newport, New Hampshire, 1, 5, 8, 12, 15, 47, 49, 50, 51, 59, 61, 87, 97, 98, 105, 113
Newton, Harriet, 74
North Clinton, Iowa, 55
Numb palsy, 75, 76
Oklahoma Cherokee Strip Land Run, 26
Old Chisholm Trail, 26
Orozimbo (ship), 11
Packard, Judson, 85
Panic of 1857, 18, 39n198, 74, 76, 83, 107
Park, Theoda, 2
Park, William, 2
Parker, Elizabeth, 31n17
Parker, Leonard, 19
Patterson Station, Putnam County, New York, 119
Perry, Van Buren, 47
Pierce, Franklin, 70
Pike, Chester, 61
Pioneering life, 17-18, 38n185, 39n214, 39n215, 41n255, 41n256, 41n258
Plainfield, New Hampshire, 1
Pond Creek, Oklahoma, 26, 42n284
Powers, Mr., 113, 114
Poweshiek County, Iowa, 101, 115, 117; population, 41n255; see also Grinnell, Iowa
Poweshiek County Central Agricultural Society, 24
Puritan Migration, 2, 7, 31n8, 31n10; values, 31

Puritans, 2, 31n10, 44n350
Reaper (ship), 9
Rehoboth, MA, 7
Riley, Glenda, historian, 30
Robbins and Lawrence, 6, 32n42, 33n69, 63, 95, 103
Robinson, Everett, 81
Root, James, 117
Rowell, George, 12
Rowell, Malvina Jerusha (Chapin), 12
Roxbury, MA, 2,
Rusco[e], Chloe, 119
Rusco[e], Emma, [Thompkins], 119
Rusco[e], Hart, 119
Rusco[e], Helen Lewis, 20, 22; 40n238, 119, 120, 123, 131
Rusco[e], Henry, 20, 22, 118, 120
Rusco[e], George, 21
Rusco[e], Gilbert, 21, 40n243
Rusco[e], Melissa, 119
Rusco[e], Nettie (Ann E.), 22, letter from, 119
Rusco[e], Sarah, 119
Rutherford, Robert, 123, 131
Sanger, Abner, 3
Santa Clara Valley, 27
Sargent, George W., 115
School teaching, Iowa, 21, 41n250, 41n251, 109, 117; mid-west, 21
Sharps guns, carbine, 6; factory, 6-7, 93, 114; rifle, 63
Sheep industry, 79, 109
Sherman, Anginette (Blanchard), Mrs. Jason, 38n180, 53, 55
Sherman, Anna May, 112
Sherman, Annginette Hall (Williams), vii, 17, 18, 20, 34n91; 37n161, 38n180, 38n185, 39n192, 50, 51, 53, 56, 59, 61, 63, 69, 70, 71, 73, 97, 98, 105, 112, 113, 114, 115, 116, 121, 131; letters from, 45, 47, 55, 57
Sherman, Clara, 19, 95, 96, 115
Sherman, Edna, 125
Sherman, Henry, 70, 96, 121
Sherman, Jane (Wheelock), Mrs. Jason, 131
Sherman, Jason, 17, 38n180, 53, 55, 121, 131
Sherman, Luke Newton, vii, 17, 18, 38n180, 53, 55, 57, 59, 63, 70, 71, 87, 97, 98, 113, 114, 115, 116, 121, 131; land deed, 89
Sherman, William, 17, 38n180, 55, 70
Sherman, Wilson, 121
Skiff, Cornelius, 121, 128, 131
Skiff, Emma, 131
Skiff, Harriet, 131
Skiff, Isabella, 131
Skiff, Roxy Ann, 131
Smith, James, 36n132
Spaulding, Silas, 101
Springfield rifle, 112
St. Albans, Hertfordshire, England, 20, 119
Stearns, Daniel, 74, 81
Stearns, Mary, 74
Stevens, Harriet, 77
Stevens, Joseph, 77
Stevens, Manson, 77, Letter from, 77
Stone, Henry, 95, 113, 114
Stone, Mrs., 113, 114
Suffrage, 27, 28, 43n311
Sullivan County, New Hampshire, 3, 9, 15
Tasker, Arthur, 65
Tasker, B. F., 73, 74
Tasker, James, 65, 111, 113, 114

www.ingramcontent.com/pod-product-compliance
Lightning Source LLC
Chambersburg PA
CBHW080614270326
41928CB00016B/3053